WHICH DIRECTION FOR
ORGANIZED LABOR?

WHICH DIRECTION FOR ORGANIZED LABOR?

Essays on Organizing, Outreach, and Internal Transformations

Edited by **Bruce Nissen**

 Wayne State University Press   Detroit

Library of Congress Cataloging-in-Publication Data

Nissen, Bruce, 1948–
    Which direction for organized labor? : essays on organizing, out-
reach, and internal transformations / edited by Bruce Nissen.
      p.   cm.
    Includes bibliographical references and index.
    ISBN 0-8143-2779-6 (pbk. : alk. paper)
    1. Trade-unions—United States. 2. Trade-unions—Organizing—
United States. 3. Labor Policy—United States. 4. AFL-CIO. 5. Labor
movement—United States—Forecasting. I. Title.
HD6508.N57 1998
331.88'0973—dc21   98-24151

Earlier versions of Michael Eisenscher's chapter were presented to the
Center for Labor Research, University of Massachusetts—Boston Working
Paper and Public Forum Series, May 2, 1996, and at the spring meeting of
the Industrial Relations Research Association in St. Louis, May 4, 1996.

To Karen, Jared, and Leif

CONTENTS

ACKNOWLEDGMENTS

The process of bringing this book to completion was a long and hard one. I hope that the result will justify the many efforts of various people to see it through. My biggest thanks go to the authors of the chapters and to the anonymous referees who read and critiqued the book, making it much better. They are at least as responsible for any merits the book may have as is the editor. Finally, a big word of thanks to Janet Witalec, a most able and productive editor at Wayne State University Press.

Introduction

Bruce Nissen

The U.S. labor movement has been in decline for at least four decades. This fact has been much documented and analyzed by those concerned with the fate of workers and unions in this country (Kochan, Katz, and McKersie 1986; Goldfield 1987; Harrison and Bluestone 1988; Moody 1988; Robinson 1988; Moberg 1989; Nissen 1990; Freeman 1992; Craver 1995; and many others). The most obvious symptom is the drastic decline in union density (the percentage of the workforce that is unionized), but almost any other measure would document the same thing.

Perhaps most striking is the decline in union *power*, however that term is defined or measured. Union bargaining power, with few sectoral exceptions, has dropped dramatically, as demonstrated by collective bargaining outcomes (Craypo 1990; Voos 1994). The same has happened with union political power (Seybold 1990; Brody 1993). On 'all fronts, the labor movement has been hemmed in by unfavorable trends in the economy, legal restraints, public image, and technological change.

One consequence of declining influence was a continuous whittling down of aspirations among union leaders and members. As less and less appeared to be possible, unionists continually readjusted downward their measure of success. Mere survival, even in a steadily shrinking form, came to be seen as success. Despite a decline in union density from around 35 percent in 1953 to less than 15 percent in 1997, and despite a loss of more than four million members since 1975, then AFL-CIO president Lane Kirkland in the early 1990s read the situation as one of achievement: "We've maintained our membership in the most extraordinary combination of adverse circumstances," he remarked (Brody 1994).

11

But a second consequence was internal ferment. At least since the early to mid-1980s, the labor movement as a whole, and individual unions, have been undergoing serious internal stresses and strains, combined with a search for new ways to break out of the impasse within which the movement finds itself. One indication is the increased tempo of union mergers. Many of these occurred in the late 1980s and the 1990s (Chaison 1996). The 1995 announcement by the United Autoworkers, the United Steelworkers, and the International Association of Machinists of their intention to merge into a "superunion" of the metal trades by the year 2000 was an indication of how seriously mergers are being pursued ("Unity Declaration" 1995).

A second highly visible public manifestation of the ferment occurred within the national federation of U.S. unions, the AFL-CIO. Dissatisfaction of some national union leaders with the leadership of then AFL-CIO president Lane Kirkland was leaked to the national press in January 1995. In February the infighting within AFL-CIO ranks burst out into the open at the executive council meeting when Kirkland publicly confronted his critics.

Subsequent events developed into the first contested election for the leadership of the federation in the twentieth century. An insurgent "New Voice" slate headed by John Sweeney of the Service Employees Union and including the Mineworkers' Richard Trumka and Linda Chavez-Thompson of the American Federation of State, County, and Municipal Employees challenged Kirkland's heir apparent, Tom Donahue, and his running mate, Barbara Easterling of the Communications Workers, for leadership of the federation.

In October 1995 the New Voice slate was elected. At the convention that month, Donahue had criticized the militant tactics of Sweeney's union, which had blocked the bridges leading into Washington, D.C., as part of its "Justice for Janitors" organizing campaign. Donahue stated, "We must worry less about blocking bridges and worry more about building bridges to the rest of society." Sweeney replied, "I believe in building bridges, whenever the shelling lets up. . . . But I believe in blocking bridges whenever those employers and those communities turn a deaf ear to the working families that we represent" (Moberg 1995, 22). This "bridges" debate became a shorthand for what many perceived to be the difference between the more aggressive and militant New Voice slate and the more cautious old guard.

While the "bridges" symbolism makes for effective shorthand in demonstrating the issues being debated and the changes in overall orientation being undertaken by the labor movement, it is important not to exaggerate the changes that have taken place, or to attribute all change to a turnover in leadership. There is much more continuity in organized labor's reevaluation of strategies than that, and it is by no means accurate to read all "old" leadership and strategies as complacent and unaware or all "new" ones as dynamic and progressive.

Thus, many of the ideas and programs being attempted today had their genesis in the years prior to the leadership turnover. To cite a few examples, the recent megamergers of affiliated unions were preceded by the return of the United Autoworkers (UAW), the Teamsters (IBT), and the Mineworkers (UMW) to the federation. The move toward a more assertive and powerful labor federation began earlier with the creation of the AFL-CIO's Strategic Approaches Committee and the federation's attempt to understand the broad changes in the political and economic landscape through the work of the Evolution of Work Committee.

The new emphasis on organizing has an earlier origin in the creation of the Organizing Institute (OI) by the AFL-CIO and some of its affiliates in 1989. And militant struggles, both successful and unsuccessful, were undertaken in the 1980s and early 1990s by unions facing employers intent on breaking the power of unions, or even breaking the unions themselves. Examples include Eastern Airlines (Machinists), Pittston Coal (Mineworkers), Ravenswood Aluminum (Steelworkers), the *New York Daily News* and the *Pittsburgh Press* (multiple unions). All of these struggles predated the changeover in leadership at the AFL-CIO, as did the creation of Jobs with Justice as a community outreach organization and the Service Employees' well-known Justice for Janitors campaigns employing "social movement" tactics to organize janitorial staff in a number of cities. All of these examples demonstrate that ferment and experimentation with new directions has been going on for some time rather than as a simple response to a changeover in leadership at the AFL-CIO.

But whatever the continuities, the changeover in leadership in the AFL-CIO has inspired a great deal of enthusiasm and rethinking among many in the labor movement. It has also led to extensive restructuring of the federation itself. The Department of Field Services has been renamed the Department of Field Mobilization. Old departments have been either abolished or changed; new departments of organizing and corporate affairs have been established. A widely publicized "Union Summer" in 1996 put 1,500 young high school and college students into numerous organizing and community mobilization situations. AFL-CIO entities with names like the Center for Corporate Affairs and the Center for Workplace Democracy have been set up. Activists from a number of unions have been brought in to replace old staff. All of which has given a sense of rejuvenation to the federation in the eyes of many activists and observers.

The new AFL-CIO also began to define a new political role for organized labor in the country. The federation has stated its intention to be more independent politically. The goal is to make issues of importance to workers the center of national discussion and debate. According to recent resolutions, the labor movement plans to shed its older role as an automatic source of checks for Democrats irrespective of their performance. Perhaps the initiative that attracted the most widespread public attention at the time this introduction was written was the expenditure of $35 million in hard-hitting political ads targeting Republican congress members in strategic districts during the 1996 election campaign. In this campaign organized labor did indeed become a more independent and important player on the political scene. To supplement the media campaign the AFL-CIO set up a permanent base of political activists in every congressional district.

The AFL-CIO also began to address the marginal role of local central labor councils. In 1996 a conference in Denver, Colorado, brought together a number of labor council leaders to develop strategies for rebirth. A new National Advisory Committee on the Future of Central Labor Councils will develop strategies to revitalize the grass roots. The new leadership has also begun to do some housecleaning in the area of international affairs, which had been notorious in some quarters for allowing U.S. government-dominated and Cold War concerns to overshadow effective efforts to build unity between workers and unions facing common employers around the world.

The new AFL-CIO has also paid some attention to the issue of diversity in its ranks and leadership. The AFL-CIO executive council has historically been overwhelmingly white and male: counting the executive officers as members, only six of its thirty-five members were either female or persons of color, and this was an improvement over earlier times. The new executive council of fifty-four includes fourteen persons who are either minorities or women. Although the change may be primarily symbolic, it is nevertheless a welcome sign that organized labor will be making more serious efforts to represent all workers at every level of the labor movement, including the leadership level. The creation of a new Working Women's Department is a similarly hopeful sign.

But perhaps the most persistent theme of the new AFL-CIO leadership is the need to increase massively the size of the labor movement. Organizing the unorganized is the top priority. Gone are the days when organized labor's top leader could say, "Why should we worry about organizing groups of people who do not want to be organized? If they prefer to have others speak for them and make the decisions which affect their lives without effective participation on their part, that is their right. . . . Frankly, I used to worry about the membership, about the size of the membership. But quite a few years ago, I just stopped worrying about it, because to me it doesn't make any difference," as then AFL-CIO president George Meany put it in 1972 (*U.S. News and World Report,* Feb. 21, 1972; quoted in Edsall 1984).

In February 1996 the AFL-CIO Executive Council established an "organizing fund" of $20 million to spend over the next year and a half. The money was used to provide assistance and funding to leverage an even bigger commitment from national member unions and their locals in major organizing drives. Unions in the recent past have spent less than 5 percent of their budget on organizing activities. The new AFL-CIO leadership wants this to be increased to around 30 percent.

In addition to gaining more resources, the goal is to use them more strategically. Rather than acting like a collection of individual unions, the labor movement would combine resources and personnel, strategically target industries and geographic areas, and develop comprehensive campaigns.

Both the massive increase in resources and the new joint strategic methods would require major changes within the unions comprising the AFL-CIO. Yet the federation has very few formal powers; national unions are completely autonomous on virtually all matters. The balkanized U.S. labor movement will face considerable obstacles in achieving the necessary consensus to carry out the needed coordination.

The labor movement is also groping toward a vague consensus that organized labor needs to reach out to the American public in new ways, ally itself more effectively with other popular forces and segments of the society, develop a prominent and powerful role for itself in the reorganized work systems sweeping the country, project a vision and role for itself in society that speaks to the goals and needs of workers, and link up with labor movements around the world to confront globalized markets and transnational corporations. Yet the further one probes the specifics of this consensus, if consensus it is, the murkier it becomes. Exactly *how* is the labor movement to accomplish those goals? Are the constraints primarily internal or external? What organizational, programmatic, ideological, or internal cultural shifts are needed?

This book attempts to explore hard questions of this nature. The authors are all knowledgeable observers of the labor movement; most are participants. All have devoted considerable attention to the details of organized labor's current predicament, giving their writings a depth that is often missing in more superficial glosses on the state of labor.

Which Direction for Organized Labor? is divided into four sections. Part 1 consists of an essay analyzing the overall state of the labor movement in the late 1990s. The sections that follow address issues that appear to be in descending order of importance to the present top leadership of organized labor. Part 2 contains three essays on the issue that is widely conceded to be the number one priority of the AFL-CIO: organization of the unorganized. Following this, part 3 contains four essays on issues that appear to be of medium importance to the AFL-CIO: rebuilding a grassroots presence in local communities and reaching out to allies, both domestic and international. Finally, part 4 contains three essays looking at an issue that is getting much less attention from AFL-CIO leaders: internal transformation of the practices and cultures of unions themselves.

Because the essays are serious in-depth studies of their subject matter, the interconnection of these three issues becomes readily apparent. It is doubtful that the labor movement will be able massively to organize the unorganized (part 2) unless it builds strong bonds within local communities, develops local political and institutional power, and creates strong bonds with workers across borders (part 3). While it attempts the above two tasks, the labor movement may need to pay greater attention to its own internal dynamics, working to develop a culture that is far more inclusive, democratic, and activist than is presently the case in most unions (part 4).

Thus, the essays in this book aim to deepen the discussion and debate over "which direction for organized labor" is best. They aim to constructively criticize past practices, review and analyze current changes, and propose directions for the future which build on the best of current trends and overcome present deficiencies.

One of the contributors sent a short note with his essay stating that he hoped the collective authorial answer to the question embodied in the title of this book would be "Forward!" Whether these essays do help provide a way "forward" for the labor movement is up to the reader to decide. They are indeed intended to provide a fuller understanding of today's labor movement and thoughtful ideas on how it can proceed "forward."

BIBLIOGRAPHY

Brody, David. 1993. "The Uses of Industrial Power II: Political Action." Pp. 199–241 in *Workers in Industrial America*. New York: Oxford University Press.
———. 1994. "The Future of the Labor Movement in Historical Perspective." *Dissent* (Winter): 57–66.
Chaison, Gary. 1996. *Union Mergers in Hard Times: The View from Five Countries*. Ithaca, N.Y.: ILR/Cornell University Press.
Craver, Charles B. 1995. *Can Unions Survive?* New York: New York University Press.
Craypo, Charles. 1990. "The Decline in Union Bargaining Power." Pp. 3–44 in *U.S. Labor Relations, 1945–1989: Accommodation and Conflict*, ed. Bruce Nissen. New York: Garland.

Edsall, Thomas. 1984. *The New Politics of Inequality.* New York: Norton.

Freeman, Richard. 1992. "Is Declining Unionization of the U.S. Good, Bad, or Irrelevant?" Pp. 143–69 in *Unions and Economic Competitiveness,* ed. Larry Mishel and Paula Voos. Armonk, N.Y.: M. E. Sharpe.

Goldfield, Michael. 1987. *The Decline of Organized Labor in the United States.* Chicago: University of Chicago Press.

Harrison, Bennett, and Barry Bluestone. 1988. *The Great U-turn: Corporate Restructuring and the Polarizing of America.* New York: Basic Books.

Kochan, Thomas, Harry Katz, and Robert McKersie. 1994. *The Transformation of American Industrial Relations.* Ithaca, N.Y.: ILR/Cornell University Press.

Moberg, David. 1989. "Hard Times for Labor." *Dissent* (Summer): 323–32.

———. 1995. "Heeding the Call." *In These Times* (November 13): 2–22.

Moody, Kim. 1988. *An Injury to All.* New York: Verso.

Nissen, Bruce, ed. 1990. *U.S. Labor Relations, 1945–1989: Accommodation and Conflict.* New York: Garland.

Robinson, J. Gregg. 1988. "American Unions in Decline: Problems and Prospects." *Critical Sociology* 15, no. 1 (Spring): 33–56.

Seybold, Peter. 1990. "American Labor at the Crossroads: Political Resurgence or Continued Decline?" Pp. 45–90 in *U.S. Labor Relations, 1945–1989: Accommodation and Conflict,* ed. Bruce Nissen. New York: Garland.

"Unity Declaration—International Union, UAW, International Association of Machinists, United Steel Workers of America, July 27, 1995." 1995. P. 3 in *UAW Washington Report* (August 25).

Voos, Paula, ed. 1994. *Contemporary Collective Bargaining in the Private Sector.* Madison, Wisc.: Industrial Relations Research Association.

I

THE STATE OF THE
LABOR MOVEMENT

1

THE U.S. LABOR MOVEMENT FACES THE TWENTY-FIRST CENTURY

David Moberg

S omething ominous happened on the road to the twenty-first century. Since the early 1970s, with only scattered protest and fragmented acknowledgment, the balance of power in American society has shifted in favor of business and away from workers. Despite opinion leaders' studious avoidance of any suggestion that social class plays a role in American life, this shift is arguably the most important change in American society during this period, notwithstanding other momentous developments such as the rising status of women and the "information revolution."

The decline of American unions is both a major cause and a major effect of this shift, which has played out across many arenas in ways that are both brutal and direct as well as oblique and subtle. The result of this growing imbalance of power is not simply wage stagnation, rising inequality, and a deterioration of both blue- and white-collar work life (longer hours, greater insecurity, heavier workloads, and more stress). It has also taken its toll on civic involvement and social cohesion, faith in government and politics, and individuals' sense of security and hope.

If the balance of power is to move toward workers, labor unions will have to grow both in membership and clout at the bargaining table and in politics. But just as it has taken many different pushes at different points on the body social to tilt power more decisively to business and the wealthy, it will take a counterattack on many different fronts for workers to win some advantage. Tipping the balance back slightly toward workers will require not only restoring unions but drastically transforming them. It will require not only recruiting new allies but creating a new political culture. It will require not only a more cohesive national strategy but also the formation of a meaningful global labor movement.

One of the most important victories for business as it has gained new influence has been ideological: there is now more than ever a tyranny of the marketplace, a deference to the "free market" as the most efficient and—therefore?—just means of making all decisions. The wave of "downsizing," for example, swept through corporations in the early 1990s despite widespread anxiety and serious doubts about its ultimate wisdom in large part because it was depicted as the unchallengeable verdict of "the market." Government, if it is not privatized, is supposed to become "market-friendly." That has often resulted in less rigorous enforcement of environmental or safety regulations, even though in many cases government protection of health and safety should have been made less bureaucratic and strengthened (for example, relying more heavily on mandatory worker safety committees to enforce workplace safety or promoting pollution prevention in redesigned factories and machinery rather than regulating emissions of exhaust pipes at the end).

This celebration of the market deliberately conceals the power relationships behind what seem to be simple exchanges of money for goods and services. It ignores the ways in which markets create and reinforce inequities of wealth, income, and power, and it denies the importance of government in structuring markets themselves. As Robert Kuttner notes about financial markets, even "this purest of all markets is unavoidably reliant on the state"[1]—for printing money, maintaining its value, reducing unnecessary and systemically threatening risk, and maintaining essential levels of trust, for example.

Re-creation of a social movement on behalf of workers would necessarily challenge the market dictatorship as well as the abuse of power by corporations and private investors. Such a movement would have to argue, once again, that workers are not simple commodities but rather people with rights that take precedence over market dictates. Whatever the merits of "the market," it is a tool—one among many institutions—for accomplishing social goals, not an end in itself. A new movement on behalf of workers would also have to demand greater democracy at work (including inside workers' own organizations, like unions) as well as in society. Over the long term, the battle for power will not be simply a question of whether unions can recruit members, strike without workers losing their jobs, or win better contracts. Rather, it will be a battle of ideas about what kind of society Americans want to inhabit.

The election of John Sweeney, Richard Trumka, and Linda Chavez-Thompson to the leadership of the AFL-CIO in October 1995 signaled a new turn for the labor movement. Many U.S. labor leaders, especially at the AFL-CIO, had long denied unions faced a crisis, even as the union share of the workforce dropped from 35 to 15 percent. When they began to recognize there was a problem, they had no strategy for revival but diffidently proffered a grab bag of potentially useful tactics, some rearguard defensive maneuvers, and an almost pathetic plea for employer cooperation, which was mainly ignored or rebuffed except when it could be exploited for management's ends.

Sweeney, who emerged from a very conventional union environment but proved supportive of risk taking and innovation as president of the Service Employees International Union, quickly brought in many impressive new staff members at the AFL-CIO and assumed a higher public profile than his predecessors. Within his first year he launched a variety of new programs, many of which drew on the most successful new ideas in the labor movement over the past decade. Most important, he committed the AFL-CIO to help spark a new wave of organizing and, despite continuing close ties to the Democratic Party, launched an independent labor political effort to educate workers about political issues and to frame the debate (most notably the multifaceted assertion that "America Needs a Raise"). But the task ahead is monumental, requiring even under the best conditions decades of hard work.

If the labor movement has a prayer for salvation, it must recognize that its overall aim has to be reversing the current growing imbalance of power between workers and employers. Cooperation with management, for example, is a secondary matter; if and when it increases workers' power, then it may be advisable, but workers in most cases first need much more power before cooperation can serve their ends. Similarly, militant but conventional strikes may be necessary and can be turned into rallying points for workers generally, but strikes in some cases actually weaken workers' hand. Building unions and winning contracts certainly are essential for winning more power, but different forms of worker organization, such as legally mandated safety committees, minority unions without official recognition, and broad-based associations of workers, need to be considered as part of an overall strategy. Unions can't survive as institutions without dues-paying members, but unions will never flourish if they are seen as working only for those members—or, worst of all, only for their leaders. Internal union politics often press leaders to assume a narrow focus, promoting the welfare of existing members or one's own union, for example. But union leaders must both adopt the outlook and make the case to their members and the general public that unions are seeking power to secure the rights of all workers. Assuming this broader social mandate not only puts unions on moral high ground, it also gives them, consequently, greater social and political power, which in the long run benefits members as well. In the 1970s and early 1980s, after unions had increased the differential between union and nonunion pay through its efforts to protect members' wages from the ravages of inflation, labor could be portrayed more successfully, albeit unfairly, as a special interest. As nonunion workers felt they had less in common with workers in unions and as employers saw increased financial advantage in fighting unionization, unionized workers became more vulnerable.

Workers in the United States have rarely had much power as a class, and for more than a century, employers in this country have typically been far more antiunion than in most of the advanced industrial countries. The period after World War II was an anomaly: the CIO organizing drive, New Deal support for labor, the wartime labor peace agreements, and the postwar boom yielded a peak level of labor membership. Labor's new affinity with the Democratic Party forged in the Roosevelt era reinforced the power that unions had in key sectors. Unions also benefited in many industries from U.S. postwar economic supremacy, a de facto protection from competition by the relative geographical isolation of the U.S. market, and regulation or oligopoly in key, heavily unionized industries.

Unions still had to fight for contractual gains, which were often replicated in nonunion businesses, but they were rarely attacked as institutions, especially if they disavowed political radicalism. Though some unions nurtured a broad commitment to social justice, there was a strong tendency toward business or insurance unionism. The union offered protection and a bigger paycheck but expected little of members and often did not tolerate members who were outspoken. The economic pie was growing, and unions helped the size of the workers' piece keep pace with the overall economy.

Workers continued to post gains during the 1960s, when war budget deficits reduced unemployment, and government took steps to reduce poverty and increase the "social wage," especially for the elderly. But by the early 1970s U.S. economic hegemony was slipping. There was new competition from Europe and Japan, and two Organization of Petroleum Exporting Countries (OPEC) oil shocks during the decade drove up inflation. Corporations felt a profit squeeze from both, as well as from demands by unionized workers, who resisted the erosion of their real wages by oil-induced inflation.

Businesses began to fight back, especially against unions. They began exploiting professional "union busters" to stymie organizing. Even big companies with a history of dealing with unions joined in the successful effort to block labor law reform in the late 1970s. With encouragement from President Reagan's actions against the air controllers union in 1981, they began using or threatening strikebreaking with permanent replacements.

Federal Reserve policies to break inflation, combined with Reagan's deficits, drove up interest rates and the value of the dollar. The triple whammy of deep recession, an overvalued dollar, and increased competition, including growing imports from very low-wage companies, overwhelmed many companies in the traditionally unionized manufacturing industries. They demanded concessions, collapsed, or fled the country.

Indeed, many American companies had already become transnational, producing overseas not only for foreign markets but for import into the United States. During the 1980s the manufacturers who remained in the United States automated heavily, cut workforces, pushed workers harder, and weakened contracts. The net loss of about 1.2 million goods-producing jobs in the 1980s weakened the bargaining power of workers in those industries and forced many new or displaced workers into lower-paying, less unionized service jobs.

At the same time, workers were under political assault. More affluent workers, pushed into higher tax brackets by inflation and an increasingly regressive tax system, were often divided from poor workers, but especially from the nonworking poor on welfare. Poor workers were often the victims, as Republicans, with some Democratic help, shredded the social safety net. For many of them that net, like the shrinking minimum wage, also served as a floor to the market. But even better-paid workers suffered as government regulation of business and enforcement of workplace laws was weakened and as Federal Reserve Board preoccupation with inflation kept unemployment unnecessarily high.

The clearest sign that workers were losing emerges in the statistics on wage stagnation and inequality. From 1947 to 1973 the earnings (hourly or weekly) of the average production worker grew by more than 2 percent per year; after 1973 that worker's earnings stagnated, then fell at a rate of about .7 percent per year. From 1977 to 1989, 70 percent of the increase in national income went to the most affluent 1 percent of the population—families taking in roughly $600,000 or more a year. As a result, income inequality in the United States increased dramatically, faster than in other industrialized countries, even though the United States had more inequitable distribution of income than its peers even in the early 1970s. As a result, the bottom fifth of families received 5.5 percent of personal income in 1973 but only 4.2 percent in 1994, declining by nearly one-fourth. By contrast, the top fifth increased its share of income from 41.1 percent to 46.9 percent, with the lion's share of that gain going to the top 5 percent.[2]

Though there was resistance for many years to recognizing what was happening, now the debate has shifted mainly to explanations of the rising inequality and stagnation. Without entering into this dispute in detail, there is strong evidence-much of it summarized in the Economic Policy Institute's annual volume, *The State of Working America, 1996–1997*—that globalization of the economy played a major role. The ravages of globalization include import-induced manufacturing job loss, global price and wage competition, capital flight (and the threat thereof), and the resulting increased competition for the jobs that were growing in services. Especially since the 1980s there has been growing competition of less-skilled immigrants for existing jobs, and the economy has been growing at a slower pace, in part because of Federal Reserve anti-inflation policies. These macroeconomic pressures—combined with management's aggressive hostility and the unions' weak response, especially in organizing—diminished the power of unions and consequently of all workers, including those not in unions. For example, with higher unemployment, unorganized workers have less labor market leverage, but also there has been a collapse of the government floor to wages, as the minimum wage, welfare payments, and unemployment compensation have diminished in value or in breadth of coverage. The diminished threat that unorganized workers might unionize reduced their bargaining power and emboldened employers. Also, a cultural and ideological shift toward harsher, untempered marketplace values made workers more anxious about their jobs, more deferential toward demands justified in terms of competition (either foreign or domestic), and more fatalistic, undermining an informal "bargaining" that exists even in many nonunion workplaces. There was a growing legitimation of managerial greed and a declining sense of responsibility of owners and managers to their employees (which sometimes resulted from industry reorganization, as when chains like Wal-Mart with its part-time, minimum-wage workforce displaced small stores more likely to provide full-time employment).

Technology—a favorite catchall explanation among many economists—does not account well for the shift. There isn't evidence of a dramatic increase in demand for better educated workers during the past quarter century compared to the earlier decades after World War II, and wage stagnation has affected the bottom 80 to 90 percent of the workforce, surely not all of whom are "unskilled." But in many cases today, as in the past, technological changes have been used to increase managerial power. In any case, technology has certainly followed a similar path in Europe as in the United States, but inequality has not increased as rapidly.[3]

Compared to their American counterparts, European workers, whose employers have historically been less geographically mobile, have been better organized, more politically potent, buttressed with a larger social wage, and more protected from imports and competition from newly industrializing countries. Yet even there workers' past gains are now under growing attack, often under the guise of meeting new European Union fiscal goals for establishing a common currency, though French and German workers have conducted massive protests and strikes in opposition.

Whether through the invisible hand of the market or the visible fist of management, the outcome of the past quarter century has been a loss of power

26

for American workers. With strategically well-organized campaigns, workers can still organize in many cases to gain power despite globalization or sophisticated antilabor tactics of corporations: janitors can organize and raise their wages if they can control a large part of local markets, for example, or they can organize small cleaning firms by pressuring the big, image-conscious corporations that hire the janitorial contractors (as the Service Employees did in Silicon Valley). But for workers to tip the balance more in their direction, they will ultimately have to win at many different levels, from influencing federal economic policy to intervening in securities markets and corporate governance debates or setting the rules of the new global economy.

Unions today are groping for new strategies on three major fronts—organizing, workplace action, and politics. There is no agreed formula for what must be done, but there is a new willingness in many quarters to take risks, to try new methods, and to dream more expansively about what is possible, as well as to recognize how much is urgently necessary.

Yet there is only a fumbling acknowledgment about how much the culture and structures of "real existing unionism" must change. Unions must become more organizations of the members, not just for the members. But even many militant union leaders seem distrustful of democracy or see it as far less important than winning victories. Democracy, of course, is no cure-all and can be troublesome. Also, it is likely that except for extraordinary circumstances only a minority of members will ever be extremely active in their union. But it is absolutely crucial to expand that minority, continually recruiting new activists. With greater membership participation and democracy, unions gain legitimacy among their members and the general public. The public is far more sympathetic to workers vis-à-vis corporations than it is to unions, and much of the skepticism about unions reflects a judgment that unions aren't democratic.[4] More important, unions gain power with democracy and participation: members are more likely to support union actions, develop a class-conscious politics, organize new members, and even represent themselves at work if they feel involved in a union that is accountable to them.

Nowhere is that more important than in the task of organizing. The union share of the workforce has shrunk for many reasons—employer hostility and changes in the occupational structure, for example—but organized labor itself bears much of the responsibility. Most unions simply have not devoted enough of their resources to organizing for the past several decades, nor have they learned how to organize effectively in a hostile climate and a new workforce. By one estimate, unions need to be spending about $300 million a year more than they recently have spent on organizing simply to keep their current share.[5] In

27

recent years most unions have spent less than 5 percent of their budgets on organizing.

The new AFL-CIO leadership has boosted its budget for organizing and for the Organizing Institute, which trains union members and young student sympathizers to be organizers, helps local unions develop organizing strategies, and encourages exchange of ideas about what works among union organizers and elected officials. More important, since the AFL-CIO money (about $20 million for the first two years) is inevitably minuscule compared to the need and will be used mainly to leverage greater efforts by individual unions, Sweeney and his organizing director, Richard Bensinger, founder of the Organizing Institute, have challenged unions to devote at least 30 percent of their resources to organizing. In most unions, where locals control the vast majority of resources, reaching that goal will mean restructuring the unions and redirecting local leaders, a task now under way. Some unions are sitting on vast, underutilized assets: unused strike funds, lavish buildings.[6] But in most cases, unions will have to spend more time and money on organizing and less on servicing members and contracts. Yet in order to do that, they will have to win members' support for organizing. They will have to involve members both as volunteer organizers and as shop stewards and activists capable of solving problems on the job with less reliance on union staff. The new model of union organizing relies heavily on volunteer member organizers calling on unorganized workers in their homes and building a core of union supporters who begin acting like a union from the start of the campaign. Those tactics not only win more frequently than old-style, less engaged organizing, they also build a stronger labor movement.[7]

Union strategists plan to target large metropolitan areas, specific industries (like hotels and tourism) or a major chain (like Wal-Mart) to take organizing to the new scale needed for a labor union revival. In 1997 the labor movement united behind an effort by the Farm Workers to organize California strawberry pickers, and both the Service Employees and a group of building trades unions joined the highly successful Culinary Workers in a campaign to make Las Vegas a heavily unionized city. Yet organizing, especially of industrial workers, increasingly must also be global. The Union of Needletrades, Industrial and Textile Employees (UNITE) and the union-backed National Labor Committee have targeted image-conscious apparel retailers, like the Gap, Disney, and the Kathie Lee Gifford line of clothes, to support union organizing and higher wages for workers in Central America. The Teamsters and the United Electrical Workers union have given support to organizing by independent unions in Mexico. By linking international labor rights, especially the right to organize, to the liberalization of international trade, unions in the

United States and other rich countries will over the long run help unions in the developing countries organize (and ultimately help themselves). Likewise, demanding and enforcing codes of conduct for corporations' global operations can strengthen the cause of worldwide labor organizing.

There will be little point to organizing—and little prospect of succeeding—if workers cannot win better wages and working conditions and secure their rights on the job. Yet as corporate power and capital mobility have grown, competition has intensified, and the political and legal status of workers has weakened, unions have had to find new ways to fight. Strikes in the United States are now as rare as they have ever been and even then often futile, partly because of the ease—and legality—of using replacement workers, more pungently known on the picket line as scabs.

Unions have made considerable progress in using other tactics. At the workplace, workers often hold demonstrations or wear red shirts and buttons to show solidarity and, even more powerfully, "work to rule" or "run the plant backwards," effectively slowing down work while avoiding legal barriers to formal slowdowns. Unions also engage in corporate, or strategic, campaigns that spread the battle to the target company's customers, suppliers, or financial allies, increase its regulatory and political problems, or hurt its public image.

In the most successful cases, unions recruit public support and organizational allies to turn a labor dispute into a community battle over social justice. Jobs with Justice and some other local union coalitions work to build cross-union solidarity so that workers are not isolated in their efforts. Most notably with Justice for Janitors, the Service Employees campaign to gain recognition and rights for janitors in big commercial buildings, unions use civil disobedience to disrupt business and even the community, making worker rights a broader political issue.

Especially in fighting transnational companies, global union solidarity has become ever more critical for workers in both rich and poor countries. Locked-out workers at the Ravenswood Aluminum Corporation in West Virginia found union allies in both East and West Europe who were willing to put pressure on the secretive power behind management, fugitive financier Marc Rich. At the small-town Illinois factory of Trailmobile, a maker of big truck trailers bought by a politically influential Indonesian family empire, the union linked up with Australian unionists and international critics of Indonesia's invasion of East Timor and successfully pressured managers who had locked out employees.

In a step toward global unionism, the long-established but typically weak international trade union secretariats, worldwide alliances of unions in particular industries, have become more active in recent years. The International

Union of Food Workers, for example, helped force Heineken and Carlsberg breweries out of Burma, where labor and democratic rights were suppressed, and it fought to strengthen the transnational corporation worker councils mandated by the European Union's Maastricht agreement. Taking advantage of publicity about Pakistani children sewing soccer balls, the International Union of Textile Workers negotiated with the world soccer federation, Fédération Internationale de Football Association (FIFA), to prohibit child labor and guarantee worker rights at all officially sanctioned contractors. Walter Reuther once dreamed that the International Metalworkers Federation councils for Ford or General Motors workers could negotiate on behalf of workers worldwide. Very gingerly, unions are moving in that direction, with the first steps involving better communication about strategies and more support of each other's struggles.

Labor unions have always had to turn to allies to make political gains, but the old alliances are growing feeble and feckless. Even in western Europe, labor and social democratic parties are distancing themselves more and more from their union base. The marriage of labor unions and the Democrats in the United States has long been dysfunctional. Yet out of inertia, nostalgia, and the realistic calculation of the lesser evil as a guardian of some past legislative gains, organized labor continued to put its money on the donkey, even if the donkey offered a braying laugh and a kick in return as it trotted off with a businessman bearing a large carrot.

Under the Sweeney regime, organized labor increased its political spending dramatically in the 1996 campaign. Rather than relying as heavily as in the past on contributions to candidates and party committees, unions said they would spend more money educating members (and incidentally other voters) and building long-lasting networks of activists who could continue to hold elected officials accountable. Though it's a legal way to circumvent campaign finance law, the strategy reflected a sober reality. In the 1994 elections unions did a poor job of turning out their members and getting them to vote Democratic, and they discovered that members trusted information on issues more than calls for party loyalty or even candidate endorsements. Labor decided to try to define the agenda, to force candidates from both parties to respond to its issues, which were typically broad working-class concerns, such as Medicare, pension security, and raising the minimum wage.

In a very tentative way, labor was becoming more politically independent, though unions still overwhelmingly supported Democrats and refrained from raising issues—like the trade policies that had been the center of hard-fought, divisive battles earlier or the continuing rise of income inequality under Clinton—that might embarrass Democrats. It was a mild version of the strategy advocated by the new Labor Party, which at least in its initial years was designed to put issues important to workers at the center of the political stage, not to run candidates.

At this point, even discounting the enormous structural obstacles to developing a meaningful new party in the United States, the labor movement is too weak on its own and lacks sufficient support among allies to break decisively with the Democrats. It would be even more isolated and exposed. Besides, there is a large bloc of Democrats, such as the Progressive Caucus, that labor unions would want to support in any case. But the labor movement does have a lot of freedom to be much more critical of Democrats, to support challengers to incumbents (either within Democratic primaries or through a vehicle like the New Party), and to develop a prolabor, progressive bloc of both voters and organizations that carry a political big stick, either to influence the Democrats or support alternatives. The danger is that the pragmatic pressures to support Democratic leaders, either in the White House or Congress, will swamp the more tentative labor initiatives to develop a more independent base of political power.

In any case, labor unions must undertake a fundamental political education chore. Most workers simply do not have a clear, simple framework to understand and analyze the world around them, according to Peter D. Hart Research political analyst Guy Molyneux, who conducted focus group research for the AFL-CIO. The old sentiments of labor solidarity and simple Keynesianism that had served well from the 1930s through the late 1960s began to fall apart, victims of many social changes—racial conflict and backlash, splits between the youthful new left and labor over the Vietnam War, and the ascendance of new movements, such as feminism and environmentalism, that often neglected or superseded considerations of class. Post–World War II prosperity left unions and workers ill-prepared to contend with the new global economy that emerged in the early 1970s. Pushed into higher tax brackets, at the same time as the tax system overall became more regressive, more affluent workers could be recruited to antitax, antigovernment initiatives. Then they became the public's villains, the reason that American companies couldn't compete. Cut off in many cases because of their own parochial narrowness from potential allies, they were more easily victimized. Yet workers themselves were often confused about who the bad guys were in the new global economy.

If the labor movement hopes to regain political influence, then it will have to convincingly tell its story about why there is wage stagnation, insecurity, and growing inequality and what government and other nonprofit organizations, like unions, can do to make the economy serve ordinary people. It will have to talk about corporate responsibility, economic democracy, worker rights, and the proper balance of national self-interest and international solidarity with other workers.

One of the foremost tasks is to develop an inclusive sense of class that demonstrates the common aspirations and interests of most working people. For example, with few exceptions, unions did nothing to fight the capitulation of President Clinton and most Democrats on Republican-style welfare reform. Yet, in the aftermath of welfare repeal, labor might be able to redress the destructive divisions between the jobless poor, the working poor, and more affluent workers. It has a big stake in developing a common agenda for universal health care, continued education and retraining, widely available child care and early schooling, and guaranteed jobs for everyone who "plays by the rules" and completes high school and subsequent training programs.

More basically, unions must make worker rights the human rights and social justice issue of the decades ahead, as Sweeney indicated in his acceptance speech on his election as president of the AFL-CIO. That involves not only educating workers about what their rights are—or should be—and how to enjoy them but also making work and class issues important in other social movements and among "middle-class" supporters. Union Summer, which recruited more than a thousand students for three-week episodes of working with unions in the summer of 1996, was important less for the work the students did than for the change in consciousness it helped create. Partly unions and workers were energized by these enthusiastic young people coming to their cause, but more important, the students took back to their campuses and their lives a new sense of social class and economic justice that is likely to influence their work, even if they never work for labor unions in the future.

If unions want to tip the balance of power back in favor of workers, then it will help if workers and the public understand that there is a class division between those who have power by virtue of their wealth, ownership of resources, and management of large institutions and those who work for them. The issue is not simply dividing the pie; it is also deciding how the pie is to be baked. Neither issue can be left to the beneficence of the powerful or the blind injustice of the powerful or the blind injustice of the market; both require a new democracy of work and economic life, the proper goals of a potentially revitalized labor movement.

NOTES

1. Robert Kuttner, *Everything For Sale* (New York: A. A. Knopf, 1997), 159.
2. Lawrence Mishel, Jared Bernstein, and John Schmitt, *The State of Working America, 1996–1997* (Washington, D.C.: Economic Policy Institute, 1996); Paul Krugman,

Peddling Prosperity (New York: Norton, 1994), 138; "Workers Take It On the Chin," *U.S. News and World Report,* Jan. 22, 1996; Anthony Atkinson, Lee Rainwater, and Timothy Smeedling, "Income Distribution in Advanced Economies: Evidence from the Luxembourg Income Study," *Luxembourg Income Study Working Paper No. 120* (Oct. 1995).

3. Mishel, Bernstein, and Schmitt, 92.

4. Greer, Margolis, Mitchell, Burns & Associates, Inc., "Being Heard," prepared for the AFL-CIO, Mar. 21, 1994.

5. Labor Research Association, *The American Labor Yearbook 1993* (New York: Labor Research Association, 1993), 6.

6. Jonathan Tasini, *The Edifice Complex* (New York: Labor Research Association, 1995).

7. Kate Bronfenbrenner and Tom Juravich, "Union Tactics Matter: The Impact of Union Tactics on Certification Elections, First Contracts and Membership Rates," working paper for the Institute for the Study of Labor Organizations, George Meany Center for Labor Studies, Silver Spring, Md., 1995; Virginia R. Diamond, *Organizing Guide for Local Unions* (Silver Spring, Md.: Labor's Heritage Press, 1992).

II

ORGANIZING THE UNORGANIZED

2

ORGANIZING LABOR IN AN ERA OF CONTINGENT WORK AND GLOBALIZATION

Eve S. Weinbaum

The 1980s were not kind to the labor movement. Changes in the structure of the economy, a conservative trend in American politics, and the increased reach and power of transnational corporations all combined to undermine the gains won by workers in previous decades. As the AFL-CIO Committee on the Evolution of Work acknowledged in a 1985 report, "the magnitude and velocity of these destabilizing changes" presented serious challenges to working people and their organizations (AFL-CIO 1985, 5). Unions have suffered from regional and sectoral shifts in employment patterns, weaker labor laws and enforcement of workers' rights, political powerlessness, and increasingly negative public opinion toward unions. Despite many workers' aggressive efforts to fight for their rights, shifts in the political economy have led to aggregate losses for the labor movement. As a result, the proportion of American workers belonging to a union fell from 35 percent in 1954 to 18 percent in 1985 (AFL-CIO 1985, 5), and the numbers have continued to drop into the 1990s.

It is true that unions still possess a strong base and represent millions of workers, but recent trends do not provide cause for optimism. Not only have unions lost members at a remarkable pace, nearly every major political reform supported by organized labor during the 1980s and even the 1990s (under the supposedly friendly Clinton administration) was defeated. Deindustrialization and downsizing have continued apace, and large corporations have been allowed to move freely between nations, states, and even cities, in search of the most generous economic development incentives—at the workers' and taxpayers' expense. Real wages of industrial workers have consistently fallen during the 1980s, and benefits are eroding even more quickly. International accords like the North American Free Trade Agreement (NAFTA) and the General Agreement on Tariffs and Trade (GATT), unanimously condemned by labor groups, have been enthusiastically embraced by Republicans and Democrats alike. Public opinion polls show that labor is considered a "special-interest group" about which most Americans—working people themselves—are more cynical than they are about big business. In the workplace, in Congress, and in communities, labor's influence has clearly diminished over the past two decades.

Analysts from both outside and within the labor movement have placed responsibility on the shoulders of the labor movement itself, condemning union leaders for neglecting organizing and eschewing aggressive political action. While that argument has some merit, this essay will demonstrate that many of the most important changes in the labor environment reflect international political and economic trends and powerful interests and cannot be blamed on organized labor itself. More important, the losses suffered by unions certainly do not indicate that the labor movement is incapable of renewal. Indeed, I will argue that there are many signs that conditions are ripe for resurgence. It is clear, however, that the time has come to consider tackling real, marked changes in labor's strategy. The labor movement as a whole must be able to admit that changing economic and political systems demand new strategies and a new plan. The most important question, as organized labor prepares to enter the twenty-first century, is "What kind of organizing program can strengthen workers' ability to control their own lives, improve the conditions of their work, and gain a larger share in the profits they help to create?"

Changes in the Economic Landscape

Since the 1970s, economists and policy makers have been documenting dramatic shifts in patterns of employment across the United States. In some ways, recent changes reflect an older, continuing pattern of "deindustrialization," geographic shifts, and the economic upheavals resulting from the decline of manufacturing and related industries. But there are signs of new patterns too, which may be even more devastating to organized labor and to workers all over the world. Two of these are particularly important and present good case studies of the challenges to unionism in the late twentieth century. First is the shift from permanent or full-time to contingent or part-time employment. Second is the globalization of the economy—in the form of both the increasing mobility of capital and the industrialization of developing countries, encouraged by international institutions like the International Monetary Fund (IMF) and World Bank, and treaties like NAFTA and GATT.

These changes have especially serious consequences for working and unemployed people and present the greatest challenge for the labor movement today.

The Rise of Contingent Work

Beginning in the early 1980s, part-time employment began to account for an increasing proportion of employment in all sectors of the economy. The most visible segment of the contingent workforce, the temporary services industry, grew explosively throughout the 1980s, expanding ten times as fast as overall employment. The number of temporary workers grew by almost 400 percent between 1983 and 1993, and the total payroll of temporary help companies increased by almost 3000 percent between 1970 and 1992 (Parker 1994; Appelbaum 1992). New methods of hiring nonpermanent employees grew in equal proportion. Some firms created their own, in-house temporary agencies or day-labor pools. Others subcontracted their hiring, paying agencies to supply them with the number of employees needed each day or week. And "temps" began to do much more than only office work. For the first time, temporary work took hold in manufacturing industries. Most industrial firms began to rely on part-time workers to do some piece of the work, and some employers replaced entire assembly lines with subcontracted casual labor forces.[1] For firms, this trend means greater profit margins. For workers, it often means a permanent place among the working poor.

This shift, especially prevalent in low-income areas of the country and in low-wage industries, has been independent of the health of the economy as a whole. Until the 1990s, employment continued its path of expansion begun in the 1950s. Although many observers remarked on the uneven nature of the recovery since the early 1980s, official unemployment rates remained remarkably low and total employment consistently increased. But closer examination of the facts contradicted this pattern of growth. Although more jobs were available, and more workers were working longer hours, expansions in employment were increasingly found in temporary jobs that provided lower wages, no benefits, no advancement opportunities, and no security. This pattern was especially pronounced in "sunbelt" states. In Tennessee, for example, deindustrialization in the 1980s led to the loss of hundreds of thousands of the best manufacturing jobs in the state. During the same period, contingent work opportunities increased over 420 percent (Gaventa and Wiley 1987; Phillips 1991).

Exact figures on contingent work in the U.S. economy are hard to find. Debate continues among economists and policy analysts on the magnitude of the trend; estimates depend upon differing definitions of contingent work and data that are not readily available. Some, for example, include subcontracted work, which may be full-time but impermanent and without benefits. Whatever the extent of contingent work, economists agree that the trend is here to stay. For most of these workers, part-time work is not a choice but an involuntary condition of employment; part-time work was the only work available. Voluntary part-time employment has actually declined since 1990, and involuntary part-time employment has accounted for the entire increase in the contingent economy (Appelbaum 1992).

Working and unemployed women and people of color suffer most from these trends. Women make up about two-thirds of the "temporary help supply" industry, as calculated by the Bureau of Labor Statistics, and more than twice as many women as men work part-time. Women and people of color are disproportionately represented within the temporary workforce—nearly double their percentages in the total workforce (Belous 1989). This correlation is most often cited by policy makers as evidence that reducing work hours has personal benefits for women and their children, as well as social benefits ranging from energy conservation because of fewer trips to work to more leisure for education, recreation, community service, and family responsibilities (Negrey 1993). But appearances are deceiving. While adult men in every age group have increased their share of part-time employment, women in the primary childbearing years of twenty-two to forty-four—the group most often assumed to be part-time workers—have decreased their rate of part-time work. In fact, studies of women with family responsibilities have shown that they are no more likely to choose temporary employment than other employees. Economists examining these data have concluded that since 1980 companies have been creating part-time jobs even though workers do not want them (Tilly 1992; Carré 1992).

As one economist concludes, "Women are taking the growing number of temp agency jobs because employers are creating more temporary positions in the fields where women typically work, and not because temporary employment better meets their flexibility needs. Rather it is the lack of bargaining power and limited employment alternatives of these workers that make this managerial strategy possible" (Appelbaum 1992, 5). As the income gap has widened, women, people of color, and workers labeled "unskilled" find it increasingly difficult to support themselves and their families. Faced with increasingly dire and unacceptable choices, they must "choose" the part-time jobs the economy has to offer. Too often, this means surviving without health or retirement benefits and living at a below-poverty wage. The only alternative, as suggested by Appelbaum's quote, is for workers to increase their "bargaining power" through collective action and to resist the apparently inexorable progression toward poverty.

The Global Economy

Another important factor in the downward spiral of wages and working conditions has been the pressure of increased international competition. "Competitiveness" in the new "global economy" is probably the most often-cited reason for companies undergoing "downsizing," "restructuring," or other processes of internal reorganization, mass firings, casualization, and concession bargaining. Corporate executives involved in cutting the workforce and reassigning production work most often argue that these changes are necessary to remain competitive in the current economic climate. If their competitors are cutting wages and benefits, subcontracting work to the lowest bidder, and basing corporate decisions on the availability of government subsidies and tax credits, it would be financial suicide not to do the same.

This has always been standard business practice. What has changed in this decade is the international dimension to this competition. Since "free-trade" policies and advancing technologies have made international production and capital mobility easier and less costly, U.S.–based firms now must consider the actions of international corporations. They must remain competitive not only with other U.S.–based manufacturers who pay minimum wage but with transnational firms paying less than this minimum hourly amount in an entire day or sometimes in a week, to workers in Mexico, Guatemala, Indonesia, the Philippines, or other developing countries.

Accordingly, the pressure of international competition and the mobility of capital bring the threat of relocation. While large, transnational corporations have long been able to expand to subsidiaries all over the world, in certain types of labor-intensive industries, the 1980s and 1990s have seen a surge in companies moving to developing countries. Unskilled production jobs are the easiest to move, as executives seek low wages, weak environmental and labor regulations, and little or no unionization. The pressures toward global reorganization, increasing corporate deregulation, and the rapid development of technologies conducive to capital mobility cause communities whose economies have depended upon labor-intensive manufacturing industries to suffer the most serious consequences of deindustrialization (Bluestone and Harrison 1982).

As with the shift to contingent work, women workers suffer the most from unchecked transnational corporate capital flight. Since companies move overseas in the first place specifically to procure a low-wage, docile workforce,

41

it is logical that they choose to hire women. In all countries, women have fewer wage-earning opportunities than men, earn less, and are often considered only supplementary income earners in their families. Managers can take advantage of this secondary status by paying women less and hiring and firing at will. For light-assembly or even service work, women are as qualified as men and are accustomed to working for lower wages in tedious, repetitive occupations. In South Korea, for example, female earnings in manufacturing in the late 1980s were 50 percent of that of males in exactly the same jobs and industries (Standing 1989). In free-trade zones throughout the developing world, where international companies have "outsourced" production work, light-assembly lines are staffed 80 to 90 percent by women.[2] The workers are also over-whelmingly young; the majority are between sixteen and twenty-five years old. Especially in industries like textiles and electronics, keen eyesight, dexterity, and physical stamina are essential. Workers over twenty-three or twenty-four are likely to be let go.

Even for the developing world's export zones, these jobs are not a stable source of economic development. When industrialization drives up wages in one area, companies routinely close up and move on to a new country. Nike, the number-one maker of sport shoes in the world, has all of its shoes made in Asia by contractors. The company has closed down twenty plants in South Korea and Taiwan and moved on to China, Mexico, and other places where wages are still low. Nike sneakers made in Indonesia cost approximately $5.60 to produce and sell in North America and Europe for up to $135. The average wage of the Indonesian girls who make Nikes, according to a 1991 survey, was 82 cents a day, or $4.92 for a six-day workweek. To promote Nike sales, by contrast, basketball star Michael Jordan is reportedly paid $20 million a year—an amount greater than the *entire* annual payroll of the factories that make the shoes (Barnet and Cavanagh 1994, 326–28).

Aside from the low cost and availability of women workers, observers have identified two other reasons for women's prominence in these factories. First, governments around the world feel less pressure to protect women work-ers than men, who are more likely to vote and to make trouble. Accordingly, in the 1980s, with the blessing of the U.S. government, many countries repealed regulations on workplace conditions, in the hope of attracting foreign investment and expanding their export sectors, and even terminated their adherence to International Labor Organization conventions for the protection of workers to which they had previously subscribed. Many stopped enforcing regulations still on the books. All of this was more possible with a workforce made up of desperate and powerless workers (Standing 1989; Barnet and Cavanagh 1994). Second, just as in the United States, women fit more easily into the "flexible" production schemes that are increasingly important to global corporations. In developing countries, this trend is even more extreme. Women work uneven hours—sometimes short shifts, sometimes all night long in buildings locked from the inside—and often take work home when asked. To refuse any of these assignments is to lose one's job.

Managers of subsidiaries in developing countries have justified their treatment of workers with claims no longer considered legitimate in the United States, precisely because popular mobilization and political pressure have led to guarantees of certain human rights. Employers, for example, justify hiring an all-woman assembly force by arguing that women have a "natural patience" and superior "manual dexterity" (Fuentes and Ehrenreich 1989). A Malaysian investment brochure declares, "Her hands are small and she works fast with extreme care. Who therefore could be better qualified by nature and inheritance to contribute to the efficiency of a bench-assembly production line than an oriental girl?" (Barnet and Cavanagh 1994; "Global Assembly Line" 1991).[3]

Managers justify frequent firings of women in their twenties, for example, by pointing out that women will quit soon anyway, to get married or have children. Transnational corporations, preferring single and childless women, routinely demand pregnancy tests of potential employees and refuse to take on the risk and expense of hiring a pregnant worker. Many firms state a clear preference for sterilized women and even offer bonuses to workers who undergo sterilization. And women workers routinely are subjected to indignities and even abuse in the workplace. An Episcopal priest from Michigan reported on the conditions in a Guatemala City *maquila* factory producing apparel for leading U.S. retailers, including the Gap and Sears: "In order to go to the bathroom, a woman needs a pass from her supervisor, which may involve sexual favors. Many women have been beaten and sexually abused. One factory [foreman] regularly beats women on the stomach every 15 days to weed out those who may be pregnant" (Barnet and Cavanagh 1994, 332).

Of course, these workers' exploitation as women is inseparable from both racial and class subjugation. Corporate executives, paying poor women a tenth of U.S. minimum wages to work and live in dangerously unhealthy circumstances, claim that the workers are thrilled with their new opportunities. One American soliciting new business for the Mexican *maquiladoras* (free-trade zone) says: "You should watch these kids going to work. You don't have any sullenness here. They smile" (Fuentes and Ehrenreich 1989, 15). Advertisements attracting American companies to move to the *maquiladora* (and, since NAFTA, to all of Mexico) tout the easy availability of willing workers and the "excellent labor relations." A primer for businesses interested in opening subsidiaries states that "from their earliest conditioning women show respect and obedience to authority, especially men. The women follow orders willingly, accept change and adjustments easily, and are considerably less demanding" (Fuentes and Ehrenreich 1989, 29–30). As an American executive in Guatemala told CBS News, "The workers here are very good. . . . American workers like a variation. But here, the people do the same thing day after day and . . . they don't mind" (quoted in Fuentes and Ehrenreich 1989, 42).

The ability of corporations to move freely in search of available, inexpensive labor has serious ramifications for American workers.[4] In many industries, especially light manufacturing, entire workforces labor under a constant threat that the company will leave if its demands are not met. Vulnerable workers, obviously, do not have the same freedom of choice. Under these conditions, workers are accepting concessions, cuts in their pay and benefits, layoffs, and transitions to segmented, part-time employment. For the individual worker and for the entire community, anything is preferable to losing all those jobs. Thus the global conditions that lead to exploitation and intolerable working conditions in developing countries have the same effect in the United States. Workers are caught in the global spiral toward lower wages and less power on the job and in the community.

BARRIERS WITHIN THE LABOR MOVEMENT

These two trends—the rapidly increasing prominence of contingent and subcontracted work, and the mobility of capital across national boundaries—have created a political and economic environment in which union organizing is more difficult than ever. Workers attempting to achieve recognition of new bargaining units or to negotiate better contracts confront companies that can credibly threaten either to subcontract their work or to move jobs overseas, in order to compete with other firms that are doing the same. Whatever the legal status of these threats, they have been very effective in thwarting unionization efforts and weakening existing collective bargaining agreements. Companies have successfully demanded wage and benefit concessions, and unions have agreed to limit their demands rather than risk a loss of work. Shifts to contingent workers and overseas production have proven formidable obstacles to local unions all over the United States.

The external challenges, however, do not mean that the labor movement must accept its powerlessness and lower its expectations. On the contrary, despite the barriers, unions have a responsibility to discover and implement new strategies that will better attain the goals of working people around the world. In order to do this, labor leaders must effectively analyze the political economy—including, but not limited to, the two trends described above—and

44

creatively design workplace-based and political organizing strategies appropriate to this evolving context. To do so requires rethinking some basic commitments and goals.

In the 1980s and early 1990s, unions responded slowly to economic and political changes, from the international level to the individual workplace. Rather than creating a proactive agenda and pushing political and private-sector leaders to respond, the labor movement was too often in the position of reacting to a set of undesirable options, and usually compromising. This was understandable, considering shifts in the economy, the failure of labor law to protect workers and to enable them to organize, and the war against unions being waged by private-sector employers in the 1980s. American unions were forced to fight not only unfair employers but also a federal government that "has done its part to encourage hostile employer actions" (AFL-CIO 1985, 11).

In this antagonistic environment, labor began to see its options as irrevocably limited by corporate power and "the economy." Most union leaders began to advocate either cooperation and compromise or technical innovations: new categories of membership, electronic media technologies, polling, more effective servicing of members. I argue that, in the long run, the labor movement suffered from this limited vision. In order to survive and grow in the political economy of the late 1990s, unions must take on a more ambitious agenda. The corporate context—shifts toward contingent labor, downsizing, and globalization—demand a strong response.

Unions cannot change international economic forces, but unions' actions—in politics and in organizing—can mitigate their effects. In particular, labor leaders in the past have paid insufficient attention to three crucial factors for labor in the global economy of the 1990s: grassroots leadership, political action, and solidarity with other groups. An examination of each principle follows.

Grassroots Leadership

In the 1980s, the labor movement's reliance on experts grew significantly. This was true of the AFL-CIO as an institution but also within many unions. Experts—including economists, academics, polling organizations, and business leaders—had a tremendous influence on organizing and policy decisions. Accordingly, the opinions of others—rank-and-file workers, activists, organizations that work with workers, or even organizers—were neglected. The people consulted on an ongoing basis were largely removed from the everyday struggles and needs of workers themselves (see, for example, AFL-CIO 1985).

This reliance on experts to tell unions what to do has serious consequences. It contradicts the spirit of the labor movement, whose success depends upon the energy, ideas, and demands of workers themselves. It suggests that workers' problems are complex, that only professionals are capable of determining their needs and preferences, and that their solutions require technical expertise. All of this is antithetical to the premise of grassroots labor organizing.

One example of the influence of expert advice is the credence given to polls. Unions of all sizes now regularly hire high-priced polling firms to study public opinion and figure out policy proposals and agendas. The AFL-CIO has led the way on polling. Its reports throughout the 1980s regularly provided information from surveys, in order to guide the labor movement in planning future campaigns (see AFL-CIO 1985). Polling, however, is based on a different set of premises from organizing. Pollsters assume that the answers workers give individually, when they are called on the telephone or visited at home, will reveal their propensity to join unions and participate in collective action. Yet any organizer would find it troubling to rely upon a poll or survey to determine workers' satisfaction with work conditions or their ability to be organized.[5] The use of polls, so prevalent in political campaigns and decision making, is in some ways the opposite of the process of organizing. Organizers, unlike pollsters, know that individuals' initial response to a question may reflect fear, powerlessness, ignorance, and/or cynicism—all of which can be overcome through collective action. The job of union leadership, in fact, is to educate workers, or to understand their fear but then to transform it into strength—not to believe that the workers' first response to a survey question is the immutable "truth."

Organizers also know that most nonunion workers have complaints about their treatment and believe that changes in their workplace could be beneficial. Workers' own ideas can therefore form the basis for an organizing campaign. Through conversations and gatherings, organizers can assess a group's coherence, anger, and strength. Polls have no way of estimating this potential. When a survey finds, therefore, that 51 percent of workers are "very satisfied" with their jobs, there is no way of knowing whether this reflects real contentment or merely a lack of other options (AFL-CIO 1985, 12–13). Indeed, since the survey also reveals that 72 percent are *not* happy with their pay or opportunities for advancement, the first number may be meaningless, from an organizer's perspective. Similarly, AFL-CIO surveys show that 65 percent of workers agree with the statement that "unions force members to go along with decisions they don't like." This would suggest a deep-seated antipathy toward unions. Yet over 80 percent of respondents believe that "unions are needed so that the legitimate complaints of workers can be heard" (AFL-CIO

1985, 13). It is hard to conclude much from these surveys. The most obvious inference is that workers have conflicting and contradictory views and questions. They can be persuaded to participate in creating an organization through which they can express their needs and meet their goals. Ironically, by asking experts to evaluate workers' opinions, the report accomplishes just the opposite.

This is part of a general undervaluing of organizing itself. The AFL-CIO itself pointed out a decade ago that there was a problem. "The costs associated with organizing are increasing while the resources available are declining," they said (AFL-CIO 1985, 11), and therefore "there must be a renewed emphasis on organizing" (AFL-CIO 1985, 27). But the organization's actions throughout the 1980s and early 1990s did not reflect the urgency of the need for organizing. Especially among those groups least represented by traditional, mainstream unions, organizing must be the first priority. Given the alarmingly high rates of reprisals for union activism—and the organized and sophisticated resistance by employers to any hint of organizing—the role of organizers is more important than ever before. Organizers must be more than mere catalysts for union drives. They must be true leaders, imparting confidence, skills, and vision in workers otherwise too intimidated to stand up for themselves. Leadership means believing that even the most oppressed and depressed workers, who do not believe they deserve better or will ever get it, can transcend their fear and hopelessness and achieve respect through collective action.

Finally, more attention must be given to improving leadership structures within unions. Members need more than "opportunities" to participate. Leaders must consider it their main responsibility to identify, bring forward, and train new leaders at every level. Rank-and-file members must be pushed to accept greater responsibility for strategy and organizing programs within local and regional unions. The success of union organizing staffs must be judged not only on their records of winning elections but also on their ability to develop local leadership that can continually organize. None of this has been a focus of the labor movement. Unions have focused more on negotiating contracts than on enlisting members themselves to take ownership in the union. Of course, both of these are essential. But more attention needs to be given to the ongoing leadership development and empowerment of workers. For if members are not taught and encouraged to take leadership in the workplace and beyond, any gains won by excellent union representation will surely be ephemeral. Unions will only have the power to challenge dominant elites if rank-and-file workers feel responsible for the union and are able to mobilize their brothers and sisters. More than representation, this requires real avenues for participation and involvement.

Politics

In addition to grassroots organizing and leadership, the labor movement must focus its energies on political action. The global economy of the 1990s is a political phenomenon, aided and abetted by political decisions and nondecisions, including deregulation, nonenforcement of protective labor laws, NAFTA and GATT, and a variety of trade policies. In this context, political organizing assumes a critical importance. If unions are to represent their members' interests, it is no longer enough to focus exclusively on shop-floor activity. The decisions that affect workers' lives are being made in the statehouse and in the halls of Congress, and the labor movement must learn to exercise influence in these realms as well.

Unions have not yet risen to this challenge. One of the most ironic contradictions of the labor movement in the 1980s and 1990s has been its aversion to conflict. The AFL-CIO argued in 1985, for example, that "confrontation and conflict are wasteful and that a cooperative approach to solving shared present and future problems is desirable" (AFL-CIO 1985, 18). Its surveys proved that workers were opposed to an "adversarial collective bargaining relationship" (18). Unions, they said, therefore should attempt to resolve conflict more quietly, through mediation when possible, or even by deciding *not* "to establish a comprehensive set of hard and fast terms and conditions of employment" (18). The AFL-CIO suggested that perhaps traditional union tactics—strikes, job actions, boycotts, demonstrations—were unreasonable and excessive. Official labor organizations presumably would be wise to renounce such unseemly behavior and instead endorse harmony and teamwork. Compromise was the word of the day.

This language echoes contemporary rhetoric of teamwork and collaboration between workers and management, so popular among the AFL-CIO leadership and many international unions in the 1980s (Parker and Slaughter 1988). This strategy does not represent much of an innovation for organized labor, and it is debatable whether it is a winning program for workers in today's climate. The irony of the drive for compromise is that not even the AFL-CIO seemed convinced that it would provide an answer to the needs of working people. When considering the possibilities for revitalization in the labor movement, the very same report that eschewed confrontation invoked the labor movement of the 1930s. That was not a movement characterized by cooperative approaches to problem solving. Rather, the rebirth of labor in that era was possible precisely because desperation and rage engendered conflict—often intense, violent, unrelenting confrontation—that eventually established the need for wide-ranging political solutions. Moreover, the conflict was not confined to a particular plant or even a set of industries but represented a broad stratum of the population challenging the dominant economic order (see, e.g., Brody 1994; Goldfield 1989; Plotke 1989; "Uprising of '34" 1994). The example of the 1930s suggests the importance of broad-based public agitation to achieving labor's goals. Rather than focusing on new technologies, research, publicity, and corporate campaigns, perhaps labor unions of the 1990s need to learn how to engineer massive community-based organizing campaigns to do just that.

The problem with the "new" model of teamwork, consensus, and compromise is that, in the long run, it doesn't work. It has not resulted in gains for workers or for the AFL-CIO. At the very best, it has allowed workers to stay where they are, and even this is becoming uncommon. As the experience of the past two decades has shown, such a narrow conception of labor's agenda is not sufficient to fight the forces of deindustrialization, deregulation, political conservatism, and a changing workforce. A broader vision is needed, one that will form the basis for a social movement for economic and social justice.

The rejection of a confrontational model illustrates a larger dilemma for organized labor in the twenty-first century. That is the question of labor's role in challenging the entire economic order. Labor unions in the United States, unlike in most other industrialized countries, have long sidestepped the question of political action. Since World War II, the AFL-CIO has endorsed Democratic candidates and spent millions on their election campaigns. It has also lobbied for improved labor law and other legislation important to workers. Other than these activities, which are conducted mostly in Washington, D.C., by a staff of political experts, the labor movement has not had a coherent political agenda.

Organized labor in the late twentieth century has not been proactive in locating broader possibilities or responsibilities for political and social change. Few unions, for example, have found a way to reach out to workers currently not covered by union contracts, to join together to organize those workers for campaigns or for political action. This is not an easy task, but it is a vitally important one, especially in an era when 82 percent of workers are not represented by unions. Labor must include all workers, not only the narrow group who happen to be employed in unionized workplaces. This raises several immediate questions. How could nonunionized workers be mobilized, either to unionize their workplaces, or to agitate for political change? How could union and nonunion workers join in a movement for economic justice?

Very few unions are asking these questions, however. Most labor unions still adhere to a traditional model of "business unionism." In this model, unions' professional staff mainly provide services to workers, and workers presumably become union members in order to improve their wages and benefits. This is not translated into larger goals, such as creating more lasting changes in power relationships between labor and management; fostering greater racial, gender, and class equality; or improving the political and economic status of working people and their communities.

One example of organizing success since the 1960s has been public-sector unionism, which grew significantly—and then retained its membership in the 1980s and 1990s—while unions in the private sector declined. There are some obvious reasons for this disparity. First, public-sector union leaders have led a campaign to defend local government against a Republican attack. They have taken a visible role as advocates for improving public services, urban aid, public education, and on other political issues (Johnston 1995). This campaign has defended members' jobs and workplaces, and it has also involved workers in politics and activism at the community level. Second, because public agencies- -unlike corporate employers—must answer to political constituencies, workers are freer to organize unions and exercise their rights. When the employer abides by the law, unions are more likely to conduct successful organizing campaigns in the workplace. Clearly, the challenge is to form a labor movement capable of holding the private sector equally accountable and equally subject to scrutiny from an entire community.

With the changes at the AFL-CIO in the mid-1990s, labor now has the potential to reverse its declining fortunes. But this will require leadership, political vision—and almost certainly a substantial amount of confrontation. Only a grassroots workers' movement of similar intensity to that of the 1930s has the potential to prove to the country the urgent need for attention to the plight of workers at the end of the twentieth century. It will require a willingness to struggle, in the most public and sustained way, about the distribution of resources and rights that has left workers without a voice in American politics.

Solidarity

Finally, the labor movement must begin a new effort to overcome not only barriers of race, region, and gender, but also national boundaries. Unions have not emphasized sufficiently the need to organize with new groups. This includes not only organizing new constituencies traditionally neglected by the mainstream labor movement but also working with groups that (at least for now) cannot be part of the AFL-CIO. This could include organizations of young people, women, environmentalists, churches—and even more conservative populist organizations. In many parts of the country, the campaign against NAFTA in 1993 was a first attempt to bring diverse groups together around a common agenda. The alliance included an array of progressive organizations, but also Ross Perot's group, United We Stand, and other more right-wing local groups interested in working people taking control over politics. Labor organizations found a wide range of people interested in an alternative analysis of the economic problems facing their communities. The anti-NAFTA campaign provides a model for labor's potential to take the lead in organizing broad coalitions around an economic justice agenda.

One of the top priorities on labor's agenda into the next decade must be international solidarity. As the discussion above indicates, the global economy presents unprecedented challenges to American workers and their organizations. With international political and economic agreements proceeding at an elite level, it is no longer acceptable for U.S. unions to concentrate solely on workers at home. Indeed, it is becoming nearly impossible to continue improving the wages and benefits of workers in highly unionized industries. These workers are increasingly being forced to compete with workers in other countries, resulting in a race to the bottom as each nation tries to become more "attractive" to business investment by cutting wages, benefits, workers' rights, and regulations. To some extent, this can be fought in the United States as labor mounts campaigns against "free-trade" arrangements that serve mainly to secure the investment rights of transnational corporate capital. Eventually, however, freer trade and greater international economic integration are probably inevitable. In that case, the only way to ensure that labor's hard-won victories in any particular country are not undermined is to be sure that workers in other countries are struggling for the same rights and privileges that U.S. workers have won.[6] This requires some serious investment in organizing campaigns throughout the countries that serve as the main production and trading partners for U.S. corporations.

MOVING TOWARD POLITICAL CHANGE

As the above discussion of economic trends demonstrates, the development and flourishing of a shifting contingent, international economy is not the function of an autonomous "free market." Rather, it depends on an array of political institutions and decisions that favor transnational corporations over workers. Purely economic tools, like strikes and consumer boycotts, are unlikely to challenge this power imbalance in a comprehensive way. The only possibility for changing the emerging direction of economic development, and to stop the race to the bottom, is therefore for workers to begin to organize across boundaries of race, gender, class, and nation, to have an impact on decision makers. Only a thoroughly politicized labor movement can have a chance of stanching the political tide that threatens to roll back a century of labor progress, creating the largest gap between rich and poor of any industrialized country in the world (Bradsher 1995).

The above examples show how economic changes affecting workers involve not only the traditional membership base of the AFL-CIO but new constituencies and entire communities. This reality brings new organizing challenges. The rise of contingent work, for example, is testing the limits of traditional union structures. Subcontracted workers, day laborers, and workers hired through temporary agencies are unlikely to win by defining a bargaining unit and petitioning for a National Labor Relations Board (NLRB) election. Often, the status of both employer and employee is vague and not legally protected. Employees in these new arrangements are not protected by labor laws, and (even more than other workers) they risk losing all opportunities to work if they are associated with workplace organizing. Instead, it may be more effective to pursue strategies that focus on outreach to other groups and build on community organizations. Community-based organizing approaches can work to find these workers and bring them together to fight.

Labor-community coalitions, discussed elsewhere in this volume, are essential in building this new political movement. Entire communities are affected when plants close, when workers have less purchasing power, or when good jobs are converted to unpredictable jobs with poverty-level wages. Accordingly, members of the community must begin to hold employers accountable for their actions. They can demand benefits to the community in return for tax incentives and other corporate "welfare" provisions, or they can join with labor unions to promote participatory decision making about local economic development and employment. These types of coalitions also make more sense from an organizing perspective. Contingent workers—largely low-income, women, and racial minorities—are likely to be more receptive to approaches that originate in their community or church, rather than a more traditional union structure. Any effort to fight against contingent work and the abuse of temporaries must include a communitywide campaign. Unions must begin to bridge the gap with communities and to consider their struggles united. Unions' survival depends increasingly on the economic survival of low-income communities, and vice versa. The future of the labor movement will hinge upon its ability to reach out to new constituencies and collectively develop new agendas for political action.

In every region of the country, there are plenty of local examples of exciting, innovative organizing programs that are doing just that. It is worth citing a few examples here.[7] One receiving a lot of publicity, especially since John

Sweeney of Service Employees International Union (SEIU) became president of the AFL-CIO, is the Justice for Janitors campaign. Justice for Janitors involves low-wage service workers, many of whom are contingent workers themselves hired through subcontracting agencies, in a visible, confrontational campaign for economic fairness. In cities where the campaign is strongest, SEIU has successfully created a communitywide coalition and generated a social movement around the issues. This is only one example of community-based efforts to improve the wages and conditions of low-wage workers. Similar campaigns have been waged locally by UNITE, Hotel Employees and Restaurant Employees (HERE), and other unions.

Another model involves direct unionization of workers not covered by the NLRB or traditional unions. One example is the recent wave of organizing drives among graduate student teaching assistants—a pool of contingent workers responsible for much of the teaching at colleges and universities. Many such unionization efforts have been successful in the 1980s and 1990s, introducing a new population into the labor movement and creating new possibilities for coalition building. Professional and managerial employees are equally susceptible to the mobility of corporations, the trend toward downsizing, and the shift to contingent work. Since professional workers are facing comparable changes in economic opportunities, there are new possibilities for organizing them and drawing the connections between them and other workers. Universities are an especially interesting place to begin, since they often represent a huge concentration of resources in communities otherwise suffering from an array of urban problems. Students and faculty may be able to contribute to union efforts—by volunteering time, research assistance, and money—and eventually to become part of the broader labor movement themselves.

Another example is a wide range of labor-community coalitions across the country. Some of these have affiliated with the Federation of Industrial Retention and Renewal (FIRR) based in Chicago. Many are working on stopping plant closings and encouraging participatory economic development alternatives. Others are hosting exchanges between local communities and workers from other countries and educating union members and other groups about global issues. Some are attempting to strategize about organizing temporary workers and other groups that have been labeled impossible to organize. Some are targeting particular industries and forming community-based coalitions to improve employment conditions and policies. There is an infinite variety of work to be done by such groups, and exciting efforts are under way.[8]

Politicization does not only involve electoral and legislative activity, which may or may not be the place for unions to start. It may begin with small, local community-based campaigns centered around workers' struggles with particular employers or industries. It may be based in solidarity work with other groups or international workers. Or it may arise as a national campaign around a particular issue of concern, as the anti-NAFTA campaign and the single-payer health insurance campaign could have been. But for workers to engage in political struggle requires many things. It requires, first, a greater proportion of workers organized into unions—or into some alternative type of organization that has the capacity to educate and mobilize its members around a range of economic issues. And second, it requires leadership from within those organizations. Leaders must provide workers with the knowledge, skills, and tools to analyze the issues and events that affect their lives. Then they must organize activities that communicate to those in power the urgency of political change and demand that workers participate in those activities. They must vigilantly promote the building of connections with other organizations and other groups, races, and nationalities, rather than allow workers to be pitted against each other. They must constantly provide an analysis of the powerful individuals, political institutions, and economic arrangements that serve to divide workers and limit their collective strength. And they must instill in workers the confidence and vision that united we can confront this order and improve the lives of working people. This is the challenge facing the labor movement.

NOTES

1. Even as these practices become more prevalent, however, management experts contest their desirability. Shifting from stable to contingent labor does produce immediate, short-term savings for firms. It cuts labor costs, fragments tasks, permits subcontracting, and makes work hours less rigid and predictable. On the other hand, it inhibits a more genuine long-term flexibility that relies on cooperation among a group of well-trained, experienced workers in an environment conducive to continuous learning, opportunity, and productivity (Piore 1989).

2. This presents a striking contrast to the fact that a full 98 percent of those currently involved in capital and financial transactions on the global level are men (Falk 1993, 43).

3. As Fuentes and Ehrenreich point out, the idea that women of color are not only happy to work but biologically predisposed to do this work is often fostered by the governments of developing countries. Under pressure from the IMF and World Bank to pursue aggressive industrialization and "structural adjustment," these governments often advertise the availability of a low-wage, hardworking, pliant workforce in order to attract business investment (Fuentes and Ehrenreich 1989).

4. On the other hand, some are benefiting extraordinarily from globalization. One study of 78 top executives of U.S. transnational corporations showed their annual

compensation averaged $2,651,825 in 1994. Executives at Ford and General Motors received raises of over 130 percent. The CEO of Allied Signal Corporation, Lawrence Bossidy, earned $12.4 million a year, an amount that exceeds the combined *total* annual wages of all of Allied's four thousand employees in Mexico (Anderson, Cavanagh, and Williams 1995).

5. This is not to say we should never use polls. They can be very valuable tools, for example, in helping determine the issues or problems that matter most to workers. Citing survey results can also be useful in convincing policy makers of the extent of support for a labor agenda. But these purposes are very different from basing organizing and strategy decisions on polling data.

6. We have already seen that this is true between regions and communities in the United States. Capital's increased mobility means that as long as workers in some states are less organized, organized workers in other states are at risk of losing everything they have won (Weinbaum 1994; LeRoy 1994).

7. For many more examples, see Brecher and Costello 1990; Rachleff 1994; Greider 1992; Byrnes 1993; Marshall 1991.

8. For more examples of labor-community coalitions, see Nissen 1995.

BIBLIOGRAPHY

AFL-CIO Committee on the Evolution of Work. 1985. *The Changing Situation of Workers and Their Unions.* Washington, D.C.: AFL-CIO.

Anderson, Sarah, John Cavanagh, and Jonathan Williams. 1995. *Workers Lose, CEOs Win (II).* Washington, D.C.: Institute for Policy Studies.

Appelbaum, Eileen. 1992. "Structural Change and the Growth of Part-Time and Temporary Employment." Pp. 1–14 in *New Policies for the Part-Time and Contingent Workforce,* ed. Virginia L. duRivage. Armonk, N.Y.: M. E. Sharpe.

Barnet, Richard J., and John Cavanagh. 1994. *Global Dreams: Imperial Corporations and the New World Order.* New York: Simon and Schuster.

Belous, Richard. 1989. *The Contingent Economy: The Growth of the Temporary, Part-Time, and Subcontracted Workforce.* Washington, D.C.: National Planning Association.

Bluestone, Barry, and Bennett Harrison. 1982. *The Deindustrialization of America.* New York: Basic Books.

Bluestone, Barry, Bennett Harrison, and Lawrence Baker. 1981. *Corporate Flight: The Causes and Consequences of Economic Dislocation.* Washington, D.C.: Progressive Alliance.

Boyte, Harry C. 1980. *The Backyard Revolution: Understanding the New Citizen Movement.* Philadelphia: Temple University Press.

Bradsher, Keith. 1995. "Widest Gap in Incomes? Research Points to U.S." *New York Times,* October 27.

Brecher, Jeremy, John Brown Childs, and Jill Cutler. 1993. *Global Visions: Beyond the New World Order.* Boston: South End.

Brecher, Jeremy, and Tim Costello. 1990. *Building Bridges: The Emerging Grassroots Coalition of Labor and Community.* New York: Monthly Review.

Brody, David. 1994. "The Future of the Labor Movement in Historical Perspective." *Dissent* (Winter): 57–66.

Byrnes, Nanette. 1993. "Blue Collar Blues." *Financial World,* November 23, 26–29.

Carré, Françoise J. 1992. "Temporary Employment in the Eighties." Pp. 45–87 in *New Policies for the Part-Time and Contingent Workforce,* ed. Virginia L. duRivage. Armonk, N.Y.: M. E. Sharpe.

duRivage, Virginia L., ed. 1992. *New Policies for the Part-Time and Contingent Workforce.* Armonk, N.Y.: M. E. Sharpe.

Falk, Richard. 1993. "The Making of Global Citizenship." Pp. 39–50 in *Global Visions: Beyond the New World Order,* ed. Jeremy Brecher, John Brown Childs, and Jill Cutler. Boston: South End.

Fuentes, Annette, and Barbara Ehrenreich. 1989. *Women in the Global Factory.* Boston: South End.

Gaventa, John, and Peter Wiley. 1987. "The Deindustrialization of the Tennessee Economy." New Market, Tenn.: Highlander Research and Education Center.

"Global Assembly Line." 1991. PBS Video.

Goldfield, Michael. 1989. "Worker Insurgency, Radical Organization, and New Deal Labor Legislation." *American Political Science Review* 83, no. 4 (December): 1257–82.

Greider, William. 1992. "Don't Count Labor Out." *Rolling Stone,* October 17.

Harrison, Bennett, and Barry Bluestone. 1988. *The Great U-Turn: Corporate Restructuring and the Polarizing of America.* New York: Basic Books.

Johnston, Paul. 1995. "New Beginnings at the AFL-CIO?" New Haven, Conn. Unpublished manuscript. In possession of the author.

Kessler-Harris, Alice, and Bertram Silverman. 1992. "Beyond Industrial Unionism." *Dissent* (Winter): 61–66.

LeRoy, Greg. 1994. *No More Candy Store: States and Cities Making Job Subsidies Accountable.* Chicago and Washington, D.C.: Federation for Industrial Retention and Renewal and the Grassroots Policy Project.

Marshall, Jeffrey. 1991. "Union Strongarms Banks." *United States Banker,* October, 14–21.

Metzenbaum, Howard. 1993. "Toward a Disposable Work Force: The Increasing Use of 'Contingent' Labor." June 15. Hearing before the Subcommittee on Labor, Committee on Labor and Human Resources, United States Senate.

Negrey, Cynthia. 1993. *Gender, Time, and Reduced Work.* Albany: State University of New York Press.

Nissen, Bruce. 1995. *Fighting for Jobs: Case Studies of Labor-Community Coalitions Confronting Plant Closings.* Albany: State University of New York Press.

Parker, Mike, and Jane Slaughter. 1988. *Choosing Sides: Unions and the Team Concept.* Boston: Labor Notes and South End Press.

Parker, Robert E. 1994. *Flesh Peddlers and Warm Bodies: The Temporary Help Industry and Its Workers.* New Brunswick, N.J.: Rutgers University Press.

Phillips, Lyda. 1991. "Full-time Benefits Sought for State's 'Temporaries.'" *Nashville Banner,* February 21.

Piore, Michael J. 1989. "Fissure and Discontinuity in U.S. Labor Management Relations." Pp. 47–62 in *The State and the Labor Market,* ed. Samuel Rosenberg. New York: Plenum.

Plotke, David. 1989. "The Wagner Act Again: Politics and Labor, 1935–37." *Studies in American Political Development* 3: 105–56.

Putz, Susan, and Nina Gregg. 1995. "Organizing Contingent Workers in a Right-to-Work State: Steps Toward an Agenda for Action." Unpublished report housed at Tennessee Industrial Renewal Network (TIRN), Knoxville, Tenn.

Rachleff, Peter. 1994. "Seeds of a Labor Resurgency." *Nation,* February 21, 226–30.

Rosenberg, Samuel. 1989. *The State and the Labor Market.* New York: Plenum.

Standing, Guy. 1989. "Global Feminization Through Flexible Labor." *World Development* 17, no. 7 (July): 1077–95.

Tilly, Chris. 1992. "Short Hours, Short Shrift: The Causes and Consequences of Part-Time Employment." Pp. 15–44 in *New Policies for the Part-Time and Contingent Workforce,* ed. Virginia L. duRivage. Armonk, N.Y.: M. E. Sharpe.

"The Uprising of '34." 1994. PBS video.

Weinbaum, Eve. 1994. "Local Economic Development, Democracy, and the State: Mobilizing Against Poverty in East Tennessee." Unpublished paper presented at Midwest Political Science Association, April, 1994, in Chicago, Ill.

3

Community-Based Organizing: Transforming Union Organizing Programs from the Bottom Up

Bruce Nissen and Seth Rosen

The top priority of the U.S. labor movement today is organizing the unorganized. The AFL-CIO lists this as "the most important of our missions" in its objectives for 1997 (AFL-CIO 1997, 3). The need is clear. Union density (membership as a percentage of the eligible workforce) has been in decline since the mid-1950s. The decline was especially severe in the 1980s; from 1980 to 1993 U.S. unions lost 3.5. million members as union density dropped from 23 percent to 16 percent (Chaison 1996, 18). By 1990 researchers were predicting that union density would drop to 5 percent by the year 2000 (Bronars and Deere 1990; Chaison and Dhavale 1990). While the decline has slowed somewhat in the 1990s, the labor movement continues to slide downward. This decline has a direct impact on the wages, benefits, and working conditions of all workers, including existing union members.

At present little over 10 percent of the private-sector workforce works under a union contract. The drastic decline can be attributed both to increasing employer hostility and to lack of union organizing efforts, both of which are more important factors than the popularly cited shifts in the economy toward the service sector or the increasing feminization of the workforce.

Many international unions are taking the organizing challenge seriously. Most organizing budgets are increasing at a rapid rate. But the task is daunting. The AFL-CIO aims to encourage member unions to spend at least 30 percent of their resources on organizing by the year 2000 (AFL-CIO 1997, 3). Such an expenditure of monetary resources would be a more than sixfold increase over averages in the past, when most unions devoted less than 5 percent to this purpose. Unions need to grow by approximately 300,000 members per year simply to stay even in a constantly growing labor force. No matter how many paid full-time organizers most unions hire and deploy, they are unlikely to be wholly successful simply by continuing to do what they did before, only doing more of it. In fact, the labor movement's most plentiful resource is not money but people. Only by mobilizing and involving growing numbers of local union activists in the organizing process can the labor movement begin to grow significantly.

Beyond simply increasing monetary resources, unions need to pay attention to the manner in which they organize. Reliance on mass mailings and leafleting at workplace entrances is relatively ineffective: grassroots "rank-and-file intensive" methods involving personal contact, a rank-and-file organizing committee, and the like are much more effective (Bronfenbrenner and Juravich 1995).

But grassroots campaigns require a great deal of time and large numbers of people. Again, a resource of potentially enormous value here is a union's own membership. Unions that are able to convince a sizable number of their members to get involved in external organizing will likely be the most successful. Volunteer organizers from the ranks constitute one of the keys to growth and healthy survival for the labor movement in the twenty-first century.

Some national unions now have programs to involve the membership in organizing the unorganized. Yet, it is unclear how well developed or widespread these efforts are. It appears to us that most programs are either very new or are only sporadically put into operation. Research into this area is also rather sparse, and most investigations to date focus on volunteer organizing from the base of the union local (Babson 1991–92; Eckstein 1991–92; Nissen 1998).

Organizing is difficult and challenging work. Local unions do not necessarily have the expertise to begin to organize effectively. Smaller locals will not have adequate resources for organizing on their own, even if they devote one-third of their resources to this task. Unions need to build support structures and link their national organizing programs with local volunteer efforts.

Regional or district structures are the potential links between national union organizing plans and the union local, which contains the membership from which volunteer organizers can be recruited. In this essay we examine a structured program by a union district that develops a comprehensive organizing program through volunteer member organizers: District 4 of the Communications Workers of America (CWA). This is one of eight CWA districts, all of which have similar programs.

CWA DISTRICT 4: AN OVERVIEW

CWA District 4 encompasses the Midwest Great Lakes states of Illinois, Indiana, Michigan, Ohio, and Wisconsin. It has 54,000 members dispersed throughout 201 union locals. About 75 percent of the members work in the traditional telephone industry: about 28,000 at Ameritech, the rest at AT&T, Lucent, GTE, SPRINT, ALLTEL, and Century. The rest are other kinds of information workers at private-sector companies such as cable and broadcast TV, newspapers, and security companies; or at public institutions, particularly universities in Ohio and Indiana.

The average size of a local is 265 members, but this average conceals a large number of small locals and a few very large ones. Only 43 percent of the 201 locals have 100 or more members; 5 percent of the total have more than 1,000 members and 2 percent have more than 2,000. Thus 115 of the 201 affiliated locals have fewer than 100 members, making them far too small ordinarily to engage in external organizing without outside assistance. Even the 74 with 100–1,000 members would need some resource support. Only the 12 with 1,000+ members, or perhaps only the 4 largest with 2,000+, could potentially be self-sufficient in organizing.

The CWA had no national organizing program during the years 1960–80. Secure in its representation of the Bell system employees, which meant most telephone workers in the United States, the union was relatively staid in its organizing activities. However, all of that changed when a 1974 antitrust suit against AT&T eventually forced the 1984 divestiture by AT&T of its 22 regional Bell operating companies. The ensuing competitive free-for-all, combined with technological and market changes, which brought closer together all forms of electronic communication, profoundly changed the environment within which the union operated (Keefe and Boroff 1994).

In 1980, after much debate on whether the union should organize outside of basic telephone, the CWA began an organizing program modeled on programs that other unions had run. An organizing director and national staff were hired. This was the beginning of CWA's national shift to becoming an organizing union. While some staff was deployed around the country, this was a headquarters organizing program where national staff would fly around the country, hiring project staff when needed and running campaigns that, in most cases, were separate from the CWA local in town. In some cases, such as the large state worker campaign in Ohio, there was open conflict between the national organizing staff and the locals and district leadership. This campaign, with open competition between CWA and other unions, resulted in a very expensive defeat. The defeat in Ohio and other factors combined to initiate a reevaluation of the organizing model and the evolution of a different program.

In 1986, CWA president Morton Bahr (elected in 1985) appointed Larry Cohen as director of organizing. Cohen, who had been CWA District 1's organizing director, brought in a new model. Cohen's belief was that organizing had to be based in local unions to succeed on the scale necessary. Since CWA locals related to the national union through the eight geographic districts, the national union program should be run through the districts, and over several years, district organizing coordinators were placed in each district. In 1990 District 4 set up the District 4 Organizing Network. This network has been operating and growing up to the present. The results have been much better than what was the case during the previous inaction or the nationally run program.

THE CONTEXT: NATIONAL CWA ORGANIZING PROGRAM

From 1987 to the present, the CWA has developed an approach to organizing that stresses a number of principles. The primary principle is that organizing is done best by local unions in their own community. When organizers have roots in the community the characterization by employers of these people as "outside" organizers is much less effective. CWA organizers may bump into workers they are trying to organize in the grocery store, at church, or at a PTA meeting. Organizing leads come from friends and families of members. Supporting organizers based locally not only is more cost effective but also allows organizers to live a more "normal" life. Organizers can have families and friends and build community ties.

Local unions need support from the national union in order to develop effective organizing programs. Since CWA locals relate to the national union through eight geographic districts, staff are put in place in each district to provide training, strategic assistance, and resources from the national organizing budget to pay for literature, lost wages, and other campaign expenses. Having the organizing program integrated into the structure of the union also makes it possible to use bargaining and community leverage to support organizing.

An additional principle is that organizing is a craft that requires time and hands-on experience to develop. Developing the skills of local organizers is an important part of the national program. Because the organizers are committed local activists, the skills that are developed stay within the organization and the labor movement.

The final principle is that part of the job of the organizer is to reproduce these skills. The role of the staff organizers is to build organizing capacity in addition to working on campaigns. Local organizers help develop the skills of other volunteers with the local, just as they help develop skills within the inside organizing committee. The work that any one individual does helps to create the work of many.

The organizing model also contains three priorities for evaluating potential projects. The first priority is the "wall-to-wall" groups; these are unorganized parts of companies like Ameritech or AT&T where the CWA already represents employees. The second priority is other information industry companies that compete with the existing bargaining units of the union. The third priority is community-based projects that help locals to expand their power in the community.

DISTRICT 4 ORGANIZING NETWORK

At its annual meeting in September of 1990, District 4 created a district organizing network. This was four years after the shift in strategy at the top of the union. Thus there was a four-year delay between national theory and local practice. In some districts it happened more quickly, but in others it took even longer. The network, according to the 1990 organizing plan, was to function as a "vehicle for mutual support, exchange of ideas and a source of recognition. Network activities should be meaningful to the people that are actually doing the work" (CWA District 4 Organizing Plan, 1990).

The district had been losing members for years. The goal was to organize new members in sufficient numbers to grow. To do that, it was necessary to increase the number of locals that were organizing and, perhaps even more important, constantly to get more locals to make organizing an ongoing part of their programs and activities. If organizing could be integrated into the routine functioning of many or most locals, a reversal of the union's decline might be possible. In addition to working on actual campaigns, the district's staff organizer needed to work on developing the capacity to organize in a systematic way. In the first year the district was able to get eighteen locals to participate in some manner within the network.

In addition to increasing involvement of more union locals, the network also aims to develop the expertise and leadership skills of individual members. To achieve this, CWA approached building the network as it would an organizing campaign. Organizing committees are built through relationships one worker at a time. The district organizing network was built the same way. The district organizing coordinator worked with local officers to identify potential organizers. Then, as leads were identified, the coordinator worked side by side with them to get campaigns started, to build internal organizing committees, to create majority support, to develop strategies to win recognition, and to carry out those strategies. Formal training programs were not often used. Instead, the staff worked with potential organizers on actual campaigns.

At first, staff needed to be present throughout every phase of the campaign. As the local organizers acquired more skills and experience, more and more of the coaching could be done over the phone with the national staff coming to town for campaign transition points. As local organizers get more experienced they operate much more independently. Just as with an organizing campaign, the district systematically tracks local organizer development over time and knows who needs attention at any particular time.

The key to making a network like this grow, and to sustaining it over the long run, is to provide support on an ongoing basis. To accomplish this, the district provides recognition to locals and individuals for their efforts and achievements, publishes a newsletter on organizing activities, holds yearly organizing retreats in the spring for training and networking purposes, and provides backup for locals in actual organizing campaigns.

Recognition is provided in a number of ways. Local leaders who join the network and pledge to attempt to organize one hundred workers per year are recognized at the district meeting. Every three years, network locals receive District 4 Organizing Network jackets. Locals that successfully organize one hundred or more new members per year are recognized at the CWA National Convention. Special effort is made in union publications to highlight the efforts of organizers.

The district's organizing newsletter, *Gettin' Organized,* began publication in October 1990. As of January 1997 nineteen editions had been published, averaging approximately three issues per year. The newsletter is sent to all organizers in the network and their local union presidents. District 4 staff also receive the newsletter. Each issue is attractively laid out on both sides of a single $8^1/_2$-by-11-inch sheet of paper. The goal is to make the newsletter brief and readable, yet packed with sufficient information to be useful to those doing the organizing.

Each edition contains a "Campaign Update" feature, which reports on the progress of a number of ongoing organizing campaigns. There are also articles for field organizers. Eleven of the nineteen published editions contain an article that is an educational "tool" piece on how to accomplish various organizing tasks. Typical topics include "learning from losses—5 lessons," "learning to pick winners," "how to make organizing committees work," "how to assess your support," "how to build an organizing committee in your local," "how to use rank-and-file activists," "tools for organizers," and the like. Finally, newsletters also contain articles on specific organizing drives or victories (twenty-two articles) and organizational news on the district's organizing retreats and workshops or organizing goals (thirteen articles).

Overall, the newsletter provides an attractive and flexible presence for the district's organizing program over time. It is an important component in maintaining continuity and constant encouragement to locals as they undertake the often discouraging task of organizing in a hostile environment.

District organizing retreats are an additional component of the network. Retreats are held every year in the spring in District 4. The retreats are by invitation only. Local organizers who worked on a campaign over the past year are invited, whether the campaign was won or lost. There are usually about thirty to thirty-five organizers invited each year with about twenty-five to thirty attending. The District 4 vice president attends, and the international organizing director attends every other year. The international union pays the entire cost of meals and lodging, with locals paying for lost time and travel expenses.

The participants are all local lead organizers and staff. Virtually none of the local organizers are engaged full-time in organizing work; most work at least part-time for the telephone company or some other employer. Though race and gender are not criteria for invitation, the participants have been very much a reflection of CWA membership. Gender balance has never been worse than 60 percent men and 40 percent women, and each retreat has included at least 20 percent persons of color.

The retreat consists of discussions of topics that are presented in groups of case studies. The case studies come from the experience of the local organizers over the past year. Every participant presents something during the retreat, and there are lessons learned from each campaign, the defeats as well as the victories.

About 75 percent of the participants return every year as a result of their consistent organizing activity. They describe the retreat as a way to "recharge their batteries" and share their wins and losses with the only people who can appreciate what was involved—other organizers. Those who are attending for the first time or who attend sporadically tend to view the retreat more as a training session where they can pick up tips from more experienced organizers.

Topics vary somewhat from year to year. There is always some discussion of employer tactics and trends. Various tactical experiments are developed in one year's retreat and evaluated in subsequent years. Most retreats will have in-depth discussions of particular industry segments such as cable TV or cellular telephone. Discussions also take place on the topic of building local organizing programs: recruiting volunteers, developing leads, and building community support for organizing through efforts like the labor-community social justice organization Jobs with Justice.

Each retreat includes an opportunity to talk informally with the district vice president about the future of the union. The final half day of the retreat is devoted to the development of a district organizing plan where local organizers identify likely projects for the coming year and collectively develop the activities that the District 4 Network will do to support those projects. The district organizing plan is sent out to every local in the district.

The retreat is an important means of sustaining local organizers in the face of difficult and frustrating work. It provides an additional support mechanism where local organizers begin to help each other in certain areas, further freeing up national staff time to develop more local organizers. The retreat also reinforces a clear sense of organizing partnership between the national union and locals.

While the newsletter, retreat, and individual support provide the basic organizer training and development, CWA District 4 also utilizes the AFL-CIO Organizing Institute. Since the inception of the institute in 1989, District 4 has sent 10–15 local activists to the three-day training. These are activists who have demonstrated a willingness to volunteer their time to do organizing work. They go to the Organizing Institute primarily as a motivational tool, but it gives them some basic skills as well.

In the past five years CWA District 4 has begun to send advanced local organizers as teaching fellows in addition to the national staff that teach at the Organizing Institute. Becoming a teaching fellow is part of the development of local organizers. They learn to communicate organizing concepts to a wide variety of participants and get to interact with organizers from other unions using different models.

Finally, the district provides backup to union locals and individuals as organizing drives progress. A growing number of district staff work with local organizers on specific campaigns. Depending on the experience level of the organizer, assistance ranges from running the campaign on the ground alongside them to consulting over the phone. Of the sixteen national staff in District 4, one is a full-time organizing coordinator, one administrative staff member spends 80 percent of his time on organizing, and six others spend between 10 and 25 percent of their time on organizing. In 1990 there was only one full-time person supporting the district organizing program. This has meant that locals at any level of expertise can now get assistance based on their need. Involving "servicing" staff in the organizing network has been accomplished by a combination of new staff coming on with an already developed organizing commitment and existing staff being motivated to become involved. Both factors are a result of leadership support to the organizing program by CWA president Morton Bahr and District 4 vice president Jeff Rechenbach.

The district organizing network has made a demonstrable difference. At its inception the district was conducting two to three organizing campaigns per year; by the late 1990s it was up to fifteen to twenty campaigns yearly. Likewise, over the years, the number of locals and organizers involved has grown a great deal. Table 1 shows the growth.

TABLE 1.
DISTRICT 4 ORGANIZING NETWORK 1990–1997

	1990	1997
# of Locals	18	46
# of Orgnaizers	26	62
Organizers by State/Sector:		
Ohio	16	21
Michigan	1	12
Indiana	6	8
Wisconsin	2	9
Illinois	0	8
PPMWS (Printing)	1	1
NABET (Broadcast)	0	3
Organizing Category:		
Full-Time	0	1
PT = Lead	5	11
PT = Beginner	8	26
Committed Volunteer	13	24

Number of 1990 lead organizers still active: 3
Number of 1990 total still active: 14

As table 1 demonstrates, the overall number of locals and organizers involved in the network has increased by two and one-half to three times in seven years. All states and all categories of organizers show substantial increases also. While there has naturally been some turnover, three of the five original part-time lead organizers are still active, and fourteen of the twenty-six original total of organizers continue to be involved.

All of this increased activity and involvement shows up in results. In the beginning the network organized a few hundred workers per year. Now approximately one thousand are successfully organized yearly. Yet, this has merely kept the district membership rolls even, as approximately an equivalent number are lost through downsizing and other forms of natural attrition in established units.

Stopping the previous shrinkage is of course important, but the goals of the district for the organizing network are more ambitious. Can the network become the vehicle for significant growth? That is the goal, still unrealized but possibly within reach if the network continues to mature.

LEADERSHIP DEVELOPMENT

Development of leaders among local activists and among the unorganized is crucial to a network such as this. Such leaders have the potential to transform the labor movement, moving it from total dependence on paid staff and a predominantly "servicing" mode of operation. They also are crucial to integrating unions into a community base, a necessity for future growth.

In the following we highlight three leaders who have developed from the ranks through the organizing network. These three demonstrate the potential within the ranks, if unions work to uncover and develop it.

Susan Baxter-Fleming was a thirty-one-year-old president of a small CWA local in Bloomington, Indiana, when she was approached by clerical workers on the campus of Indiana University who were interested in organizing. Susan was a telephone operator at Indiana Bell and part-time president of the 300-member Local 4818. She had handled grievances and represented members for a number of years but had no organizing experience. She needed help organizing 1,800 clerical and technical workers who were not covered by any collective bargaining law.

She contacted the International Organizing Department, thinking that they would do it for her. She found, much to her surprise, that the national organizers wanted to organize in conjunction with her. She also involved two other telephone operators and local activists. It was a difficult and complicated campaign that resulted, four years later, in an overwhelming election victory, recognition, and a contract for the 1,800 workers. Susan had the opportunity to work side by side with experienced organizers and learned quickly. She became the lead organizer on the project. She found that she liked organizing more than being a local president and certainly more than being a telephone operator.

A long-term campaign like this was carried out relatively inexpensively because CWA could use organizers like Susan in their own community. More important, a long-term campaign goes through just about every organizing tactic known, so that Susan got the opportunity to participate in a wide variety of activities and strategies. After the Indiana University victory in Bloomington, CWA took Susan off the job temporarily to spearhead successful campaigns at Indiana University Northwest in Gary, Indiana, and the technicians at Indiana Bell Communications (IBC) across the state of Indiana. In the IBC campaign she coordinated volunteers from three locals. This prepared her for her current position, coordinating organizing full-time in District 4 as part of CWA's national organizing staff. A well-respected leader who started out as a telephone operator, Susan has been the primary force behind the growth of organizing activity in the western part of District 4 (Indiana, Illinois, and Wisconsin).

Shannon Kirkland was an unorganized cable TV worker in Detroit when he showed up at CWA Local 4100's office in the spring of 1994. An African-American father of five daughters, he knew that he needed to take action to make his life and standard of living better. Working with Local 4100 officers and CWA organizing staff he became part of an organizing committee on the inside at the cable company. CWA ran an open campaign, where Shannon and his fellow committee members stood up and publicly supported the union effort. Over the next few weeks they signed up their coworkers on petitions and "unity pledges," statements that workers signed giving permission to use their name on union literature. With 65 percent publicly supporting the drive, they won a two-to-one victory in the one-hundred-person unit in June of 1994.

Shannon served on the bargaining committee that achieved a first contract in May of 1995. He also was elected to the Local 4100 Executive Board as a representative of the Comcast CATV unit. The outside technicians like himself at Comcast Detroit saw their conditions improve dramatically. However, Shannon recognized that the existence of nonunion Comcast workers both in Detroit and in surrounding communities was a threat to all the gains that they had made.

Despite this increased hostility and pressure from management, Shannon began to work with district organizing staff to mount campaigns at other Comcast groups. In the first effort, which involved the "inside" workers in Detroit, Shannon had District 4 organizing staff working side by side with him. That campaign led to the filing of a petition for an election, and later its withdrawal. Although the exact contours of the bargaining unit were determined, it was clear that it was not possible to win. About eight months later, CWA tried again. This time Shannon and Local 4100 officers ran the campaign mostly on their own. When workers felt afraid of Comcast management they could look to Shannon, a fellow employee also taking great risks. The CWA won the election for the Detroit inside group in the fall of 1996.

In 1997, Shannon learned other valuable organizing lessons. The CWA lost a campaign for representation of the workers in the Comcast operation in Flint, Michigan, by a six-vote margin, in part because of racial conflict within the potential bargaining unit. The union also blocked another election with an unfair labor practice charge against the company because Comcast moved all but one of the workers to a vacant building outside the area for this particular unit a few days before the election. These experiences are part of the realities of organizing in the United States today. Shannon also spent four months on an "organizer exchange," organizing telecommunications workers and cable TV workers in Great Britain for the Communications Workers Union (CWU) in the United Kingdom. These activities have all been on a lost-time basis while he continues to work at Comcast as a field engineer.

Jim Cosgrove was a thirty-year-old printer in a commercial shop when the International Typographical Union merged into the CWA in 1987. He was an officer in his local when it merged with a Cleveland, Ohio, CWA local a few years later. He was put in charge of servicing the several hundred printer members in the three-thousand-member Local 4340. Most of his members were retirees, and the future was not bright for those who were still working. Jim realized that organizing was the only way that part of the local could survive. Local 4340 had a long history of organizing both telecommunications workers and public workers. Jim was able to work with both experienced local organizers and District 4 staff.

Soon he was working with a variety of workers, from printers to county emergency dispatchers, cable TV workers to alcoholism counselors. Over time his organizing skills improved, and he learned to deal with diverse employee populations. As the part-time lead organizer, he had his share of successes and failures. But overall the results have been positive. Local 4340 has been recognized for organizing more than a hundred workers in four of the last seven years.

In 1997, as part of an increased commitment to organizing, Local 4340 appointed him as a full-time organizing director for the local. He works with a growing number of part-time local volunteers and helps them develop organizing skills, just as he developed them. He is involved in the community through coalitions like the Jobs with Justice group and as a central labor council delegate. This has given him opportunities to utilize community strategies as part of his organizing campaigns.

Our brief descriptions of these three organizers and leaders coming from the ranks illustrate how such individuals develop into important resources for the union in its organizing efforts. But they must be systematically sought out and cultivated. When they are, a union's effectiveness and power multiply many times over.

COMPARISONS WITH OTHER APPROACHES

There are numerous "models" or approaches to organizing the unorganized. Many different tactics and strategies are being tried as the labor movement attempts to reverse its previous neglect of organizing. No one model will fit all situations or unions; maximum tactical flexibility is advisable.

Most union organizing programs rely heavily on paid full-time organizing staff. Frequently organizers move rapidly around the country (or area of the country), moving from campaign to campaign. They may focus exclusively on campaigns rather than also focusing on developing organizing capacity. Entirely different people are involved in organizing than in other phases or aspects of the union's work. Workers who are already in organized units play no role in organizing, or at best, a very small number of them play an extremely minor or subsidiary role for a brief period—for example, house-calling during a "blitz."

We are not arguing that this is never an appropriate way to organize. But alternatives should be considered in light of recent difficulties. This model, with its focus on building capacity as well as campaigns, may contain certain advantages. The advantages stem from being rooted locally, developing organic links between different aspects of the union's work, internal leadership development, and development of the union's capacity to mobilize internally or for community coalitions or alliances.

The CWA's structure is somewhat unique. CWA is one of the most geographically dispersed unions in the country, with locals in virtually every community. CWA also has a significant number of its staff located in state or district offices as opposed to its Washington, D.C., headquarters. Because of these differences, parts of what we have related above may not be applicable to other unions. Nevertheless, certain elements of the above "model" should be applicable in any union.

First, the District 4 Organizing Network develops member lead organizers, and does so in a systematic way. This takes time; to develop within a member the full range of skills necessary to occupy a lead position in organizing drives requires a real investment of the union's resources in that member over time. But the payoff is enormous: the union contains ever-growing numbers within its ranks capable of taking charge of organizing duties. These lead organizers are dispersed geographically and are available as needed. They can be used in place of national staff in regional or national campaigns such as the recent CWA US Airways campaign for representation of ten thousand passenger service employees. They also develop into more versatile and devoted union activists, as other research has demonstrated (Nissen 1998).

71

Second, the organizing is done from a community base. This has multiple advantages. Locally based organizers know their communities. They can constantly search for organizing projects with minimal cost. They can be rooted with families, friends, children, churches, and so forth. They can relate to unorganized workers as part of their community rather than as "outsiders." Local organizers who come from the ranks demonstrate, by example, that it is workers who run their unions. Local union-based organizing allows CWA to support long-term strategic campaigns where there is not a "hot shop." Local organizers can stay in touch with contacts indefinitely, waiting for the time to be right.

Third, locally-based organizing allows community support for organizing to take a long-term approach. Many CWA locals participate in ongoing Jobs with Justice coalitions that provide support for organizing. When such efforts are part of an organizing strategy it is not necessary to create a community coalition—it already exists.

Finally, this model helps workers become leaders. Building strong unions that improve the lives of working people is not simply a matter of winning elections or getting contracts. Without the development of workers into leaders it is not possible to build an effective union. Becoming an organizer of unorganized workers helps to develop a leader with a democratic understanding of leadership. Leadership should not be a finite commodity. The labor movement needs as many leaders as it can get to step forward. That is a lesson that an organizer learns over and over again. The labor movement needs to organize all workers, high-skill and low-skill. Worker-organizers can show, by example, the value of union activism in their personal development as leaders.

Organizing workers in the United States will continue to be a difficult task. Employer opposition continues to grow more vicious and more sophisticated. The legal framework continues to be ineffective at restoring any balance to the process. The need for unions greatly to increase their efforts could not be more clear.

But often lost in the discussion of increasing the resources devoted to organizing is the point that people are the most plentiful resource in the labor movement. The CWA District 4 Organizing Network demonstrates some of the potential of that resource. We do not want to romanticize or overstate the positive aspects of this network. It is important to note that it has not yet been successful at organizing consistently on a scale that would produce growth. But it has kept membership relatively constant during a period of massive downsizing among the CWA's core employers. Perhaps more important, it points in the direction of making organizing a way of life for local unions rather than a separate program that members pay dues to fund. Only when organizing is integrated into the daily life of most local unions will the percentage of the workforce that is organized begin to grow significantly.

BIBLIOGRAPHY

AFL-CIO. 1997. "Building a Movement of American Workers: Federation Objectives for 1997." P. 3 in *AFL-CIO Program and Budget*. Washington, D.C.: AFL-CIO.

Babson, Steve. 1991–92. "'Come Join Us': Volunteer Organizing from a Local-Union Basis." Pp. 60–71 in *Labor Research Review #18*. Chicago: Midwest Center for Labor Research.

Bronars, Stephen, and Donald Deere. 1990. *Union Organizing Activity and Union Coverage, 1973–1988*. Cambridge, Mass.: National Bureau of Economic Research.

Bronfenbrenner, Kate, and Tom Juravich. 1995. "Union Tactics Matter: The Impact of Union Tactics on Certification Elections, First Contracts, and Membership Rates." Working paper of the Institute for the Study of Labor Organizations. Washington, D.C.: AFL-CIO.

Chaison, Gary. 1996. *Unions Mergers in Hard Times: The View from Five Countries*. Ithaca, N.Y.: ILR Press/Cornell University Press.

Chaison, Gary, and Dileep Dhavale. 1990. "A Note on the Severity of the Decline in Union Organizing." Pp. 366–73 in *Industrial and Labor Relations Research Review #43*.

"CWA District 4 Organizing Plan." 1990. Cleveland, Ohio: CWA District 4.

Eckstein, Enid. 1991–92. "Using People Power: A Successful Member Organizing Program Builds New Unions, Strengthens Your Own." Pp. 72–81 in *Labor Research Review #18*. Chicago: Midwest Center for Labor Research.

Keefe, Jeffrey, and Karen Boroff. 1994. "Telecommunications Labor-Management Relations after Divestiture." Pp. 303–71 in *Contemporary Collective Bargaining in the Private Sector,* ed. Paula B. Voos. Madison, Wisc.: Industrial Relations Research Association.

Nissen, Bruce. 1998. "Utilizing the Membership to Organize the Unorganized." Pp. 134–49 in *Organizing to Win,* ed. Kate Bronfenbrenner et al. Ithaca, N.Y.: ILR Press/Cornell University Press.

4

LETTING MORE FLOWERS BLOOM UNDER THE SETTING SUN

Wade Rathke

There is a cultural and social change going on within institutional labor today. The symbols of the blocked bridge over Fourteenth Street in Washington, D.C., are now permeating the halls of labor. The march line has started to compete with the buffet line as a staple of many international conventions. Labor leaders have caught on quickly that if they want to stay at the front of the march, they are sometimes going to have to be the first to go to jail, rather than the first to catch the limo back to the hotel.

We are not nearly there yet, but finally, the times "they *may be* a-changin'!" One can remember again the liberating commitment of Eugene Debs's famous assurance that victory was inevitable and was ours with continued struggle, as certain "as is the setting of the sun."

From my perspective as the chief organizer of a local union—Local 100 of the Service Employees—which was founded from nothing in the hard-scrabble south of Louisiana, Texas, Mississippi, and Arkansas, I found special hope and comfort in the changing situation of institutional labor, even while realizing that we are still mainly nibbling at symbols rather than feasting on the results of such changes.

As unionists, we are no doubt closer to the "setting sun" spoken of so eloquently by Debs than we might like, while the inevitability of our victory continues to be more illusory. The strategic choice made over the years has been to continue to attempt to undergird the status quo by relying most on the bankrupt prospects of the servicing model of organizing. Servicing has been the "heart and soul" of most unions, and institutional labor has hunkered down in the bunkers with the remaining members to try and weather the assault. Unfortunately, this is neither a prescription for growth nor a palliative for the membership, since most membership satisfaction surveys still report that though unions mean well, they can't deliver.

These results were perhaps more likely than the prophesied victory. Having made the conservative choices and lost one-third of the AFL-CIO membership and even more in terms of overall power among the American workforce, perhaps labor, with its new look and leadership, will be able to use the remaining light from this setting sun to allow at least a few new flowers to bloom while there is yet time in the day.

FINDING A DIFFERENT HEART AND SOUL

There is no bible anymore, even if some might argue that there once was. It is also axiomatic that virtually anything, if done consistently, might in fact work. Even the standard National Labor Relations Board (NLRB) model would in fact win against certain firms in certain situations if practiced with high skill and constant resolve. The problem is clear; though from the current record of representation elections filed before the board, organized labor simply must either develop or rediscover some methodology that allows great gains through quick actions, or alternatively reduces the perpetual burden of defeat that is now the hallmark of union organizing under the NLRB.

Some strategies would increase the prospects of organizing's success and ability to move mass organization among unorganized workers. Reviewing the constraints in the present practice helps make the case that the course advocated here is prudent, or at the least no more foolhardy than the path most plodded now.

Currently unions lose a little more than half of all representation elections conducted under the auspices of the NLRB. The win rate unfortunately is disproportionately favorable in smaller rather than larger units, with the highest win rates for unions being found in elections with fewer than fifty workers eligible to vote in the bargaining unit. Some take comfort from the fact that some of the fastest job growth in America is in exactly this sized firm and bargaining unit, but such grasping for straws ignores the relative powerlessness that flows from such a strategy of "small-scale" organizing, as well as the high failure rate of smaller business enterprise. But, even worse (and given how badly this is already breaking, one hesitates to say "worse"), less than 80 percent of these workers will end up being covered by collective bargaining agreements between the unions and companies.

Of those workers who have survived thus far to continue to be represented by a union, the most optimistic (see AFL-CIO 1985, 29) would have it that 90 percent would finally then become full-fledged dues-paying members, while 10 percent would ride free. One would not want to depress and complicate this already horrific picture by looking at the job increase in right-to-work states and the downward trend of these figures as labor, particularly in the private sector, is found to be increasingly waning. The uninitiated would also not even want to contemplate the fact that additional significant percentages of these contracts expire and terminate in increasing numbers three and five years from execution as businesses fail; second contracts do not always follow the first; and decertification efforts accelerate.

If this is an "organizing model" then it is certainly one that seems to roil together troubled economics and difficult organizing in a treadmill of tangential relevance designed at best to harass temporarily a limited number of firms and expend maximum resources from unions in the pursuit of diminishing returns. This model, if not created by business, is certainly perfected by them and adapted to their needs.

This is not to say that there are no situations in which an NLRB process may not be appropriate. This can, and should, be one of the blooming flowers under the setting sun, but it must be one planted more carefully and nurtured more fully.

In looking at future strategies, several alternatives, not mutually exclusive of all other efforts, are worth serious implementation and activity. Among such strategies that come immediately to mind are ones that involve "members-only" or "minority representation" and more concentrated locally based drives.

Campaign Versus Organizational-Driven NLRA Models

At best the National Labor Relations Act (NLRA) has only been with us a little more than fifty years, while unions have organized through better and worse times for closer to two hundred years. The concepts of secret ballot elections, showings of interest, exclusive recognition of one union versus many labor organizations, and the other more or less institutional components of structural representation are all relatively more recent organizing phenomena than iron laws of organization. The history of the organization of labor unions is a rich one with many variables, twists, and turns, as expressed by the plethora of job sites, classifications, and workers themselves. That fact alone should inspire organizers to look more strategically at other possibilities. There is an indisputable common sense to a model of "members only" nonexclusive representation when compared to an NLRA model of union organization, but first one has to understand the conflict of theory and practice in the NLRA-focused organizing world.

The classic articulation of an NLRA model drive is that the union is the bond formed in the community of the workplace by its worker participants. Once support and adherence for this collective vision and experience establishes a solid majority of support among workers, then an NLRB–conducted election simply *certifies* the union already built in the workplace. It follows that the results of the election simply *record* numerically the level of strength held by the organization built by the workers. In the same logic the contract achieved along with the quality of terms is a final *recognition* by the employer of the organization's strength. The process under such an NLRA theory is seamless and flows directly at all points from an analysis of the strengths and weaknesses of the basic organization.

In confronting the basic organizing choices between being *campaign-driven* or *organization-driven,* the NLRA model drifts from the primary organizational theory into deep and drowning seas. A campaign-driven practice builds to events as opposed to constructing organizational strength, and therefore when done well is building first toward an organizational formation sufficient to file for and win an election. After succeeding with the election campaign—sometimes implemented by specialized organizers and other technicians—the campaign-driven model then moves to a contract campaign to activate workers in other ways to pressure the bosses to achieve the most favorable agreement available under the particular circumstances. Such campaigns are in many unions pursued by yet other individual craftspeople, such as negotiators, researchers, lawyers, and publicists. Though such resources are not generally available in local-land, needless to say, the culture still dominates.

If an institutional victory is achieved, the task then becomes to build a *permanent organization* in the workplace. Such a responsibility is often the assignment of a union representative or business agent disconnected to the other phases of this campaign-driven developmental model, who then constructs a *servicing representation model* which may or may not rely on any of the same workers who were (or were not) activated in the earlier but dramatically different sequences during the election and contract struggles.

The contrast between proper theory and common practice occurs naturally in the ebb and flow of organizing, rather than through any more mysterious circumstance. There are no evil people deliberately pushing unions down dead-end paths, yet the results unfortunately yield many unintended consequences. The most obvious is that the NLRB campaign model only inadvertently builds power at the workplace. A campaign model is more tactical than strategic, and therein often lies its strength and weakness as well. The campaign model unfortunately depends too much on intervention from outside the workplace at critical points to succeed, which not only puts too much emphasis on such expertise and resources but also increasingly limits such a model as a means to achieve mass organization.

The advantages of the campaign model are its relative speed and surety over the organization-driven model: campaigns have discernible timelines and fixed points along the road—elections, negotiations, or grievances—while organizations dedicated to building power at the workplace are evolutionary. With campaigns there are fixed battlegrounds, and therefore also—whether for right or wrong ultimately—fixed spaces of peace. In organization-building models there is constant struggle along a hundred fronts in an ongoing guerrilla war in which time and attrition are ultimate allies but never necessarily short-term friends, and though there may be lulls there is no peace until victory is complete. A campaign model is designed to win battles, while an organization-driven model is designed to win wars.

MEMBERS ONLY AS A MEANS TO MASS ORGANIZATION

Following an organization-driven NLRA organizing model, the NLRA can be simply utilized as a measurement or barometer of organizational strength and power. The NLRA can be detached from the organizing itself as a merely tangential and tactical component of the overall strategy indistinguishable from the tactical use of regulations and laws governing discrimination, health and safety, pension rights, wage and hours, or any number of other local, state, or federal protections that might become useful organizing handles. That is precisely the proper placement of the NLRA and the NLRB in an organizational-driven model.

The task of building organization in a workplace does not inherently infer an election or even a collective bargaining agreement. An organization by definition has to have adherents, and there is simply no better way to determine such support, participation, and loyalty than by first requiring as a precondition to all other activity the joining and paying of full membership.

"Full membership" means exactly what it implies. One of the emptiest achievements of institutional labor has been the creation of "associate members." "Associate" membership was available in either nonbargaining situations or prebargaining circumstance. Such "members" would pay minimal dues and would receive some benefits accessible through the AFL-CIO exclusively because of their membership. Such a membership classification was designed to catch people either before they were in the church or after they were pushed outside of the church.

This has made the concept of collective bargaining even more inappropriately hallowed. Associate membership in effect became a form of *second-*

class union citizenship, though in some cases the differences between the contract member and noncontract member were overestimated and exaggerated way past any realistic expectation. Unions that recruited associate rather than full members diluted the impact such workers sought in the active life of the workplace in order to keep such "members" disenfranchised in the political life of the union itself. This has been a bad bargain that has undermined the organizing potential of the entire program.

All actual organizing experience indicates that to a worker-member there is no automatic equation that equates collective bargaining with payment of full membership dues and the absence of collective bargaining with minimal or no dues, yet this was a fundamental premise of the associate membership experiment. In effect social work and political judgments substituted for organizing judgment.

In Local 100 both in public- and private-sector work sites workers were not only willing to pay dues at the full and usual rate in nonbargaining situations but desirous of the full participation and collective membership status offered by full dues payment. Certainly this experience is not unique to our own local but in fact is common and shared in a vast number of situations, particularly in the public sector in states and local jurisdictions where formal bargaining laws or regulations do not exist by the American Federation of Teachers (AFT), National Education Association (NEA), and state employee associations both independent and affiliated.

The threshold of an organization-driven model is membership and the activity, energy, and rewards that flow from and to that membership. Examples for successful development abound in unions, as well as in pathbreaking community efforts, like those of the Association for Community Organizing for Reform Now (ACORN), which has built a membership of close to 100,000 families on direct dues payment, including almost $.5 million per year in bank-draft dues. Though unions may not have access to payroll dues deduction in such community efforts or workplace organizing drives, advances in banking technology have developed so rapidly that membership dues can be deducted or "drafted" directly from any of a variety of accounts a potential member may have.

In a members-only organizing model we need to be able to conceive of the organizing constituency as *unorganized workers* rather than simply discreet unorganized workplaces. Once we have moved workers to see themselves as a union and as union members, we need to have them see themselves as able to act not only collectively within the context of a specific work site but individually as organizers and as members regardless of the work site. This conceptual framework must be the base from which any new mass organizing model

80

is built. At the heart of any future prospects for rekindling a real labor movement there must be such a radically different conception of members and membership within a culture of collective action, activity, and activism.

NECESSITY CREATES ITS OWN INVENTIONS

In any careful reading of the pre-NLRA history of various unions or any discussion with old-timers, one quickly sees that a common organizational strategy was predominantly one of building membership in the union and acting collectively as a union either in exemplary fashion or to demonstrate majority membership. One finds myriad dues-collection strategies that were employed in the absence of payroll deductions, from the now outlawed closed shop to the membership pins that changed colors on a monthly basis so that stewards would know you were up to date (see Freeman 1989). There are also very contemporary examples of "members-only" or "minority" unionism, though most of the more successful are in the public sector in noncollective bargaining situations.

There is no major public sector union that has not had extensive experience in "members-only" organizing and representation. The more than two-million-member NEA organized teachers in many non-collective-bargaining states and continues to do so on a "members-only" basis. Certainly, this is also the situation as well in education-based organizing for the AFT. One should not jump to a conclusion that this is a "professional phenomena," since support personnel units of everybody from janitors to teachers aides have also been organized this way by Local 100 in Texas and Louisiana, as well as by other Service Employees International Union (SEIU) locals in the country.

American Federation of State, County and Municipal Employees (AFSCME), SEIU, and the Communications Workers have all had extensive organizing projects in the public sector among state workers that were based on membership-only representation. The almost ten-year organizing struggle waged by the Texas State Employees Union (TSEU), a branch of the Communications Workers of America (CWA), in the 1980s that culminated in their winning payroll dues deduction in 1991 under then governor Ann Richards, was one of the seminal drives using such an organizing model. For TSEU in Texas, Georgia State Employees Union (GSEU)/SEIU Local 1985 in Georgia (which won payroll deduction in 1994), and Local 100 SEIU's Arkansas project, there were often long periods of time in which dues were hand-collected or collected by bank drafts in building long-term organization among such workers.

The ample demonstrations of success in public-sector organizing where no choice was available demonstrate that the demand was most clearly articulated *for organization*—pure and simple. This has been obscured by the "social worker" ideology that has suffused union organizing with the bread-and-butter objectives of collective bargaining agreements. Nevertheless, it is surprising that there have not been more efforts to build direct members-only organizations in difficult organizing environments where there is arguably no simple NLRA alternative.

Ideological Obstacles to Members-Only Organizing

Experiments with a "members-only" model will work best in large units rather than small ones. Approaching a critical mass threshold of 10 percent or so of the available constituency is much different if that means the first one hundred members of one thousand workers than if it means simply five of fifty. One hundred workers acting together can see and feel the power of the union they are creating. Conceivably so can five of fifty, but there is no getting around the problem that five still know they are only really five. Fortunately, existing NLRA organizing's best success is in units of fifty or fewer, so there is no reason to believe that "members-only" organizing should compete with campaign-based work in micro-organizing rather than projects of scale.

Some might argue that the long time frames involved in large-scale "members only" drives may make such drives too expensive. Certainly, these drives will not be cheap, but conversely neither are NLRA drives in large units. An investment in organizing a unit of one thousand or more workers (where current win rate percentages are the most abysmal for unions) is extremely high risk under any NLRA driven model. Unless such a drive is already white-hot, it is going to take some time and some talent to reach 70 percent on such a unit, and the odds of such a drive ultimately failing are better than fifty-fifty. However, with a "members-only" model there is some income immediately when one triggers dues collection. The drive can continually pay a substantial part of its own way. More important, as the membership and organization expand, the power and income grow correspondingly. As long as the union has the will to organize in that work site, one will have a union, as opposed to an NLRA–based model where failing to file or to win implodes the fragile collectivity immediately.

Another obstacle revolves around the inability to practice the standard "servicing" model in "members-only" organizing. Generations of business reps who have run the routes faithfully to fly the flag for the union would have some difficulty operating without formal recognition, formal work site access, formal payroll deductions, and other standard assumptions of existing servicing. The union cannot be built, nor can it survive on the backs of the "expert" union agent coming in and thumping the table on a grievance to prove the

82

value of the union. The union has to be built in this model on the strength and backs of stewards and membership activity in the workplace. Leadership has to be developed and activated not in a simple "representation" system but in a strongly participatory system.

Direct action at the work site, not external intervention, is key to building organization and power. Local 100's "kitchen cabinet" in the Dallas Independent School District often marches 25–30 workers into the supervisor's office to file a grievance, and attempts to resolve it on the spot. Ironically, almost all organizers can recount stories of workplace direct and collective action before the union was organized, when workers took matters into their own hands to resolve issues and grievances. It is often organizers in the modern institutional labor organization who are constructing the legalistic system to replace the organic experience of the workers, without even realizing the impact. Nonetheless, one has to build deep, and not simply wide, to construct organization and eventual success. The culture created has to be an "organizing" culture, not a servicing culture, and it must depend on direct, collective action in the workplace, rather than individual, external representation. Long-term, these are assets, though, short-term, such situations are outside so much of contemporary experience that they pose ideological constraints about what is presumed to work or not work. This may be a "better" way to go, but to many it will feel "harder."

Finally, in making a short list of obstacles to wide-scale implementation of this model, it is fair to say that such organizing models will have to be dominated more by locals than by national and international organizers. International organizing staffs, many of which are unionized themselves, are not going to line up to be assigned to x, y, or z place around the country for two to ten years until one wins, even if it may mean organizing five-, ten-, or twenty-thousand workers at a clip. Organizers who are "project-" and campaign-oriented are hardly going to favor "members-only" organizational development. To the degree that many, if not most, organizing staff are increasingly consolidated at national and international levels, this militates against any but isolated implementation of this model, unless such work is driven by locals, which by jurisdiction, charter, and necessity have to eat where they live rather than going from opportunity to opportunity. Strategically, international and national unions have to develop the ways and means of decentralizing organizing so that the maximum number of locals in the optimum number of locations can effectively organize and win, but politically this is not the current trendline, even though our very existence is in peril.

In the same way that one might read in *Business Week* or *Forbes* that long-term investments in market and product development are not the norm for enterprises having to show immediate returns, an analogous problem exists for national and international unions politically. Leadership needs to be very secure in developing, funding, and staffing projects where, despite the high probability of ultimate success, the timeline may run from five to ten years. It is difficult politically for many institutional bureaucracies to develop programs and results that may not mature until terms of office have expired.

Strategically if we are to build mass organizing models again for organizing unorganized workers there will be failures and there will be long struggles. We need institutional and collective support to ensure that this is possible. Such support requires not only the ways and means but also the will, which still does not quite exist to support mass organization.

TARGETS FOR MASS ORGANIZATION WITH A MEMBERS-ONLY MODEL

In order for there to be a labor movement again, we must target huge firms in industries that, because of our own inactivity and their growth, are becoming more unorganized daily. Organizers and labor leaders can look back at the massive AFL and CIO drives to organize basic industries in the 1930s and 1940s and take it as a first principle that the size of these enterprises demanded an organizing solution that could tackle them effectively. How could one not go after a Ford or GM or US Steel, when these firms had more than 100,000 workers under hire in those times, we say? How could the labor chieftains of that era have been so asleep at the switch?

But in truth we are also getting quite a bit of nap time in our generation. There is no shortage of companies with more than 50,000 and even more than 100,000 workers that are virtually as "union-free" as any modern management seminar would ever promise. This is especially the case in any modern firm founded after 1950 whose growth has created mass employment. "New" industries in "new" areas have successfully resisted standard organizing techniques. Examples abound in modern telecommunications and manufacturing, semiconductors, computer components and assembly, and other high-growth, high-tech, new industrial segments. A Motorola or a Texas Instruments is a huge employer operating almost union-free.

The booming service industry has produced the most expansive job growth in recent years and has produced employment giants working without anything more than the faintest traces of unionization. The explosion in tourism as a major postwar employer cannot easily be reconciled with the plummeting membership figures of the Hotel Employees Restaurant Employees (HERE) in any other way than as a major opportunity being forfeited. Corporations like Marriott, Holiday Inn, and others each have more than 100,000 workers under hire. Other hotel chains like the Hilton and Hyatt are presumed by many unions to be "friendly" to organized labor, yet these firms are able to operate carte blanche with a majority of their workers unorganized.

Despite the current downsizing in the acute care side of the health care industry, total employment is huge and some of the employers are giants by any standards, yet union density is small. Even a downsized Beverly in the nursing home segment of the industry (a more than ten-year organizing target of the Service Employees and United Food and Commercial Workers) continues to be as large as Chrysler, with more than 93,000 workers. Hospital chains that are rapidly integrating along with many other nursing home companies are largely unorganized. Columbia/HCA has considerably more than 100,000 workers, and despite its avaricious gobbling of market share and hospital beds in many areas of the country, particularly in the Sun Belt, it remains virtually union-free. Houston-based nursing home operator, Living Centers of America (formerly a piece of ARA Services), continues to be union-free within the top five largest national chains, but others in this range are also virtually unorganized.

In general services ARAMARK (formerly ARA Services), which handles all manner of services from janitorial to entertainment concessions to school sub-contracting, has considerably more than 120,000 workers and is increasingly nonunion in major growth sectors of its business. ARAMARK, like the Hyatts and Hiltons, is an interesting example of a company that has been aggressively antiunion for a decade but, because it is unionized in some of the large remaining union strongholds like New York, Chicago, and San Francisco, is presumed to be a friend. The real business of an ARAMARK is essentially as a low-cost labor contractor. Home health care companies, which are currently mushrooming, are little more than that, except with a health care twist. Like janitors, clericals, and nurses' aides, home health aides are among the top ten fastest-growing job classifications. There are increasingly significant employers like Staff Builders, Kimberly, and others becoming larger employers in this still largely fragmented new growth industry of 700,000+ workers.

In many of the jobs in the lower-wage service sector, because of the part-time nature of much of the work, "multiemployers" and "coemployers" are also very common, offering additional opportunities on a direct "members-only" model, since one is organizing the worker rather than the company first. It is certainly common to find a hotel worker by day becoming a janitor or home care attendant by night or by weekend, or a nursing home worker who is also doing home care or may be a part-time school cafeteria worker "in season."

The highly transient nature of modern service employment has made such workers both ubiquitous and fungible. Organizing the firm often means that the union is simply manning the turnstile at the job. SEIU Local 880 in

Chicago estimates that in winning its 8,000-worker home health care unit, they did more than 50,000 home visits over the last several years to sign up the majority of these workers. This time around mass organizing may mean following the worker, rather than the job, in order to build the organization.

In many of these "new" industries, union avoidance has become highly sophisticated in utilization of the NLRA and the NLRB's case law and precedents to increasingly minimize the likelihood of successful organization through the classic campaign-driven model. Living Centers of America, for example, aggressively seeks to combine units in entire metropolitan areas so that they can resist being organized on a "home-by-home" basis, which is common in the rest of the industry (see ARA Living Centers NLRB decisions, 1978, 1984). In the same way, Columbia/HCA is designing dominance of their employees through their personnel system. Reading a series of corporate confidential personnel memoranda distributed from their Houston-area operations upon the consolidation of Columbia's Health Trust merger in 1994, starting with registered nurses and moving "down" the line to other classifications, Columbia was systematically constructing a single bargaining unit scenario for their 15,000 workers in the Houston metro market across Harris County. Assignments were being shifted between hospitals; workers were being hired "from one hospital" and assigned to other hospitals in the chain; job classifications of "roving" employees in specialized areas were being created; policies, hiring, firing, and other systems establishing terms and conditions of employment were being unified and centralized—all of which combined creates the argument for a single appropriate bargaining unit on an NLRB petition.

A classic NLRB model directed at a chain with 286 hospitals (one is union by acquisition) in units that might run from 10,000 to 20,000 in different markets would be wild. We cannot guarantee that a "members-only" approach would be the only one that would work, but we can absolutely assert that—barring a miracle—we will never organize HCA under a classic NLRB driven model. Columbia/HCA is arguably one of the Ford Motor Companies of our generation.

At the rate we are going, given current conditions, the same statement is unfortunately true of virtually any large-scale employer. Yet with patience and practice, we could begin hunkering down now in industry after industry with firm after firm to begin the process of developing real organization to win, just as was done by unionists in America time after time in the past.

The Atomized Workplace and Minority Representation

Modern organizing does not find the concentration of workers "under one roof" where drives can spark and blaze like spontaneous combustion when the proper ingredients are available for such a conflagration. It is undeniable that America was a slightly simpler place fifty years ago than it is today. Many of the larger employers have disparate workplaces stretched throughout the country. There are more than 800 stops to make on the way to reaching the 93,000 workers of a Beverly Enterprises and more than 300 stops to reach the 125,000 of a Columbia/HCA Hospital operation. Some indeed are close together, where, with a mighty plan and excellent resources a union could go after huge hunks of individual firms, but, even if successful, a union would then have been built on only a way station along the road to organizing the entire company, much less the industry.

Worth noting as well, particularly in the service industries, are the wide variety of diverse job classifications and the shrewd utilization of cultural, class, and racial differences to control workforces and provide unionization obstacles. In a hospital one may find more than 1,000 workers under a couple of roofs, but one is also going to find more than a 100 different job classifications in what is now eight possible NLRA bargaining units. In a hotel, from the back of the house to the front, one confronts systematic differences in many facilities, with limited contact between the various departments, though unfortunately power for the workers really is more likely wall-to-wall than in any other individual slice of bargaining units.

Suffice it to say that there are organizing problems galore in trying to wrap a strategic, winnable organizing plan around any major firm or significant unorganized industry on the current corporate and national landscape. We are too often following the blind man around the elephant, facing choices that are unreal: going after a piece of a company rather than the whole firm; going after limited localities without the will or resources to organize nationally; going after one unit since we lack the plan that would allow us to go wall-to-wall.

REAL LOCALS AND REAL INTERNATIONALS

Whether one moved toward an organization-building offensive utilizing nonexclusive representation on a members-only basis or not, strategically one begins from the dismal day currently dawning. As a rule, institutional labor has little current *national* economic strength other than in industrial exceptions or historical aberrations. What we have left is some level of spatial power generally in urban/metropolitan areas and some regions of the country such as the Pacific Northwest, Great Lakes, and mid-Atlantic states (Rathke and Rogers 1998).

Embarking on campaigns to build mass organization among the unorganized either on an enterprise or industrial basis, we must build on what is left of our existing strength, because it is in these zones of continued union presence and power that our potential leverage still lies. At the same time we have to go after the related operations throughout these segments or entire industries simultaneously.

In the main the habit and practice of both national/international unions and local unions has been to divide these responsibilities in an unfortunate way. There has been a presumption that most local unions handle the organizing that manages to work its way into the hall through phones or feet but it is the national/international union that initiates, staffs, and finances "big" drives. Local unions under the dominant servicing model disproportionately have hired nothing but servicing or business reps, with local after local having no staff positions for organizers. On the national/international level one finds organizers, though there are not nearly enough, no matter the plan.

Organizing has become an increasingly high-skill but low-prestige job within the largely politically-driven hierarchy of institutional labor. (Perhaps in labor's new desperation even that is starting to change; note Andy Stern's election as the new president of the Service Employees after a dozen years as SEIU organizing director.) The current confrontation of personalities and national/international unions is ripe with the rhetoric of change for organizing, but resolving the structural and political organizing problems is a prerequisite for successful organizing, and that will require tremendous political will, as new president John Sweeney is finding at the AFL-CIO.

We need locals that in concert with other locals—regardless of the particular organization or natural work jurisdiction—are able fully to organize on a firm and industrial basis within a spatial environment. We need a different conception and leadership of central bodies that sees its role as coordinating and spearheading such mass organization within the range of its jurisdiction (consider the experience of the Chicago Federation of Labor in the early twentieth-century meatpacking drives, a good description of which is found in Barrett 1987, and the Atlanta AFL-CIO effort to move jobs from the 1996 Olympics). We also need the political and institutional resources that are available to protect and promote such organization building. Such local efforts must be national in scope with permanent resources and dedicated and trained local organizing staffs, rather than impaled in the impotence of voluntarism, lobbying, and irrelevance.

We need national/international unions not only to support the locally driven efforts against industrial and enterprise targets but to be able to "fill in the gaps on the map" and mount serious and concentrated organizing efforts where there are strategic holes based on historical inequalities of organization and resources. We have to be a national labor movement to survive, not simply a paint-by-numbers ad hoc effort, trying to jump from organized island to organized island. Internationals need to develop organizing and other staff that know how to build locals where none now exist and to mount and bring together local efforts *across union lines* to go after mass organizing targets in the methodical and systematic way that models like "members-only" will require. International organizers have to be able not simply to win an organizing campaign but to leave something behind in local structure and capacity other than a hotel and bar bill.

In the current rethinking about a direction for the AFL-CIO the most encouraging development is the notion that the AFL-CIO also might play a role by coordinating and aggregating the organizing efforts of the federated unions to produce major organizing initiatives. To the degree this is done in a new and different way it creates something that holds more promise if it moves unions to consolidate resources and staff from the local level up to the national level, and activates the latent central body and state federation resources toward organizing as well.

Change in this area may require rethinking jurisdiction and how it affects local and national/international unions. The changing complexity of commercial enterprise indicates that such a reinvention of jurisdiction is long overdue, since the notion is passé that corporations operate only within local geographies, yet that concept of local unions remains a cornerstone of institutional labor strategy and practice. Additionally, though virtually all kinds of work and workers are found in community after community around the country, individual locals with conventional jurisdictions do not represent such workers effectively in such an array of locations. Yet, that premise is exactly what currently propels much of the national and local federation's conception of jurisdiction. We need a more holistic and practical jurisdictional model for organizing.

The strongest organizing locals in local demographic and economic markets could act as coordinating bodies to bring other locals together into *organizing councils* to organize the unorganized on coordinated national organizing campaigns *regardless* of the usual or traditional jurisdiction but solely on proven *organizing ability*. If a council is not workable, then individual local unions—regardless of international union jurisdiction—that have proven themselves skilled and successful as *organizing locals* should be encouraged and supported in expanding their organizing range to other targets that need organization. We cannot continue to play internal labor politics when the stakes include the survival of organized labor. One hopes that new institutional leadership will be visionary, brave, and willful enough to push past artificial jurisdictional and structural lines to create the organic organizing machinery that can really produce results and new organization from place to place.

Real locals need to be multidimensional enough not only to service what they have left but to organize all the rest. *Real* national unions need to go after national targets and build unions out in the vineyards where the work still desperately needs to be done. Such interests transcend the particular model employed. A realignment of institutional resources to produce the scale of organizing necessary to enroll the unorganized into unions is necessary.

FROM DUSK TO DAWN

The history and practice of nonexclusive members-only representation has been an important one that continues to bear important results, particularly in the public sector. Such a model might be an antidote to institutional labor's current organizing malaise. This model would take time, people, and resources. It would involve some changes in the way institutional labor is currently doing "business as usual." The changes might be as sweeping as the strategy, yet these are times when radical surgery is the prescription—not a couple of pills or some cosmetic touch-ups.

While I advocate members-only organizing as a primary approach to national targets and mass organization, I also believe that such a strategy of organization building accommodates many other strategic and tactical options. Building sufficient organization in individual workplaces would not bar having the government or some third party certify the result. Any enterprise and industry under organization through such a model, with its constant internal and external struggle in the workplace and throughout the community, will eventually *want* unions to return to pure and simple collective bargaining. This is part of the lesson of the successful direct-action tactics with which the Justice for Janitors campaign has prevailed. Nothing historically or contemporarily would bar collective bargaining in the future, if that is seen as the wisest and most appropriate means for building the organization.

The urgent demand is not one of degree but of orientation. We need to realign to organize workers, not workplaces, and to vitally involve them as organizers and leaders of mass organizing drives. We need to rethink the way we work as unions at all levels of the organizational chart, to see if the bureaucracies and job classifications are strangling organizing or accelerating growth. Making a long story short, if we could combine forces and resources into organizing, we could even do the wrong thing, and, as Debs offered, if we do so persistently, we will inevitably succeed. Right now we can't seem to win for losing, and our traditions are not helping us realign to face the challenges of the future. That is a situation that has not been changing but must change immediately if labor is to find organized unions in our future.

Works Cited

AFL-CIO Committee on the Evolution of Work. 1985. *The Changing Situation of Workers and Their Unions.* Washington, D.C.: AFL-CIO.

ARA Living Center NLRB decision. 1978. 1984. NLRB Region 16 (San Antonio, Tex.) decision regarding United Food and Commercial Workers, 1978. NLRB Region 15 (New Orleans, La.) decision regarding SEIU Local 100, 1984. Contained in ACORN collection, Labor Organizing Files, within the Social Action Archives of the State Historical Society of Wisconsin, Madison, Wisc.

Barrett, James R. 1987. *Work and Community in the Jungle: Chicago's Packinghouse Workers, 1894–1922.* Urbana: University of Illinois Press.

Freeman, Joshua B. 1989. *In Transit: The Transport Workers Union in New York City, 1933–1966.* New York: Oxford University Press.

Rathke, Wade, and Joel Rogers. 1998. *Labor Strategies.* Ithaca, N.Y.: ILR Press/Cornell University.

III

REACHING OUT

5

WORK, ORGANIZED LABOR, AND THE CATHOLIC CHURCH: BOUNDARIES AND OPPORTUNITIES FOR COMMUNITY/LABOR COALITIONS

John Russo and Brian R. Corbin

The election of John Sweeney as president of the AFL-CIO has been characterized as signaling the renewal of the American labor movement. Since his election in the fall of 1995, Sweeney has moved rapidly to restructure the federation and to shift financial resources in ways that reflect a renewed emphasis on organizing and political action. While it is too early to judge overall effectiveness, there are indications of a tactical shift and that the labor movement is about to engage in more aggressive advocacy and coalition building.

Of course, the issues upon which labor/community coalitions can be built are both varied and complex, but one that has currently emerged in the public consciousness involves modern worklife. A growing body of primary research has developed around the issue of work and has been popularized by mainstream magazines and journals devoted to such themes as contingent work, restructured work, alienated work, virtual work, overwork, the future of work, the end of work, and the impact of changes in worklife on the overall quality of life. At the same time, individual labor and community groups (including women's, religious, and environmental groups) have sought to develop policies to address the changing work environment. Yet, these same groups have frequently failed to develop the types of coalitions that might have a broad impact on the growing worklife debate.

To understand better the basis for community/labor coalitions, it is important to look at the issue of work using Catholic social teaching and its connections to organized labor. To do this, a brief analysis of the relationship between changes in worklife and community building will be provided. This will be followed by a summary of Catholic social teaching on work and unions. Finally, I will discuss the boundaries and opportunities presented by labor-church coalitions.

JOHN RUSSO AND BRIAN R. CORBIN

WORK, TECHNOLOGY, AND COMMUNITY

Work is the dominating element in most people's lives. Work can be stimulating and creative or boring and stifling to individual development. (Work is defined here to include both time paid for and unpaid domestic labor.) While work can be seen as a cultural act (artistic and other forms of creative and investigatory activities) that nurtures the development of the whole individual, over the last century the production process has increasingly fragmented work, centralized knowledge, and separated the individual from what is produced. Despite some positive claims by postindustrial theorists concerning knowledge workers or the future of work, as in the past, work in developed and developing countries remains largely monotonous, boring, repetitive, and ultimately depressing. It is also expanding.

Economist Juliet Schor in *The Overworked American* has documented that the average employed person is now on the job an additional 163 hours per year. This is roughly equivalent to working an extra month a year. This phenomenon is largely the result of employer preference for longer hours and consumer consciousness (the expansion of consumer debt and the acceptance of the work-spend cycle). The overall impact of expansion of work on employee health and family has been dramatic. Increases in stress-related disease, sleep disorders, marital distress, and child neglect all have been associated with changes in worklife (Schor 1992).

Of course, conventional wisdom has suggested that technology ultimately would reduce the most unsatisfactory elements of work and provide more leisure time. No doubt, technology has increased productivity and, in many situations, improved work environments. However, as Jeremy Rifkin has suggested in *Time Wars,* technology—especially computers—has introduced new forms of temporal measurements (nanosecond) to our consciousness and enabled employees to be increasingly tethered to their work even when not in the workplace (Rifkin 1987). Clearly, the technological revolution in the last twenty years has coincided with the intensification of work.

The quid pro quo for demeaning and intensified work was supposedly an increased standard of living and more leisure time. However, just the opposite has happened. Since 1974 the standard of living of the average American has declined while leisure time has been reduced. That is, in order to maintain living standards, there has been an expansion of overtime, moonlighting, and multiple contingent employment situations; simultaneously there has been a shrinkage of vacation, holiday, bereavement, and sick time for the average worker.

While the impact of the expansion of work and decline of leisure on the individual is well confirmed, less understood is the impact of changes in work-life on ideas of community. Community institutions (economic, political, religious, gender-based) are at the heart of any civil society. From Alexis de Tocqueville (*Democracy in America*) to Francis Fukuyama (*Trust: The Social Spiritual Values and the Creation of Prosperity*), various authors have recognized that community institutions help create public-spirited citizens, who sustain a healthy and dynamic democratic culture and society.

These community institutions form and flourish as intermediate organizations between family and government in what feminist scholar Sara Evans calls "free spaces" in a society (Evans 1989). In these "free spaces" between the private and the public spheres, identities, ideas, approaches, and skills (speaking, hearing, and negotiating) are formed and honed for later participation in a civil society. For example, the role of the African-American Churches and more progressive labor unions with minority memberships in the development of the philosophy, leadership, and membership in the civil rights movement has been well established.

Similarly, labor educator Ruth Needleman has suggested that within intermediate organizations themselves "independent spaces" and "structured opportunities" must exist where the dominant organization's customs, values, and perspectives can be discussed free from organizational sanctions (Needleman 1993). Furthermore these independent spaces are loci where diversity can be encouraged and nurtured and where new voices (women and individuals of color) can gain leadership experience. That is, breathing room must be created where new ideas, methods, and leadership can be developed without being seen as dissident or disloyal. Some examples within the labor movement and Catholic Church include the Coalition of Black Trade Unionists, Post Office Women for Equal Rights (POWER), and many organizations funded by the Catholic Campaign for Human Development such as the Farm Labor Organizing Committee, Nine to Five, and the Association for Community Organizing for Reform Now (ACORN).

But free spaces require free time and therein lies a problem. With the expansion of work and consumer consciousness, participation in intermediate organizations is withering. Like the democratic political process itself, participation in most organizations has been reduced to mere voting. Less participation results in weak organizational affiliation, and circularly, weak affiliation results in apathy and even less participation.

Some might disagree with this formulation and suggest that the communications revolution has merely changed the form of participation. More specifically, E-mail, chat rooms, talk radio, cable TV, and the emerging interac-

97

tive television have changed the form and scale of participation even within intermediate organizations. It is true that new communication technologies do hold promise for new forms of cooperation and partnership. (The communications revolution has made it possible instantaneously to transmit pictures, talk, music, and advertising throughout the world.) But, on balance, it would seem that time that might be spent engaged in political discussions, community affairs, or institutional activities is currently being spent passively by couch potatoes. That is, the overworked are largely entertainment voyeurs rather than active participants in the communications revolution, often collapsing in front of the television, radio, or computer.

To summarize, the increase in hours worked, technology, and consumer consciousness has resulted in an intensification of work. The intensification has not been accompanied by the expected increases in the standard of living and leisure time. Consequently, the alterations in worklife have contributed to the loss of affiliation within intermediate organizations (including labor and religious groups) while forming the basis for possible future alliances by these same organizations.

These contemporary discussions about the nature of work have some historical antecedents in Catholic social teachings. Catholic social teaching on work provides a basis in the present context to assist in the formation of labor, community, and church coalitions. Contemporary discussions not only are informed by Catholic social teaching but can also provide the foundation for labor, community, and church coalitions. In the next section, we will provide a brief overview of the theological principles regarding labor unions and work, and discuss some practical ideas for labor, religious, and community coalitions suggested in the tenets of Catholic social teachings.

CATHOLIC SOCIAL TEACHING AS A BASIS FOR LABOR/CHURCH ALLIANCES

The Catholic Church, through the voice of the Vatican and the pontiffs, began its modern economic and social-ethical analysis in earnest with the publication of *Rerum Novarum*, or *On the Conditions of the Working Classes*, in 1891 (NCCB 1985). Pope Leo XIII responded in this "magna carta" to the plight of the working-class population in Europe and America as it underwent radical transformations wrought by the Industrial Revolution. Many church leaders feared two critical issues: first, that the church would lose contact with its working-class adherents if it refused to deal with modern realities; and second, that working-class laborers would find solace, comfort, and organizational strength in radical labor parties, communism, and anarchist movements. These major issues are akin to current concerns by church leaders about dwindling participation, social apathy, and materialism of its members. Many church leaders believed that the church had no choice, based in its own ethical tradition and its immigrant populaces, but to speak on behalf of the working classes. It could ill afford to alienate so many of its believers, then and now.

In response to the changes faced by the church and its working-class adherents, Leo XIII challenged core values and assumptions about work in the economic and political paradigms of his day. The church officially committed itself "to a rejection of a central thesis of the prevailing capitalist 'realism' of the Western world, namely, that labor is a commodity to be bought at market prices determined by the law of supply and demand rather than by the human needs of the worker" (Dorr 1983; Russo and Corbin 1991; *Rerum Novarum* [RN], par. 61–66).

Leo XIII also criticized socialist tendencies regarding violence and the secularization of society. However, Leo incorporated some tenets of socialist thought in his insistence that the state, or government, play an active role in the redistribution of wealth, property protection, and workers' rights in the name of justice and not just charity. Leo further legitimized the rights and duties of workers to join and form workers' mutual associations or trade unions (RN, par. 68–69; 73–74; 76) in order to protect themselves against the powers of employers and even of the state. Finally, Leo XIII established the church's continuing insistence on the interdependence and interrelationship of labor and capital. *Rerum Novarum* called for a mutuality between the forces of labor and capital, since "each needs the other; capital cannot do without labor, nor labor without capital" (RN 28).

Throughout the one hundred years since *Rerum Novarum,* pontiffs and conferences of bishops,[1] especially in the United States, have continued the social-ethical reflection on work, capitalism, and unionism. In the modern context, the church does not just deal with a moral analysis of the existing economic and social structures but calls for a normative framework for what laborers should want from work, organizations, companies, and society: in other words, there is an awareness of the practical implications of the religious and spiritual nature of work. This is most clearly seen in John Paul II's encyclical *Laborem Exercens* (LE), published in 1981.

In *Laborem Exercens,* John Paul states "that human work is a key, probably the essential key, to the whole social question" (LE, sect. 3). In that light, John Paul II strives to articulate a new spirituality of work based on a deep theological principle, namely, that God made humans in the divine image. That divine image, taken from the Book of Genesis, is a creator. Therefore, labor and work are essential cocreative features of human spirituality. As God creates, so too do individuals cocreate with God through work. This spirituality further dictates that work is not only needed for our human material condition (food, family, leisure, savings) but is also part of our subjectivity, creativity, and artistic personality. Labor gives food for our bodies and meaning to our lives. Therefore, work must be available to all, labor must be subjectively meaningful to the worker, and everyone's labor must be seen as beneficial to the common good.

Since labor has both objective and subjective meanings, John Paul II asserts clearly that not only are labor and capital interdependent but, more important, labor has priority over capital. He writes: "This principle directly concerns the process of production. In this process, labor is always a primary efficient cause, while capital, the whole collection of means of production, remains a mere instrument or instrumental cause. This principle is an evident truth that emerges from the whole of human experience" (LE, sect. 12). It is now clear: the struggles of laborers are primary over the concerns of capital.

John Paul II further claims that work is not an individualistic enterprise; rather it is social. Solidarity between workers and with workers is as critical today as it was during the industrial revolution. The church again reclaims its historical position regarding the rights of workers to form and join unions and to bargain collectively. Just as important, John Paul II states that the purpose of unions is to defend "the vital interests of those employed in the various professions . . . [as] the mouthpiece for the struggle for social justice, for the rights of working people in accordance with their individual professions" (LE, sect. 20). Regardless of the rights of workers, John Paul II reminds all that "it is characteristic of work that it first and foremost unites people. In this consists its social power: to build a community" (LE, sect. 20).

In the American context, the U.S. Catholic Bishops have extended John Paul II's thinking in their 1986 *Pastoral Letter on Economic Justice for All* (NCCB 1986).[2] In that statement, the bishops argue that all economic systems must be judged on how the system affirms the dignity of the human person, and especially all workers. The bishops state three fundamental normative questions about economic life: "What does the economy do *for* people? What does the economy do *to* people? And how do people *participate* in the economy?" (1).

These normative questions, once raised in the political realm in American history, according to the bishops, are now to be asked in the economic realm. They state their argument clearly:

> For over two hundred years the United States has been engaged in a bold experiment in democracy. . . . The nation's founders took daring steps to create structures of participation, mutual accountability, and widely distributed powers to

100

ensure the political rights and freedoms of all. We believe that similar steps are needed today to expand economic participation, broaden the sharing of economic power, and make economic decisions more accountable to the common good. (295–97)

The bishops call this economic normative and practical challenge "the unfinished business of the American experiment," which requires "new forms of cooperation and partnership among those whose daily work is the source of prosperity and justice of the nation" (296). Here the bishops have clearly joined together ideas shared by other commentators about the interrelationship of political democracy, workplace democracy, and the economy.

These key normative positions reaffirm the church's constant call for the government and economic actors to respect the right of workers to form unions, to bargain collectively, and to "encourage a stronger role for unions in economic decisionmaking" (104). The bishops state further that "labor unions themselves are challenged by the present economic environment to seek new ways of doing business. The purpose of unions is not simply to defend the existing wages and prerogatives of the fraction of workers who belong to them, but also to enable workers to make positive and creative contributions to the firm, the community, and the larger society in an organized and cooperative manner" (304). The bishops also raise fundamental concerns about the "acceptability" of high rates of unemployment and the great needs of communities that are left unmet. Workers, businesses, and governmental entities are required to ensure that work is made available to fulfill both objective and subjective meanings of one's life and the common good.

In chapter 4 of the pastoral letter entitled "A New American Experiment: Partnership for the Public Good," the bishops discuss their core theme of expanding economic democracy in firms and in society. They state that "new forms of partnership between workers and managers are one means for developing greater participation and accountability within firms. . . . The organization of firms should reflect and enhance this mutual partnership" (299).[3] The bishops suggest the following structures and organizational models: profit sharing by the workers in a firm; enabling employees to become company stockholders; granting employees greater participation in determining the conditions of work; cooperative ownership in the firm by all who work within it; and programs for enabling a much larger number of Americans, regardless of their employment status, to become shareholders in successful corporations (299).

The bishops continue that "Catholic social teaching has endorsed on many occasions innovative methods for increasing worker participation within firms. . . . The appropriateness of these methods will depend on the circumstances of the company or industry in question and on their effectiveness in actually increasing a genuinely cooperative approach to shaping decisions" (301). More important, "cooperative ownership is particularly worthy of consideration in new entrepreneurial enterprises" (301). But at a minimum, firms should develop labor-management relations that are family-friendly and non-exploitative. Further, firms must furnish early warning systems for plant closures, with proper training and education for displaced workers and communities. They must provide for the right of workers to negotiate alternatives and ensure that management and stockholders equally share the burdens of economic decline or transformation (303). The bishops state that even the churches themselves must become creators of, or investors in, economic opportunities for persons unable to find meaningful work.

Given the foregoing, Catholic social teachings on economics and labor can be summarized in terms of three themes: creation, community, and covenant (Corbin 1989). These themes form the foundation of its principles, and its normative call for what workers should want from their objective and subjective work lives.

First, the creation theme is rooted in the Genesis theology John Paul II discussed in *Laborem Exercens*. As created beings made in the image of a Creator God, we too share in the enterprise of cocreation. Our lives are tied to this creative activity through both our reproduction and our production. We continue creation through our sexual acts and through our work and labor. This theme helps to explain the "deeper" spiritual understanding about work that many are seeking.

Second, the theme of community is tied to the basic understanding that our work and labor are social and not just individualistic pursuits. Our work and labor aim to build community, not only of workers alone but of the entire social common good. It is a fundamental premise that we have the duty, and the right, to be active participants in our community. Social and economic institutions must enable and empower people to be active agents in society or the workplace. There is a commitment to work not only for the workers' sake but also for the benefit of building community. This is sometimes called the Catholic "communitarian vision."

The third theme of covenant is tied to the church's social and communitarian vision. A covenant relationship goes beyond mere contracts and agreements. Rather, there is a basic justice in the work relationship that goes beyond wages at market rates. In this sense, there is a covenant between labor and capital insofar as both are interdependent. This theme enables the church to call for a "living" and "family" wage. The theme of covenant also has another relationship: between workers. There is an essential solidaristic local and global relationship between laborers themselves, between laborers and nonlaborers, and between social institutions and workers. In essence, the covenant extends to the establishment of labor, community, and church coalitions.

As we can see, the Catholic Church's labor theory is rich in normative values and themes that challenge contemporary understandings about work and labor movements. Further, these religious viewpoints about a just society and workplace translated into a progressive social and political agenda more aggressive, in some instances, than the New Deal itself. But when it came to practical, community-based alliances between organized religion and organized labor, did these values and social policy prescriptions translate into concrete solidarity? What were the boundaries? What were the opportunities? In this next section, we will discuss some of these organizational relationships.

BOUNDARIES AND OPPORTUNITIES FOR ALLIANCES

The politics of religion and labor institutions intertwine in various ways. Alliances between organized religious and labor institutions frequently create boundaries that can either promote and transform or hinder and block the political ideas, goals, and strategies of the institutions and the workers, in society or at the workplace. Interinstitutional alliances between organized labor and religion can become either political liabilities or strengths when it comes to organizing workers or improving working conditions.

American religious institutions and labor unions have worked together in the past, both formally and informally, especially in the industrial sector. In a previous work, we discussed the uneven, and sometimes conflict-ridden, relationships between the Catholic Church and organized labor through three case studies, involving the Youngstown Ecumenical Coalition, the Pittston Coal Strike, and the Los Angeles cemetery workers' organizing campaign (Russo and Corbin 1991). Currently, new cases are developing for church-labor alliances: the National Interfaith Committee for Worker Justice is working with local church-labor alliances throughout the United States by sponsoring church-based programs on faith and work, while the AFL-CIO "Union Summer" project has engaged religious seminarians and rabbinical students in organizing projects during the summer months of 1996. Various conferences sponsored by religious bodies, including the United States Catholic Conference, and by other academic groups, such as the Industrial Relations Research Association, have reintroduced sessions on forging alliances and relationships between religious bodies and labor unions. Academics, religious leaders, and labor leaders, along with rank-and-file workers, have begun to rethink their historical formal and informal relations, reanalyze their institutional and ideological boundaries, and reenter into more organized dialogues.

On balance, according to our case studies, the Roman Catholic Church has been perceived as an activist institution in the realm of labor politics. The support of trade unionism, collective bargaining, and an activist regulatory state on the behalf of workers has been central to universal Catholic social teaching and has been echoed by the U.S. Catholic leadership and workers. In the past, organized and unorganized workers called upon the political and moral power of the Catholic Church to assist in gaining workplace rights and social protections and rethinking their understandings, meanings, and values about work.[4]

It would seem that in times of labor crisis, such as now, the Catholic Church and other like-minded religious organizations engaged in politics could again provide a powerful resource for labor organizing, labor politics, and the regeneration of a deeper sense of work as more than employment. Yet, like any institutional and ideological relationship, boundaries between groups—real or perceived—can hinder alliances as well.

In the past, the acceptance of business unionism of the American labor movement has acted as a boundary between organized labor and community groups. With its emphasis on bilateral collective bargaining, business unionism focused narrowly on job-related issues. Simply put, labor organizations were often indifferent to community-wide issues such as environmental, health care, educational, and social concerns.

This was not simply a matter of philosophy. There is evidence that individual union members did not want their leadership heavily involved in civic activities that would distract from their primary duties at the workplace. This perception only grew with the complexity of the social/moral issues involved, and with the increased recognition of individual identity. For example, major splits occurred within the labor community as to their level of leadership commitment to labor/community coalitions vis-à-vis the affirmative action, abortion, and antiwar movements.

The reliance on business unionism had another detrimental effect. Business unionism relies heavily on a hierarchical leadership and service structure; members pay their dues and call if they have a problem. (Clearly, this approach is shared with other institutional organizations, such as many religious institutions.) This philosophy differs greatly from that of community activists and labor organizers. That is, community and labor organizers focus on grassroots organizing and empowerment strategies. This often puts them at odds with the institutional leadership, who fear rank-and-file involvement and the loss of institutional control. Unwillingness to share power and responsibility by leaders can undermine the basis for community/labor alliances. On the other hand, sometimes grassroots activists are reluctant to engage institutions as their allies in community struggles. It should be remembered, however, that institutional structures can provide needed resources, communication networks, legitimacy, and support to grassroots groups and emerging leaders. It is not always an "either/or" proposition between grassroots organizing and empowerment, and institutional structures and hierarchies. Intermediate organizations and relationships can be developed.

Consequently, the acceptance of business unionism has reduced most labor/community coalitions to crisis situations where immediate needs overcome philosophical concerns. Put differently, labor/community coalitions have largely been ad hoc reactions to crisis situations rather than well-established and systematic planned alliances (Craft 1990). Given the inadequate foundation, these alliances have been easily undermined by employers and political figures or have produced feelings of resentment by community groups of having been used. Overall, it is fair to say that organized labor's involvement in community affairs has been largely isolated to participation in local community-service programs.

As suggested earlier, the current reciprocal crisis involving work and declining memberships in both unions and the Catholic Church provides an important opportunity to renew the coalition between these often forgotten allies. Further, the crisis itself has forced these institutions to reexamine and abandon outdated formulations, relationships, and philosophical approaches and methods regarding participation and coalitions. For example, in 1995 at a special church meeting of groups funded by the Catholic Campaign for Human Development, there was a great deal of discussion about coalition building among various institutions.

Any new labor-church alliance will require the acceptance of differences between these institutions and their membership on many issues without reducing these variances to mere identity politics. What is most important in coalition building will be the focus on unifying principles and the sense of common cause between these institutions. To be sure, the central question is no longer whether these organizations should respond institutionally, educationally, economically, geographically, and culturally but rather how these institutions might intervene in more intelligent and supportive ways.

RECOMMENDATIONS

The changing situation of workers and their labor and religious institutions provides a basis for possible alliances in the next decade. The intensification of work and corresponding reduction in leisure time has reduced opportunities for democratic participation in our political, economic, and religious institutions that are essential in maintaining a democratic society and spiritual life. In essence, both labor and religious institutions have a moral and vested interest in working together for substantive change in working and economic conditions. In this context, the following recommendations are being made to the respective institutions.

First, the revitalization of organized labor is contingent upon building a grassroots social justice movement for the twenty-first century. To do this, local and national unions must make a fundamental and substantive commitment to build coalitions with community organizations, especially those in the religious community that are addressing issues of poverty and racism. It is important for trade unionists to remember that five of every seven Americans belong to Christian churches and that their social justice networks could be natural allies in the struggle for justice and equality in the workplace and society.

Second, common concerns about culture can lead to new relationships. Both secular and religious leaders have presented their critiques of the overwhelming individualistic and materialistic culture evident in Western society, especially in the United States. The perceived lack of worker-community solidarity, which is in part fueled by this self-interested ethos, enables individuals and groups to focus on their own needs, identities, and "private" concerns (Piore 1995). Church members, as well as labor unionists, have tended to be taken over by this materialistic consumer-driven culture with little critical reflection. The "privatization" of life, faith, and work has been challenged by leaders in both the labor movement and religious institutions, most notably by Pope John Paul II. Many agree that there must be some "deeper" meaning to work and life.

Some religious leaders have entered, again, into the foray about recovering the deeper meaning and value of work itself. In this light, religion and spirituality have increasingly become points of interest in the current discussions about work. Some religious thinkers, many of whom were longtime labor advocates, have called upon the leaders of faith communities to revitalize their understanding and commitment to the community and social movements. Churches, synagogues, and mosques are challenged to reaffirm their commitments to the labor movement, renew their understanding about the deeper nature of work, recreate opportunities for persons to participate in economic life, and rediscover the social and political dimensions of their religious lives (Fox 1994; Higgins 1993, 1994; Holland 1989). These religious thinkers, however, are not again calling for a "spiritualization" of the workforce or the religious education of labor unions, as many had done in the past. Rather, the challenge is to tap into the spiritual sources of work of all people and to create partnerships between institutions that advance a more humane society. This is a call for religious leaders to connect again to the everyday life experiences of their communities, thereby eliminating the reductionism of spirituality to one's "private" life while ignoring the social world.

Religious and labor leaders' reflections on contemporary culture are oftentimes analyzing a similar reality: that is, the materialism of believers and workers tends to reduce the subjective meaning of work into only its objective outcomes (wages for more purchases). This call for a spirituality of work and cultural critique raises a number of challenges. First, the need to forge alliances in order to help workers and believers share a common vision of a "public" life leading to a just society. The common good for all people is a common language shared by both religious and labor movements. Second, labor-community coalitions must directly challenge the ideology of a materialist society. Not just an issue of spirituality, this also leads to natural coalitions with the environmental movement.

Third, labor/community coalitions must immediately begin to address the issue of work and worklife. As has been suggested earlier, both labor and community groups have a vested interest in increasing the standard of living and free time. Nearly a third of all working Americans earn wages that on a full-time schedule would not lift them out of poverty. Low wages only encourage moonlighting, overtime, and multiple-earner families in order to make ends meet. Inequality of income creates inequality of time in society. For all but the leisure class, the inequality of time impairs the quality of life and community participation in various institutions. As Juliet Schor has suggested, changes are needed to improve the wages for the lowest paid—by creating gender equality, by altering employer incentives to expand work hours, by establishing time's value independent of price, and by short-circuiting the work-spend cycle (Schor 1992).

Fourth, church-labor-community alliances can be formed and strengthened around the issues of job creation, job retention, and community development. Coalitions and networks composed of labor activists, unionists, and community and church leaders, such as the Ecumenical Coalition in Youngstown, the Federation of Industrial Retention and Renewal in Chicago, and the Tri-State Conference on Manufacturing in Pittsburgh, have established early warning systems for plant closures and have advocated for new forms of worker ownership. The time is ripe for organizations to join forces to continue to analyze mergers, acquisitions, and plant closings, and more important, to develop and invest in worker-owned businesses, like Employee Stock Ownership Plans (ESOPs), and cooperatives.

One of the mechanisms available is a program of the U.S. Catholic Bishops. In 1970, the Catholic leadership created the National Campaign for Human Development (CHD) to address the organizing of low-income people and the creation of economic enterprises that address ownership and participation issues. CHD has become a significant funder of low-income controlled and/or worker-owned and managed cooperative enterprises in the United States, with over $200 million invested over the past twenty-five years. Through this program, the Catholic Church, along with many others, has become a lead agent in funding and supporting various community-based economic development projects that create jobs and empower low-income and disenfranchised persons (Corbin 1989). These CHD programs are not unlike those used by the construction industry, which have been involved in the financing of new construction using pension funds and other sources of capital.

The challenge is for community, labor, and religious organizations to support these community economic-development endeavors. Small and medium-size worker cooperatives and flexible networks, both in manufacturing and in services, should be investigated for their feasibility in each community. Local community coalitions should support such ventures by purchasing these firm's services and investing financial resources into these businesses. The issues of wages and representative labor organizations in these firms need to be addressed, not out of some reactive and negative campaign to prevent these businesses from succeeding but in terms of being developers of jobs that pay just and living wages. There are plenty of locally based, flexible networks and cooperative models in operation, many of which have been funded by the Campaign for Human Development. These models are worth exploring and replicating within the context of each community; but they require solidarity, problem-solving attitudes, and supportive coalitions and alliances between many factions of the community.

Fifth, both organized labor and religion, especially the AFL-CIO and the Roman Catholic Church, have sophisticated legislative networks of grassroots people and access to policy makers. Many issues are held in common. There has been a tendency, however, for each group to request legislative and political assistance on very specific matters, only after much critical time has passed. Sometimes collaboration on various social policy matters seems to come as an afterthought; and, if the other group does not respond immediately or even favorably to the request for advocacy, feelings are hurt and old wounds are reopened.

It would seem important for local, state, and national community, labor, and religious organizations to meet to plan annual legislative campaigns and social policy educational events for their members. Certainly, there may be some very critical and non-negotiable issues that may generate fissures in the alliances, but the groups and coalitions can concentrate on several local, state, and national issues that are held in common. Truly, these coalitions already do exist and function very well. Such experiences need to be shared and, more important, reproduced on various levels.

To close, these recommendations involving the Catholic Church suggest a possible starting point for a new dialogue between labor, religious organizations, and community coalitions. Instead of competing or being indifferent to one another, these groups must work together based on shared concerns for human life, economic justice, and participation in social and religious institutions.[5] Without new coalitions and alliances, organized labor, religious institutions, and community groups will continue to be marginalized in an increasingly competitive and individualistic society.

NOTES

1. See also Pius XI, *Quadragesimo Anno,* 1941; John XXIII, *Mater et Magistra,* 1961; John XXIII, *Pacem in Terris,* 1963; Vatican Council II, *Gaudium et Spes,* 1965; Paul VI, *Populorum Progressio,* 1967; Synod of Bishops, *Justice in the World,* 1971. The United States Catholic Bishops have published the following statements on economics and labor issues specifically: *Program for Social Reconstruction,* 1919; *A Pastoral Letter,* 1919; *Statement on Unemployment,* 1930; *Statement of Economic Crisis,* 1931; *Present Crisis,* 1933; *Statement on Social Problems,* 1937; *Statement on Church and Social Order,* 1940; *A Statement on Man's Dignity,* 1953; and *The Economy: Human Dimensions,* 1975.

2. This statement was not written in a vacuum. Like the Vatican, the U.S. Catholic Bishops published numerous statements and pastorals on the labor question. For instance, in the bishops' 1919 *Program for Social Reconstruction* statement, they called for state-provided public employment programs; the continuation of labor boards; a stable and family-based living wage; public housing; federal laws to control monopolies; worker cooperatives; established and enforced state minimum-wage laws; social insurances against unemployment, sickness, and death; laws and policies to promote greater worker participation in the firms for which they work; the provision of more vocational training for youth; enforcement of laws against child labor; and the legal protection for workers to organize. Any labor organization has called for the same.

The U.S Catholic Bishops continued their practical policy implications of their moral theory in their *Statement on Economic Crisis* of 1931, their 1933 *Statement on the Present Crisis,* and their 1937 *Statement on Social Problems.* In those documents, they reaffirmed their call for a living, family wage; they called for alternative types of industrial production and distribution mechanisms, like cooperatives; they continued their support for labor unions and collective bargaining; they demanded policies to ensure that all people can work; and, they challenged industries to provide a proportionality in wages between sectors, that there be an equitable share in profits between workers and owners, and more important, that there be mechanisms for copartnership and co-ownership between labor and management in firms. In these statements, the U.S. Catholic Bishops further annunciated that workers should be empowered to participate in the decision making of the firm, as well as to become more self-determined.

These pastoral-moral policy prescriptions, echoed throughout the forties, fifties, sixties, and seventies in terms of poverty, racism, and international economic concerns as well; the church's continued concern for working-class issues; and the rise of liberation theology aimed at providing privileged perspectives from the point of view of the poor and working class in third world countries provide the basis for the U.S. Catholic Bishops' Pastoral Letter of 1986 called *Economic Justice For All: Pastoral Letter on Catholic Social Teaching and the U.S. Economy.*

3. Concretely, the church leaders assert various models for such labor-management cooperation based on a simple statement articulated by John XXIII in his 1961 *Mater et Magistra* [MM], in that "employees are justified in wishing to participate in the activity of the industrial concern for which they work" (MM 91), and in their own conference's 1919 statement that "the full possibilities of increased production will not be realized so long as the majority of workers remain mere wage earners. The majority must somehow become owners, at least in part, of the instruments of production."

4. The Catholic Church has a long tradition of activist "labor priests." In the last half century some notable labor priests include Msgr. George Higgins, Msgr. John Egan, and the Rev. Patrick Sullivan. See Higgins 1993.

5. For example, in Chicago, the National Interfaith Committee for Worker Justice "calls upon our religious values in order to educate, organize, and mobilize the religious community in the U.S. on issues and campaigns that will improve wages, benefits and working conditions for workers, especially low-wage workers." See National Interfaith Committee for Worker Justice 1997, 2.

BIBLIOGRAPHY

Corbin, Brian R. 1989. "Unfinished Business: Community Economic Development and the U.S. Bishops Economic Pastoral." *Social Thought* 15, no. 2 (Spring): 35–47.

Craft, James A. 1990. "The Community as a Source of Union Power." *Journal of Labor Research* 11, no. 2 (Spring): 145–60.

Dorr, Donald. 1983. *Option for the Poor: A Hundred Years of Vatican Social Teaching.* New York: Orbis.

Evans, Sara. 1989. *Born for Liberty: A History of Women in America.* New York: Free Press.

Fox, Matthew. 1994. *The Reinvention of Work: A New Vision of Livelihood for Our Time.* San Francisco: Harper.

Higgins, George, with William Bole. 1993. *Organized Labor and the Church: Reflections of a "Labor Priest."* Mahwah, N.J.: Paulist.

Higgins, George. 1994. "Subsidiarity in the Catholic Social Tradition: Yesterday, Today, and Tomorrow." The Albert Cardinal Meyer Lectures, Mundelein Seminary, University of St. Mary of the Lake, Chicago.

Holland, Joe. 1989. *Creative Communion: Toward a Spirituality of Work.* Mahwah, N.J.: Paulist.

John XXIII. 1961. "'Mater et Magistra': Christianity and Social Progress. Pp. 219–85 in *Seven Great Encyclicals.* New York: Paulist Press, 1963.

John Paul II. 1981. "'Laborem Exercens': On Human Work." *Origins,* September 24, 1, 227–43.

Leo XIII. 1891. "'Rerum Novarum': The Condition of Labor." Pp. 1–36 in *Seven Great Encyclicals.* New York: Paulist Press, 1963.

National Conference of Catholic Bishops (NCCB). 1985. *Justice in the Marketplace: Collected Statements of the Vatican and the U.S. Catholic Bishops on Economic Policy, 1891–1984.* Washington, D.C.: United States Catholic Conference.

———. 1986. *Economic Justice for All: Pastoral Letter on Catholic Social Teaching and the U.S. Economy.* Washington, D.C.: United States Catholic Conference.

National Interfaith Committee for Worker Justice. 1997. "Mission Statement." Chicago. *Faith Works,* 2.

Needleman, Ruth. 1993. "Spaces and Opportunities: Developing New Leaders to Meet Labor's Future." *Labor Research Review 20* (Spring/Summer): 5–20.

Piore, Michael J. 1995. *Beyond Individualism: How Social Demands of the New Identity Groups Challenge American Political and Economic Life.* Cambridge, Mass.: Harvard University Press.

Rifkin, Jeremy. 1987. *Time Wars.* New York: Henry Holt.

Russo, John, and Brian Corbin. 1991. "A System of Interpretation: Catholic Social Teaching and American Unionism." *Conflict* 11, no. 4 (October–December): 237–66.

Schor, Juliet. 1992. *The Overworked American: The Unexpected Decline of Leisure.* New York: Basic.

6

THE CONCERTED VOICE OF LABOR AND THE SUBURBANIZATION OF CAPITAL: FRAGMENTATION OF THE COMMUNITY LABOR COUNCIL

Philip J. McLewin

C ommunities and capital have an uneasy relationship. Sometimes for the better, inevitably for the worse, forces of the market system disrupt communities. Guided by the profit motive and motivated to maximize their own returns, employers initially change green fields into work sites only to desert them, leaving workless brown fields. People in those communities prosper or founder depending on which phase of the metamorphosis is dominant and whether they are willing to struggle collectively for their interests.

This essay focuses on the role of central labor councils in suburban communities. Very little is written about them. More than ten years ago a reflective report from the AFL-CIO began: "The nature of work, the organization of the workplace, and the size, *location,* composition and background of the workforce have been changing at an especially rapid rate in recent years and that process of change is continuing unabated" (AFL-CIO 1985, emphasis added).

Location is an important way change is occurring. This includes location both of the worker and of the workplace because it is this mixture (even disjuncture) that contributes to the weakening of the labor movement.

The most obvious and dramatic form of jobs in new locations results from the globalization of capital. The negative impact of capital flight on U.S. labor unions is widely understood (Bluestone and Harrison 1980, 1982). The threat of closing plants and moving them to other countries, or even to other regions within the United States, has been one of the most effective tools in keeping trade unions on the defensive over the past two decades. The availability of lower-paid labor and, in most instances, a more docile workforce overseas has reduced labor standards here. The transportation and communication revolutions have allowed corporations to extend their reach and become more integrated worldwide. These same forces have left workers more fragmented along racial, ethnic, and national lines and (where they exist) their unions in stages of disintegration and impotence.

Worldwide decentralization of their operations has given corporations more flexibility in production and autonomy from local communities. The very expression "export platform" suggests an elevated and distinct position. This fundamental process of worldwide corporate integration against local community fragmentation has its parallel within the United States.

International capital flight is a visible and dramatic example of the processes draining the power of labor. The suburbanization of capital is another, and it involves merely moving jobs outside city limits. This is the glacial movement of capital, as slow and undramatic as it is sustained and powerful. When U.S. corporations have relocated in the postwar period, it has been principally from the cities to the suburbs and not to other regions (Jackson 1985, 269).

The growth of suburbs around major U.S. cities has been among the most important social and economic changes of the twentieth century (Ashton 1984, 54). It has occurred in three stages. The earliest phase established residential suburbs for the elite who could afford the time and money to commute by steam railroad into the central cities. In the second phase, residential suburbs for working families were created based on the streetcar between the wars, followed by the automobile suburbs after World War II. The third stage is the suburbanization of capital. In 1963 more than half of industrial jobs were in the suburbs; by 1981 the number had grown to two-thirds. Between 1963 and 1977 the twenty-five largest central cities lost nearly 20 percent of their manufacturing jobs while their suburbs gained 36 percent. At the same time that jobs were being moved to the suburbs a transformation from manufacturing to service employment occurred. Suburban manufacturing jobs fell from 46 percent of suburban employment in 1972 to 36 percent in 1982; consumer services jobs expanded during the same time from 41 percent to 51 percent (Jackson 1985; Schneider and Fernandez 1989; Garreau 1991; Logan and Golden 1986, 430).

When businesspeople relocate jobs to the suburbs, they do it to gain an economic advantage. Labor is the most important operating cost in running a business, so this will play a pivotal role in the decision to expand into the suburbs. Corporate leaders are aware, too, of the sociopolitical context in which they function, and its impact on their private costs and ability to influence public policy. A strike by workers, for instance, has a far greater chance of success if there is local community support for the union. One issue raised by the suburbanization of capital is the role of the social control of labor. Are location decisions made primarily as a response to labor unrest? Are workers "entrapped" by the purchase of houses in the suburbs, both limiting intergenerational social mobility and reducing labor militancy? Is the labor movement fragmented in the suburbs, and thus weaker both in collective bargaining and political action?

There are strong arguments to support this explanation (Gordon 1977; Harvey 1976; Edel, Sclar, and Luria 1984; Tabb and Sawers 1984). But if sub-urbanization of capital is so powerful, why is it characteristic only of the United States and not of other capitalist countries (Gottdiener 1983)? There are several structural features in the United States that point to tantalizing answers to explain this puzzle.

First is the uneven distribution of suburbanization within the United States. When looked at carefully, suburbanization is more prevalent in the northeastern and midwestern regions. In the South and Southwest, metropol-itan regions grew by central cities annexing surrounding land. As measured in square miles, each Texas city, for instance, was ten times larger in 1960 com-pared with 1900. The territorial size of cities like New York, Philadelphia, and St. Louis barely grew at all. According to Jackson, "under the guidance of a determined business community, Dallas followed an aggressive postwar annex-ation policy, and it took in a huge reservoir of unincorporated county land in anticipation of rapid suburbanization" (Jackson 1985, 154).

On its surface this seems no more complicated than open, undeveloped space annexed by a central city, where none was available in the Northeast and Midwest. But it does raise questions as to why a "determined business com-munity" wished to avoid suburbanization in places like Texas, and why equally powerful corporations did not attempt to force consolidation of existing sub-urbs in the Northeast.[1] If the issue is social control of labor, then in "right-to-work" states like Texas the union movement is already weak and fragmented. Not only is the potential for worker unrest comparatively low, but of equal sig-nificance, there is little threat of labor union influence on city hall. By contrast, the unity and militancy of the labor movement in urban centers of states with-out "right-to-work" laws make suburbanization of employment a more attrac-tive alternative. The impetus for suburbanization of jobs as an antiunion strategy is too strong to ignore.[2]

The other piece of the puzzle involves the structure of the AFL-CIO, which is the focus of this essay. A defining feature of the United States labor movement is the dispersal of power (Barbash 1972). As of March 1996, sev-enty-seven "international unions" had chosen to affiliate with the AFL-CIO. Each retains control over organizing, contract negotiations, and contract enforcement. In contrast to the labor movements in Germany, Austria, Sweden, and the Netherlands, collective bargaining in the United States is fragmented and decentralized. The major exception has been "pattern bargaining" in a few key industries, but even this is now on the wane.

The organizational structure of the AFL-CIO itself is complex and diffused. Housed in the Washington headquarters are nineteen "AFL-CIO departments," which provide such basic services as accounting, economic research, community services, political education, and legal counsel. In addition there are nine other "trade and industrial departments" such as the Food and Allied Services Trade Department and the Building and Construction Trades Department, each with a president and secretary-treasurer. There are four "international institutes," including the Institute for Free Labor Development, and thirteen other constituency groups and AFL-CIO–sponsored programs, from the A. Philip Randolph Institute to the Organizing Institute.

Until John Sweeney was elected president, the AFL-CIO supported two sets of directors with local offices in each of twelve regions spread throughout the United States. One director maintained contact with the field (operated by the Department of Organization and Field Services); the other coordinated election activity (operated by the Committee on Political Education). These twelve regions were reduced to four in 1996, and the staff unified under the direction of the Department of Field Services. There are plans to assign state field directors designated to work with state and community labor councils.

The key to the presence of the AFL-CIO in communities is the local labor council. When corporations decentralize jobs in the suburbs, they continue centralized control through a bureaucratic hierarchy. By contrast, the AFL-CIO simply replicates itself first as fifty-one state federations and then again as six hundred community-based central labor councils. Each of the state and community AFL-CIOs seeks affiliations from local unions with work sites in its respective jurisdiction. Each establishes a dues structure based on affiliated membership to fund its operations. With each succeeding replication, the proportion of unions affiliating, dues revenue, and staff fall dramatically. There are only eighty full-time officers and full- or part-time paid staff in all of more than six hundred central labor councils.

Power in the structure flows from below—from the affiliated local unions—not from the AFL-CIO in Washington. One consequence is that the AFL-CIO field staff works with leaders in state federations and community labor councils who marshal the resources for their own AFL-CIO organizations. The state and community AFL-CIOs function with a good deal of autonomy, except in the matters of foreign policy, national elections, and national legislation. Under extraordinary circumstances the national AFL-CIO can impose its will by pulling a charter, but this hardly affects the day-to-day activities of these organizations (Catchpole 1968, 129).

Central labor councils are the "vital link" in the structure of the AFL-CIO (Connecticut State AFL-CIO 1985). By combining the strength and discipline of individual local union affiliates, labor councils form the basis of the community's labor movement. For that reason I prefer to call them community labor councils. They engage in a variety of activities, including community and human service programs, assistance to affiliates (such as food banks, boycotts, rallies, strike support), and education programs (worker training, scholarships). As the collective community voice of labor, councils help establish the conditions for positive industrial relations within the workplace and a supportive environment within the community. According to an AFL-CIO pamphlet, "The Central Labor Council is the foundation of labor's action structure" (AFL-CIO Department of Field Services 1992).

The key function of community labor councils is political action. They coordinate the panoply of election activities directed toward rank-and-file members, including endorsements, telephone banks, literature distribution, volunteer recruitment, mailings, door-to-door visits, election day transportation, and so on. Also, because endorsements serve to legitimate a political candidate, financial contributions from individual locals can hinge on the position of the community labor council.

Sometimes large local unions will operate their own political action program independently of the labor councils. The Autoworkers (UAW) supports "Community Action Program" (CAP) councils to coordinate the efforts of many locals, much the way they did before reaffiliation with the AFL-CIO. But suburbanization increases the importance of the community labor council because union membership is more widely dispersed over smaller work sites. The community labor council has an impact on elections and legislation by coordinating and focusing the efforts of many local unions.

Election activities are not limited to county races. Politicians who represent local districts at the state capitols or in Washington also depend on the support of the community labor councils. The principal means by which the AFL-CIO mobilizes rank-and-file support of presidential candidates is through them.

Thus, decentralization describes a key component of the AFL-CIO's political operation. It is up to the community labor councils to mobilize trade union members for elections—both as volunteers and as voters. Critical to the argument in this essay, a transfer of jobs to the suburbs moves collective bargaining and especially union political action into a different sociopolitical context. Yet there is little or no research on the particular challenges confronting organized labor in the suburbs. Until recently these were places where people lived, not where they worked. As jobs have shifted to the suburbs it is precisely this environment that is dominant for most local unions and their members.

If the purpose of community labor councils is concerted grassroots action, then the greatest threat to their effective functioning is fragmentation. The obvious export platforms of the Philippines or *maquiladoras* of Mexico do not exist in the U.S. suburban environment. The very invisibility of suburban capital is more a problem. The fragmentation that exists is not because of separation from the community but the dispersal within it.

Fragmentation strains local unions because smaller collective bargaining units are more expensive to organize and, once certified, require more resources to service members. For unions these units are going to require the development of a cadre of voluntary shop stewards at the work site. Otherwise, union staff will be stretched so thin as either to jeopardize enforcement of the contract or to lose the bargaining unit itself through decertification.

This situation presents a challenge for local unions both to integrate for strength against employers and to decentralize for effective presence in the workplace. When the local union is facing the challenge of attempting to combine its own resources for concerted action at the workplace, affiliation and active participation with one (or more) community labor councils may appear a luxury.

The corporate strategy of job dispersal through decentralization has an enormous and direct impact on the community labor councils since they must rely on the local affiliates for all their financial resources and delegate participation. The suburban setting of new jobs contributes to fragmentation because a significant number of people work and live in different communities.[3] For unionized workers this means that collective bargaining and workplace issues are separated from political and community issues. Workers experience alienation between their workplaces and living spaces.

The AFL-CIO rules of affiliation are based on the workplace. Local unions choosing to affiliate with a community central labor council calculate their per capita fees on membership working in the jurisdiction. This works when a labor council aids a local in its negotiations or with strike support. But the AFL-CIO Committee on Political Education (COPE) membership lists used for electoral and legislative action are, for obvious reasons, based on residency in the community not the workplace. The community central labor council is left with the task of attempting to mobilize a labor constituency for electoral work when many union members living there belong to unaffiliated locals. This contributes to the weakening of labor's political voice.

Local unions, too, have divided community identities. Their leaders quite correctly see themselves as operating at a regional, state, or even multistate level. County-based political action, community involvement, and participation with other locals are either ignored, or (more commonly) delegated to a

118

subordinate member in the local's organization. The requests of community labor councils for funds, volunteers, and delegates can become tiresome if a local union operates in several county jurisdictions.

As a result, the leadership pool available to suburban labor councils is thin. In a single suburban county that is part of a mosaic of similar counties, union leadership in the community is fluid because individual leaders must decide where to place their priorities. The top leadership in locals simply cannot participate personally in every labor council their bargaining units may encompass, and that is just where they have work sites. If there is a representative or delegate active in the community labor council it is often not the principal decision maker for the union. The effective communication of labor council initiatives to the locals' leadership and ultimately to their membership is unpredictable and uneven.

The problem is compounded because officers of suburban labor councils usually volunteer their time and have no staff. Most have full-time jobs, either with their local union or at the work site. When job pressure mounts the business of the labor council becomes secondary. Only the officers who are retired can devote full time to council activity, but (a fact of life in the labor movement) their influence with other trade unionists is low.

There is a more subtle effect on leadership. Some unions function by integrating their industry. This is especially true in the construction trades and the garment industry. In a variation of this pattern, northeastern grocery chains have been organized by huge locals of the United Food and Commercial Workers.[4] Dispersed employers are brought together under a uniform contract negotiated with the union, defining a community of interest. The suburban pattern of job decentralization is no obstacle to these unions. Indeed, they gain strength from it. Thus, building trades unions and (where it exists) UNITE! International Ladies Garment Workers (ILGWU) and Amalgamated Clothing and Textile Workers Union (ACTWU) have the potential to set the political and legislative agenda of community labor councils. At least with respect to the building trades, their principal interest is more suburban growth, especially commercial development, because it adds construction jobs. The social agenda of industrial and public sector unions must compete for inclusion in this environment. In many communities the building trades council simply acts as a separate political entity, further fragmenting the local labor movement.

The trade union movement depends on concerted action and forming coalitions with other likeminded community groups to press for the interests of working people. The workday inflow and outflow of workers/citizens, the fractured identity between workplace and living space, and the broader regional commitments of many local unions make the task daunting.

119

Consequently, the effectiveness of labor councils in political and community affairs varies widely from place to place. This uneven performance makes it more difficult for the AFL-CIO to put community labor councils on the front line.[5]

The role of the labor councils must not be overemphasized. The basic organizing of new workers, collective bargaining, contract enforcement, and other forms of workplace participation will continue to reside with the local/international unions, whether jobs are in the city or the suburbs. It is also important to recognize that not all city-based labor councils function as powerful magnets to pull the labor movement together for concerted action (Bok and Dunlop 1970; Kelber 1990). Yet the basic point remains cogent. Corporations, by shifting jobs to the suburbs, have placed suburban labor councils in a new strategic role for the U.S. labor movement. The very dispersal of jobs that enhance their importance also reduces their ability to function effectively.

An effective labor council is a grassroots organization that can mobilize local union leaders and members for concerted action. The unrealized genius of the AFL-CIO's organizational structure of replication is that it renders central bureaucratic control ineffective, thereby facilitating this kind of solidaristic activity by community-based labor councils. "Solidarity works," as the theme of the guidebook for central labor council delegates stresses.

In the early history of the labor movement city-based labor councils played an instrumental role in bringing local unions together for concerted action. During the 1880s, for instance, the twenty-two affiliates of the Chicago Central Labor Union fought for the eight-hour day, including with a strike of eighty thousand workers. During the same period, the New York City Central Labor Union developed a powerful organization in support of striking workers and boycotts (Rayback 1966, 166, 169). As the U.S. labor movement consolidated itself in the post–World War II period into a single national federation, a top-down leadership developed issuing policy statements and action directives to "the field." During the same time many community-based union activists—some of whom were socialists—were replaced as leaders in central labor councils. The result was that the command-from-above-practices of the AFL-CIO were incompatible with its replicative structure that depended on a committed local leadership mobilizing through influence from below.

The challenge today is to realize the potential of the AFL-CIO's unique structure and build on it in the context of fragmented suburban communities. I will offer several specific, if modest, recommendations to strengthen them. These are practical suggestions within the capacity of the AFL-CIO to reform itself. As with all reforms, these can be self-limiting and ultimately operate

120

merely to mitigate the current crisis of the U.S. labor movement or they can be the initial stages of a revitalization and radical restructuring of the labor movement. Which of these possible outcomes is more likely depends on the commitment of the national AFL-CIO leadership to community-based trade union activism.

In 1985 when the AFL-CIO considered major reforms, very little was offered about community labor councils. "The Changing Situation," a report by the AFL-CIO Committee on the Evolution of Work, included nothing about them under the general sets of recommendations involving new methods, increased members' participation, improved labor communications, and improved organizing activity (AFL-CIO 1985, 18–29).

The report suggested that the Executive Council Committee on State and Local Central Bodies develop a funding system so that "each affiliate should be required to make a per capita payment to the AFL-CIO for the state federations and local central bodies" to be distributed to the councils. The AFL-CIO bylaws were subsequently modified to include state (not community) central bodies in such a financing arrangement, but only three internationals have adopted this policy (AFL-CIO 1994). No action was ever taken to include the community-based councils. They still rely on voluntary affiliations and good-faith reporting of the membership on which locals pay "per capitas." Affiliation rates continue to be low, around 55 percent for state federations and even less for community labor councils.[6]

In spite of the low affiliation rates, the community-based labor councils are expected to deliver "grassroots" support for AFL-CIO initiatives and programs (AFL-CIO 1994). Communication comes down from the Washington headquarters to community labor councils on national issues and from the state federations on state issues. There is no direct participation of the community labor councils in the formulation of national/state agendas and issues. There is little opportunity for timely participation in the other direction. This carries greater significance than the ordinary observation that two-way communication is often weak in corporate bureaucracies, for the AFL-CIO community-based organizations have an independent power base. What is not understood, is impractical, or is out of touch with grassroots leadership sentiment will simply not be acted on. Potentially even more threatening to the national leadership of the AFL-CIO are labor councils that, either consistently or sporadically, take local action in direct conflict with stated policy. Without bureaucratic control, a weak set of community-based labor councils can appear very attractive from the national office when policy is determined at the top.

The labor council "oversight" function of the Department of Organization and Field Services is weak and largely procedural. As reported by the department itself, the oversight consists of approving changes to constitutions and bylaws, dissolving or merging labor councils, and receiving an annual report. The first two events rarely occur, and the annual report is filed and forgotten by the local leadership.

Looking at alternatives involves the longstanding debate over bureaucratic control from the top versus voluntary participation from the bottom. Bureaucratic control makes it possible to maintain discipline with a united front while decentralized decision making encourages broad and enthusiastic participation. Happily, the choice is less stark for labor. This is because there is no well-defined bureaucratic spine spreading out from headquarters to the community labor councils. In effect, the structures for effective bureaucratic control are absent and with it the capacity to command action. This leaves only the option of encouraging local participation through influence. The problem is, of course, how best to encourage local action.

Currently AFL-CIO action is guided by the question, How can it increase the willingness and ability of the community labor councils to mobilize grassroots activism to carry out the programs conceived and planned in Washington? The labor movement would be opened up and strengthened if an alternate question were posed: What can the AFL-CIO learn from the community labor councils about the issues and actions that excite grassroots activism? Health care reform and privatization are examples of local issues that became "hot" far in advance of their emergence on the national agenda.

With this context in mind, I offer suggestions for change:

1. *Funding:* Full-time officers lead about 10 percent of the community labor councils. These are principally in major cities with budgets ranging from fifty thousand dollars to over one million dollars per year. The remaining 90 percent, which are outside the central cities, are led by volunteers or part-timers. The Department of Organization and Field Services has reported, "their efforts are often hampered by low local union affiliation rates." Optimistically, I calculate these 90 percent average about ten thousand affiliated members with an annual income of twelve thousand dollars. Until this is changed, we know the international unions making up the AFL-CIO have no serious interest in establishing a strong community-based labor movement.

Many community labor council leaders think mandatory affiliation of locals in their jurisdiction is the solution. I disagree. Ultimately, the AFL-CIO itself survives through voluntary affiliations, so why should the community labor councils function differently? This is also a funding approach consistent with the notion of community labor councils as the organizers of voluntary grassroots activism. But there are important changes to consider:

(a) *Incentive rebates:* Under this program a portion of per capita dues paid by a local into one or more community labor councils is deducted from membership dues paid to the international. Whether this is done as a percentage of the total or fixed fees per member would be a matter of policy determination. The important elements are that affiliations would still have to be recruited in the community, but the international union would be clearly indicating its preference for local participation.

(b) *Challenge grants:* Under this program the AFL-CIO would establish a Fund for Community Labor Councils. It would issue requests for proposals (RFPs), similar to those from foundations and government agencies, to fund projects important to the labor movement. Competition for these grants, establishing performance standards, subsequent evaluation, and publicizing outcomes would help energize local participation. The particular projects to be supported are open to the imagination. They could include projects for extending community alliances, experimenting with new voter registration drives, developing local delegate and leadership training programs, conducting affiliation campaigns, and establishing local retiree councils. Specific performance measurements and other contractual provisions would help ensure accountability yet maintain the independence of community labor councils flowing from the replication structure of the AFL-CIO. This is a type of "indicative planning," in which policy goals established from the top are transformed into practical operations locally.

If 5 percent of the labor councils received an average of thirty thousand dollars per year, this would cost about one million dollars. Part of an individual grant may be in kind, with, perhaps, one day per week of an AFL-CIO staff member devoted to the special project. This is a substantial commitment of money, but it would support thirty experiments in community-based union building on projects conceived and evaluated by the AFL-CIO. Significant sums of money are spent by the AFL-CIO on international programs as globalization extended the reach of U.S. corporations. Meanwhile the suburbanization of capital remains largely unanswered. The value returned to the AFL-CIO in volunteer time would be in multiples of the original investment in the Community Labor Council Fund.

(c) *New rules for affiliation:* Community labor council officials know that all locals do not fully report their membership for purposes of paying per capita dues. Presumably, the rebate plan would help reduce this problem. But beyond this is the troublesome problem of workplace versus residential affiliation. I have discussed this issue above, and here suggest new rules for affiliation to include both work site and residential affiliations. The formula for figuring out the proportions is a matter for policy determination. This would allow a community-based labor council to approach locals with work sites outside their jurisdiction to affiliate based on residential membership within it. Electoral and lobbying activities depend on residence, not the workplace.

2. *Information:* Expressions such as "we live in an information age" or "power is knowledge-based" are clichés about modern society. The AFL-CIO provides plenty of information via U.S. mail, keeping labor councils informed about emerging issues, current campaigns, and contexts. However, it is rare for information to flow the other way in any structured manner.

(a) *LaborNET:* The one-way flow is changing a bit. In 1994 the AFL-CIO opened LaborNET on CompuServe to community labor councils, further increasing accessibility to materials and reports generated in Washington. Of greater potential significance, however, the system has an open E-mail discussion section and allows users to upload files from the "field." Compared to internet discussions, much of the exchange on LaborNET is chitchat. The few substantive comments that invite an open discussion of the labor movement bring little response and inevitably draw unofficial rebukes for raising the point in the first place.

At the end of May 1995, LaborNET had just over one thousand subscribers, including thirty-five community labor councils. Considering the potential, the base of the union electronic community is still very thin. Suburban labor councils clustered around central cities will especially benefit from LaborNET for exchanging information. As LaborNET evolves it could make an important contribution by sponsoring a forum devoted to community labor councils, much like the "labor editors" discussion group that exists today.

(b) *COPE Lists:* Access to databases remains restricted. Then president Lane Kirkland was quoted after the 1994 winter meeting as saying labor has a third party and it is called COPE. Unfortunately, as a matter of policy, the COPE list of current and retired union members is not directly available to community labor councils to conduct local campaigns. Control is tightly held in Washington, and the COPE lists are distributed through the state federations to areas "targeted" for political action by them. If centralized mailing is done, or special districts set up, it is possible that community labor councils will have no role in statewide or federal elections and no COPE lists for local elections.

COPE lists involve very sensitive issues of power and responsibility. The lists can be misused or misappropriated by, for instance, being copied and given to a local political party or candidate. But they are also the raw material of what the AFL-CIO knows is its ultimate power over capital—the capacity to mobilize people. Access to those lists should be like a driver's license. You pass tests to earn it, and if you abuse the privilege you lose it. The current policy leaves the community labor councils without any right to COPE lists based on a locally developed plan for political action. If the COPE department is not now equipped to handle requests from community labor councils, here is an opportunity to allocate resources in a new direction to encourage local initiative and volunteerism.

(c) *Membership on state-federation and national executive boards:* The two-way flow of information possible on LaborNET will always be inadequate. Currently, community labor councils have no right to a place at the table where policy decisions are made by either state federations or the national AFL-CIO.[7] This is such an obvious way to open the AFL-CIO that many outsiders, and some trades unionists as well, are surprised to find out this is not current practice. There is no formal way for community labor council leaders to deliberate on issues at the national policy level. The communication back-channels through the regional directors, the Washington departments directly affected, or even the international affiliated unions, are inadequate for effective participation on matters of policy.

3. *Regional Association of Community Labor Councils:* Organized labor has no organization of community labor councils. In suburban areas the formation of a regional association of community labor councils would help to strengthen the concerted voice of labor. It would provide a forum for sharing information, sponsoring educational programs, focusing the energies of local union leaders, coordinating political and legislative action, and fostering alliances with other community groups to advance the goals of working people.[8]

Once a year the Department of Field Services sponsors a leaders' conference for the sixty or so labor councils that have full-time officers. Some state federations organize special conferences for labor councils.[9] However, I am not aware of any program within the AFL-CIO to establish peer or horizontal networks of labor council officers. Community labor council presidents are insular. They are not in regular contact with their peers, who deal with similar issues in isolation. A regional network would be of immense value, especially to suburban labor councils that must deal with overlapping political jurisdictions and diffused communities of interest based on work site and residence. A community labor council network, if granted legitimate standing by the AFL-CIO, would help solve mutual problems that result from fragmentation.

4. *Grassroots activism:* The Department of Field Services is clear in its goal of "energizing and activating grassroots action." What does "grassroots activism" mean? As practiced by the AFL-CIO it includes some very important activities such as volunteering for election telephone banks, getting out the vote, making individual telephone calls to Congress, letter writing to congressional and state politicians, and attending events such as Workers Memorial

125

Day. These support the electoral and lobbying strategies of state federations and the national AFL-CIO.

Much less rarely is the practice of grassroots activism extended to public demonstrations or other overt mass actions. During the most recent phase of rising corporate warfare against working people in the 1980s and 1990s, the AFL-CIO sponsored only two mass demonstrations in Washington. I cannot remember last when coordinated mass regional demonstrations were organized across the entire country.

Of course there is nothing to prevent a community labor council from sponsoring its own local events in support, say, of a striking local union affiliate. There are many examples of these. My point is that rarely does the national AFL-CIO commit its organizational resources to sponsoring grassroots community demonstrations. If an organization can prove power in the streets, then every politician is a friend when it seeks to change public policy.

5. *Change the name to community labor council:* This is a matter of perception that has real consequences.[10] The term *"central* labor council" conveys the impression of a distant bureaucracy, and *"local* labor council" is often confused with local union. Neither name captures the essence of the labor council as the grassroots, concerted voice of organized labor in the community. It would be a relatively simple matter to change the generic reference now used by the AFL-CIO. That may be sufficient. A cursory review of the directory of "central labor councils" published by the AFL-CIO shows none with "community" in their official name. Here is an opportunity to open a dialogue between the national leadership and the community leadership about how to improve the "action foundation" of the AFL-CIO.

The public campaign for election of the president of the AFL-CIO resulted in one set of proposals that included "creating a strong grassroots political voice for working people" by restructuring and supporting central labor councils as the "front line of labor's political effort" (Sweeney, Trumka, and Chavez-Thompson 1995). The essentials of the proposals advanced are not as important for this essay as the fact that they were distributed to central labor councils for comment and reaction "as the beginning of a dialogue among all of the movement."[11]

Since becoming president, Sweeney has created a national Central Labor Councils Advisory Committee composed of twenty-four labor council leaders. The committee is working with the national leadership on the role, structure, and programs of the community labor councils. Additionally, a historic central labor council conference with the theme "Organizing for Justice" was held in July 1996 in Denver, Colorado. For the first time officers from all labor councils were invited to participate in discussions about revitalizing the labor movement at the community level. The result of these activities is the *Union Cities* initiative. It is too early to tell if this will be a transforming framework for mobilizing the labor movement in hundreds of communities across the country, or if it is just another program calling for ambitious goals unlikely to be achieved. Based on the analysis in this chapter, it is one of the boldest and most significant moves the AFL-CIO has taken in recent years. The appendix to this chapter contains an elaboration of *Union Cities*.

The suburbanization of capital has fragmented and weakened labor at the community level. The AFL-CIO response to this will determine how powerfully workers in suburban jobs and communities can express their concerted voice. An AFL-CIO handbook for community labor council leaders began with the observation, "Local central labor councils played a vital role in the early history of the labor movement in the United States and were responsible, more than any other single institution, for the development of organized workers into a true labor movement" (George Meany Center for Labor Studies 1989, tab. 1:1) This is a lesson that should not be forgotten in the current attempts to revitalize the U.S. labor movement.

NOTES

1. Central city growth by annexation and consolidation (the absorption of an existing municipality by another one) was the common form of urban growth in the nineteenth century. According to Jackson, "in many cases, the cry for efficiency was a mask for the desire to exploit and to control; it might be termed the local or downtown brand of urban imperialism" (Jackson 1985, 145).

2. Public employers share this impulse to weaken labor when they can. Throughout the 1960s in the U.S. Postal Service, blacks, Latinos, and women made major gains in the workforce. Then came the 1970 nationwide strike keyed by major cities, especially Chicago and New York. In wake of this, Congress passed the Postal Reorganization Act, and the USPS turned to a network of twenty-one bulk mail centers that were named after cities but located in suburbs (or at least outside the city core). The effect was that while inner-city post offices were 67 percent African American and Latino, new bulk mail centers were only 25 percent so. Argument could be made (using quotes of postal officials) that they were consciously turning to what they perceived as a more docile workforce. This example also introduced the factor of race in the suburbanization of capital. (Source: Jeff Perry, Secretary-Treasurer, Mail Handlers Local 300, New York, N.Y.)

3. For example, in 1980, nearly 40 percent of Bergen County, New Jersey, residents commuted outside the county to work, roughly split between New York and other New Jersey counties. At the same time, more than 35 percent of Bergen workers came from outside the county, mostly from Passaic County (11 percent),

Hudson/Essex counties (8 percent), and New York City/State (10 percent). Each of these counties had its own central labor council (County of Bergen 1988).

4. Piore 1985. United Food and Commercial Workers Local 1262, centered in North Jersey, has more than thirty thousand members in three states.

5. According to an AFL-CIO reference manual for labor council officers, "While it is clear that there is wide variation in the strength and effectiveness of local labor councils, it is also clear that where they are strong and effective, local unions within their jurisdiction, and workers generally, fare much better" (George Meany Center for Labor Studies 1989, tab. 1:3).

6. According to a recent report by the Executive Committee of the AFL-CIO, "The state central bodies continue to face serious financial difficulties. The major source of these difficulties is the relatively low rate of state body affiliations. To date neither the national affiliation fee nor the other AFL-CIO and state body efforts to encourage new affiliations have produced the desired results" (AFL-CIO 1991). The Executive Committee recommended a system of establishing targets for state federation affiliations and imposing a penalty payment on those unions that failed to achieve the level established.

Publicly reported affiliation figures are notoriously inaccurate, generally overstated for political purposes and understated when money is paid out. Based on reports of the Department of Organization and Field Services, all state federations had 7.2 million members affiliated in 1994, or about 55 percent of the total AFL-CIO membership (AFL-CIO 1994). When I asked for the affiliation rate for community labor councils, the Department of Organization and Field Services was unable to provide it.

7. At least one state federation has extended this right to community labor councils in their jurisdiction.

8. Since the 1985 report was issued, the number of labor councils was reduced from 750 to about 600, through mergers. This is not the kind of regionalization I am suggesting here.

9. The Wisconsin State AFL-CIO sponsors a two-day Central Labor Council Conference each year. In 1989 workshops were conducted on preparing news releases, legislative action committees, motivating delegates/members, financial officer training, affiliation identification, telephone trees, and so forth.

10. The AFL-CIO's Department of Field Services changed its name during 1996 to the Department of Field Mobilization. This is symbolic of an emphasis on community activism by the department.

11. Quote is from a cover letter from John J. Sweeney, President SEIU, June 28, 1995. The following is an excerpt from the proposal itself, calling for restructuring of central labor councils: "Provide direct [financial?] support for labor councils that are re-tooled as effective political operations. Encourage the building of community coalitions and alliances. Provide training and technical assistance to the leadership and boards of these labor councils through the Political Training Center. Develop the

restructuring through a consultation process with labor and council leaders, aided by an *Advisory Committee of Central Labor Council leaders* from both large and small councils. Assign to each member to the Executive Committee (and to other national union presidents) a group of state and local labor councils where they would act as *Executive Council Liaisons* on behalf of the Federation to ensure that the views of these councils were considered by the council and that Federation programs were carried out by the councils" (Sweeney, Trumka, and Chavez-Thompson 1995).

BIBLIOGRAPHY

AFL-CIO. 1985. "The Changing Situation of Workers and Their Unions." A Report by the AFL-CIO Committee on the Evolution of Work.

————. 1991. "Statements Adopted by the AFL-CIO Executive Committee." Detroit, November 7 and 14.

————. 1997. "The Road to Union City." *America@Work,* March.

AFL-CIO Department for Organization and Field Services. 1992. "A Guidebook for Central Labor Council Delegates." Publication 236: 5.

————. 1994. "State Federations, Local Labor Councils." LaborNET file *sf11c.4fs.*

Ashton, Patrick J. 1984. "Urbanization and the Dynamics of Suburban Development Under Capitalism." Pp. 54–84 in *Marxism and the Metropolis,* ed. William K. Tabb and Larry Sawers. New York: Oxford University Press.

Barbash, Jack. 1972. *Trade Unions and National Economic Policy.* Baltimore: Johns Hopkins Press.

Bluestone, Barry, and Bennett Harrison. 1980. *Capital and Communities: The Causes and Consequences of Private Disinvestment.* Washington, D.C.: Progressive Alliance.

————. 1982. *The Deindustrialization of America.* New York: Basic.

Bok, Derek C., and John T. Dunlop 1970. *Labor and the American Community.* New York: Simon and Schuster.

Catchpole, Terry. 1968. *How to Cope with COPE: The Political Operations of Organized Labor.* New York: Arlington.

Connecticut State AFL-CIO. 1985. "Vital Links: A Handbook for Connecticut Local Central Bodies' Officers and Delegates." Hamden, Conn.

County of Bergen. 1988. "Planners Data Book." Hackensack, N.J.

Edel, Matthew, Elliott Sclar, and Daniel Luria. 1984. *Shakey Places: Homeownership and Social Mobility in Boston's Suburbanization.* New York: Columbia University Press.

Garreau, Joel. 1991. "Edge Cities." *American Demographics,* September, 26.

George Meany Center for Labor Studies. 1989. "Local Central Bodies: Leadership and Leverage." Silver Spring, Md.

129

Gordon, David. 1977. "Capitalist Development and the Stages of Urban Development." Pp. 55–82 in *The Rise of Sunbelt Cities*, ed. David C. Perry and Alfred J. Watkins. Beverly Hills: Sage.

Gottdiener, M. 1983. "Understanding Metropolitan Deconcentration: A Clash of Paradigms." *Social Science Quarterly* 64 (June): 234.

Harvey, David. 1976. "Labor, Capital, and Class Struggle around the Built Environment." *Politics and Society* 6, no. 3: 265–95.

Jackson, Kenneth T. 1985. *Crabgrass Frontier: The Suburbanization of the United States*. New York: Oxford University Press.

Kelber, Harry. 1990. *A Vision for New York Labor.* New York: Union Leadership Training Institute.

Logan, John R., and Reid M. Golden. 1986. "Suburbs and Satellites: Two Decades of Change." *American Sociological Review* 51, no. 3 (June): 430–37.

Piore, Michael J. 1985. "Computer Technologies, Market Structure, and Union Strategic Choices." Pp. 193–204 in *Challenges and Choices Facing American Labor,* ed. Thomas Kochan. Cambridge, Mass.: MIT Press.

Rayback, Joseph. 1966. *A History of American Labor.* New York: New Press.

Schneider, Mark, and Fabio Fernandez. 1989. "The Emerging Suburban Service Economy: Changing Patterns of Employment." *Urban Affairs Quarterly* 24, no. 4 (June): 540.

Sweeney, John J., Richard Trumka, and Linda Chavez-Thompson. 1995. "Rebuilding the American Labor Movement: A New Voice for American Workers: A Summary of Proposals from the Unions Supporting John J. Sweeney, Richard Trumka and Linda Chavez-Thompson." SEIU, Washington, D.C., June 28.

Tabb, William K., and Larry Sawers, eds. 1984. *Marxism and the Metropolis.* New York: Oxford University Press.

APPENDIX

The Union Cities Framework

"A Union City is a place where workers earn a living wage and have time to spend with their families. It's where employers respect the contributions of workers and where elected leaders are held accountable to working families. It's where unions are organizing, mobilizing and reaching out to community allies—and building the power to change workers' lives" (AFL-CIO 1997).

The U.S. labor movement has been losing membership since the early 1970s, and with it the power to create or sustain workplace democracy and political accountability. The causes of this decline have been much speculated about, including globalization, the communications revolution, failure of labor law reform, the end of work, hostile management, and so forth. Whatever these external forces, the unions of the AFL-CIO themselves have failed to organize aggressively. The resources devoted to organizing are less than 5 percent in most unions, compared to 30 percent or more during the period when union membership was expanding. In order to stay even, the AFL-CIO must organize about 300,000 new members per year. Like politics, all organizing is local. That is to say, it is done in a community where the environment can either support an organizing campaign or render it ineffective. Also the largest proportion of union resources remain with the local union, and organizing is done by the locals or through some kind of regional organization.

The *Union Cities* initiative grew out of an understanding that community labor councils were strategically situated to foster a "change to organize/organize to change" environment within their jurisdictions—for both local unions and the community at large. Specific elements of the framework were developed between the summers of 1996 and 1997 through a series of steps, including a telephone survey of all labor councils, the Denver conference, several meetings of the National Labor Council Advisory Committee, and endorsement by the AFL-CIO Executive Committee.

Union Cities challenges community labor councils to adapt eight specific goals to their local circumstances over a period of time (AFL-CIO 1997):

1. Organizing to change: to recruit half the local unions in the community to join the "Organizing for Change" program to shift resources to organizing.

2. Mobilizing in the community: to recruit at least 1% of unions in the community for a rapid response team.

3. Building political power: to recruit 100 activists in key legislative districts for grassroots lobbying and political action.

4. Promoting economic growth, protecting our communities: to reach out to community allies to promote worker- and family-friendly economic development strategies.

5. Paycheck economics education: to sponsor an AFL-CIO economics education program for a majority of local unions in the community.

6. Generating support for the right to organize: to persuade city or county councils to pass resolutions supporting the right of workers to organize and insist that political candidates support these resolutions as a condition of endorsement.

7. Mirror the membership: to ensure that leaders and officials of the AFL-CIO labor council are as diverse as the membership of affiliated unions.

8. Membership growth: to reach an annual membership growth rate of 3% by the year 2000.

131

According to internal reports from the Department of Field Mobilization, in late May 1997 approximately 130 labor councils had requested information about applying for *Union City* status. To achieve that status they would have to adopt an enabling resolution (about seventy have), develop a specific plan with measurable goals, and engage in at least one mobilization. Additionally, eleven international unions had sent letters to their locals urging participation in central labor councils developing a *Union City* framework.

7

EXPANDED ROLES FOR THE CENTRAL LABOR COUNCIL: THE VIEW FROM ATLANTA

Stewart Acuff

After the congressional election debacle of 1994 where a well-organized group of right-wing ideologues following Newt Gingrich won under the banner of the Contract with America, eleven leaders of national unions decided to change the leadership of the AFL-CIO. The AFL-CIO, America's umbrella organization of unions, had never had a contested election for its leadership. That changed in 1995.

John Sweeney, president of the Service Employees Union, Rich Trumka, president of the Mineworkers, and Linda Chavez-Thompson, a local leader from Texas of the State, County, and Municipal Employees, offered themselves respectively for president, secretary-treasurer, and executive vice president, pledging to focus their campaign and subsequent administration on organizing; mobilization and militancy; effective political action; and coalition building with natural allies.

Because that program would require much more intense and effective local, grassroots activity, the New Voices campaign of John Sweeney, Rich Trumka, and Linda Chavez-Thompson focused new attention on and interest in labor councils across America.

Central labor councils (CLCs) are the local-, city-, or town-centered federation of labor. Some, such as in San Francisco or New York, are large, well-funded, well-staffed, active, and powerful. Others, because of low affiliation or moribund leadership, lack the ability to do much more than go through the motions of meeting regularly and giving paper endorsements to political candidates. All, however, have the potential to focus labor's power in a relatively compact area and political jurisdiction, build a sense of movement in a local labor community, and serve as the tool or vehicle for building more power at the lowest level for workers and their organizations.

Perhaps, for that reason, central labor councils were not a priority for the previous leadership of the AFL-CIO. But the New Voices campaign made central labor councils a significant part of their electoral strategy and of their program for the revitalization of the labor movement.

Reaching out to CLC officers, getting CLC delegates to the convention in New York, and organizing them once there was key to the campaign's convention floor and electoral plan.

Beyond that, the New Voice's program calls for active, energized, and engaged CLCs. Arguably, the New Voices program cannot be successful without a network of effective CLCs across America.

Local unions typically pay dues to their local central labor council and turn to the council for assistance when on strike or in any public dispute, for leadership in local electoral politics, and to be the public face of organized labor in their community.

What is an effective CLC and how is one built? It starts with an understanding of power and its dynamics. It must have an electoral strategy that produces real electoral influence, be comfortable with membership mobilization and militancy, be committed to solidarity, and believe in the value of active coalitions with nonunion groups and the importance of community allies.

POWER

Power is how things get done. It is how unions produce improvements in wages and working conditions for their members, how people collectively make politicians respond, and how the labor movement wins victories for unions and working people. Central Labor Councils and CLC leaders who don't understand power, its development and use, or who are uncomfortable with it, are doomed to ineffectiveness. A monthly meeting of a CLC afraid of the concept of power is a deadly boring ritual of habit.

Power is like a muscle. It is built with wise exercise. The smart use of power builds more power, gains more effectiveness, and wins more victories. Inactivity, overreaching, or the careless use of power erodes it.

The power of a central labor council is exercised and built when a CLC and its affiliates practice solidarity, are willing to mobilize their members and embrace militancy when necessary, develop a political strategy that can produce tangible electoral influence, and are committed to nurturing active coalitions with nonunion groups and community allies.

The most effective CLCs will weave all these elements into a program that produces victories that, in turn, increase the level of power. Building power in a CLC requires the leadership to think and plan strategically, to weigh the consequences of each fight, to understand how militancy or power in the street helps one consolidate electoral power—by holding accountable the politician one got elected, by respecting one's allies and honoring their struggle, and by continually asking how we compete with the corporate power arrayed in our community. Building power begins with strategic thinking.

The Atlanta Labor Council's effort on the 1996 Olympics is an example of weaving all the elements into a powerful and victorious campaign.

THE ATLANTA OLYMPICS

When the International Olympic Committee announced in September of 1990 that Atlanta had been awarded the 1996 Games, the building and construction trades were in decline. The Georgia Dome, home of the Atlanta Falcons, had just been built almost entirely nonunion. Indeed a homeless man who had been part of a labor pool had died while doing work for about six dollars an hour that required a highly skilled ironworker. More and more large commercial projects were being done nonunion. The membership of Laborers Local 438 was about 60 percent unemployed. The membership of all the Atlanta building trades combined was about 40 percent unemployed. One labor official when notified of Atlanta's winning Olympics bid said it didn't matter to organized labor—we wouldn't get the work anyway. And as building and construction unions lost influence, the Associated Builders and Contractors (ABC), representing the antiunion construction industry, increased theirs. The ABC seemed determined to make Atlanta a "merit shop" town.

Construction wasn't the only segment of the labor movement the Olympics would affect. Experts predicted eighty-five thousand jobs would be created. The Games would cost $1.6 billion and generate about $4 billion in economic activity. It wasn't hard to understand that the Olympics would have a huge impact on the local economy, wages, union density, and working conditions. Almost thirty venues would either be constructed or altered. Five hundred million dollars was to be spent just on construction, with half of that going into the Olympic Stadium.

The Olympics would not have a static effect on the working people of Atlanta and Georgia, union and nonunion alike. The Games would either lift us up or pull us down. Early in 1991 the leadership of the Atlanta Labor Council changed, and we decided that as much as possible we would make the Olympic work union work. We met with both the Olympic Committee president, Billy Payne, and the chief operating officer, A. D. Frazier. They explained matter-of-factly that these would be the first Olympics funded completely by the private sector, that no prevailing wage law was applicable, that no political pressure would be useful, that they had a responsibility to the sponsors to do the work as cheaply as possible, and that since Georgia is a right-to-work state, we had nothing to talk about.

This was clearly a campaign that would require every bit of power the local labor movement could muster and a full complement of the tools of that power: electoral action, solidarity, mobilization, militancy, and coalition strength.

Because we wanted to build a large and strong coalition and because we wanted plenty of room to escalate, we began a long lobbying campaign. By April of 1991 both Mayor Maynard Jackson and the Atlanta City Council had said repeatedly and publicly, the council by resolution, that the Olympic work should be done at least at prevailing wages with benefits and training and that the work should uplift the people and communities of Atlanta and the surrounding area.

We began a yearlong process of developing relationships and getting the support of community organizations and constituency groups. By the spring of 1992 we had built a relationship with activists at the Poverty Rights Center and the Emmaus House in the neighborhood where the Olympic Stadium was to be built. We had fashioned stadium construction demands that included union wages and benefits, a preapprenticeship training program for people from the community, and 10 percent of the jobs to be set aside for local residents. That coalition helped us get the support of the Concerned Black Clergy, the Southern Christian Leadership Conference (SCLC), and the city's formal coalition of community groups, the Atlanta Planning and Advisory Board (APAB). The Atlanta Committee for the Olympic Games (ACOG) still wouldn't budge.

That same spring we heard that the Olympic flag would come from Barcelona, Spain, on September 18, 1992, marking Atlanta as the home of the Olympics. By June the labor council was putting together the heads of all the city's construction unions and activists from the labor council's Jobs with Justice committee every Friday morning at a local hotel for breakfast to plan a huge demonstration to greet the flag and disrupt ACOG's celebration.

Coalition-building activities were stepped up. We put together a statewide mobilization strategy. Every possible union affected by the Olympics in Atlanta was recruited, most in Georgia. At our Friday meetings we explored every possible way to mobilize and increase turnout. We set turnout goals for every affiliate of the Atlanta Labor Council. We printed 100,000 leaflets, which were distributed at union and nonunion work sites, public transit stations, and churches. We bought radio time. And we promised that the September 18, 1992, flag arrival would demonstrate our ability to stop the Olympic Games if we didn't get an agreement.

On Friday, September 18, every union construction site in Atlanta was quiet. Ten thousand people gathered a mile south of downtown at the

International Brotherhood of Electrical Workers (IBEW) parking lot and, marching behind Rev. Jesse Jackson and Dr. Joseph Lowery of the SCLC, shut down downtown Atlanta and completely overwhelmed ACOG's celebration of the arrival of the flag. It was one of the largest displays of union force in the history of the South. It made the front page of the *New York Times,* and it signaled a willingness and the ability to use militancy and the mobilization of enough people to disrupt the city and ACOG's plans.

Our next meeting with ACOG was with A. D. Frazier and Shirley Franklin, senior vice president for external affairs, who had been one of Andrew Young's top lieutenants when he was mayor of Atlanta. This meeting in November of 1992 was decidedly more friendly but still not productive. So, in early December, Duane Stewart, representing the Emmaus House and the Poverty Rights Center, met with me and Charlie Key, head of the Atlanta Building Trades Council, in Key's office. We planned a Christmastime demonstration at the ACOG offices.

On December 22, eighty-five construction workers and fifteen community residents walked into ACOG's offices and took them over, chanting through bullhorns and stopping the normal daily flow of business for about two hours. The action forced another meeting with Frazier and with ACOG board cochairman Andrew Young. We had escalated yet another notch.

As we explained in a subsequent meeting with ACOG we were determined to do whatever it took short of hurting people or destroying property to keep Atlanta workers from being exploited by the Olympics.

The groundbreaking for the Olympic Stadium was scheduled for June 10, 1993. We began mobilizing in April for a demonstration that would stop the groundbreaking ceremony. We said, in effect, there would be no stadium groudbreaking, no Olympics, without an agreement.

The week before the scheduled groudbreaking we set up a tent city with allies from the community. A handful of us moved in around the site of the planned stadium. Every newscast that week had at least one remote from our tent city with us reaffirming our commitment for it to be done right or not be done at all.

The Building Trades Council led by Charlie Key began intense bargaining with the general contractor. At 6:30 P.M. on June 9 the contractor and the building trades signed a union agreement for the construction of the stadium with union wages, benefits, and training, and 10 percent of the jobs set aside for local residents.

Although we announced the agreement, more than a thousand union members showed up Saturday morning, June 10, for what turned out to be a celebration. Both Andrew Young and A. D. Frazier spoke, promising a new era of cooperation. But the campaign was far from over. The stadium was only half the construction work, and there was a lot of other work as well.

Maynard Jackson had decided not to seek another term as mayor because of health problems. Atlanta's business community had drafted two candidates to run: Fulton County CEO Michael Lomax, who had built $900 million worth of county construction nonunion, and city council finance committee chair Myrtle Davis. The third candidate for mayor was a city councilman with a perfect labor voting record but only 42 percent name recognition, Bill Campbell.

On July 22, 1993, the Atlanta Labor Council endorsed Bill Campbell for mayor—two full months before qualifying day. Determined to exercise our power, we pulled out the stops. I went inside the campaign as deputy campaign manager. American Federation of State, County and Municipal Workers (AFSCME) ran a fifty-instrument phone bank for two months, calling every union member three times. Campbell and I spoke at local union meetings. We had union volunteers walking precincts and leafletting churches on Sundays, grocery stores and shopping centers on Saturdays. We mailed to all twenty thousand union members in the city three times. We had union volunteers on Campbell's phone banks. We made the election of Bill Campbell the number-one priority of the Atlanta Labor Movement.

On November 23 Campbell won the runoff with 73 percent of the vote. I stood at his shoulder that night when he declared victory and thanked organized labor for his election.

Two months after his inauguration he came back to the Atlanta Labor Council—press in tow. That night he said he wouldn't be mayor were it not for organized labor, and as a token of his appreciation he was appointing me to the board of directors of the ACOG. After a two-year fight in the streets, we were at the table with at least some decision-making influence. Had Campbell not won, we wouldn't have gotten to that table. But, with only one member on a thirty-one-member board, had we not demonstrated power in the streets, there would have been no power in those suites.

Since that appointment we have gotten union members on every ACOG construction project. The communications were handled by members of the Communication Workers of America. The transportation was provided by members of the Amalgamated Transit Union. Much of the printing was done by members of the Graphic Communications International Union (GCIU), and for the first time in the history of the South, the International Association of Theatrical and Stage Employees (IATSE) had a wall-to-wall agreement for all the staging work for the whole Games, including opening and closing ceremonies.

We won more on the Olympics than we ever thought possible because we thought strategically about power and we used all the tools at our disposal: electoral action, solidarity, mobilization and militancy, and coalition.

ELECTORAL ACTION

There are a number of labor councils that have very effective electoral programs. Electoral action was always encouraged by the AFL-CIO, especially phone banks to members during federal elections. But with organized labor's dwindling base we need to reach beyond just our membership to influence the voting decisions of wider chunks of our communities. We have the potential to define not just the political interests of union members but the political interests of working people. Central labor councils can help guide parts of the American electorate back to class-based politics from the mushy center of the Democratic Party and the scary right of the Republican Party and the corporate agendas of both.

One of the biggest frustrations of the American electorate in general, and workers in particular—especially union members—is that our interests are not adequately represented. While Democrats and Republicans argue over issues like gun control and abortion, all we hear is the silence of a conspiratorial consensus over issues like trade and job loss, downsizing and privatization, workers' rights to organize, and corporate CEOs who make more in a day than they can spend in a lifetime while their employees work two and three jobs to scrape together an existence. These are the issues that affect our lives every day, all day long. But we won't hear about them until we return to class-based politics. And we'll do that only when unions speak for more than 16 percent of the workforce.

Of course, the best way to represent more workers is to organize more workers. But, in the short term, we can take a shortcut by expanding our political influence beyond just union members.

If, through the use of union volunteers and effective paid media, we can influence larger groups of workers than just our members we can begin to define workers' interests and mobilize workers around those interests—both union and nonunion.

That is what we in Atlanta did with the election of Bill Campbell, and it is what the labor council in San Francisco did in the election of Willie Brown. Led by Walter Johnson and Josie Mooney, the San Francisco Central Labor Council developed a Labor-Neighbor strategy that had seven hundred union volunteers knocking on the doors of their neighbors for Willie Brown.

Bruce Colburn at the Milwaukee Labor Council is attempting a similar effort. But he goes even further. Working with New Party cofounder Joel

Rogers of the University of Wisconsin, Colburn is trying to develop a political strategy that reaches beyond just union members, involves union volunteers in direct voter contact, but is also independent of the two dominant political parties, allowing the Milwaukee labor movement the space to create their own political agenda with their allies instead of just accepting or rejecting what is handed to them.

Effective electoral action requires thinking strategically about power: how do we use ballots to build it, what does it mean to win, how do you translate electoral victory into a stronger labor movement and changes workers can feel and touch, what tools does labor have to make a real difference in electoral campaigns?

Every effective political program begins with a definition of victory and a strategy for achieving it. Clearly, workers care much less about the personal fortunes of political leaders than about their actions. The goal, then, real victory, is not the election but the consequences of the election. So the effective CLC begins with a set of goals or demands that workers will feel, that will also increase the power of organized labor.

Then effective political action requires a CLC to assess its ability to help build the constituency for the endorsed candidate, persuade uncommitted voters, and get out the vote. That realistic assessment must be matched with the candidate's needs. Finally, after the election is won, the CLC must have the victor accountable to the goals and demands set in the beginning of the process.

In Atlanta in 1993, we endorsed Bill Campbell very early in his campaign—two months before qualifying—after he had promised to support us in our Olympic fight, to oppose privatization, and to sign a Memorandum of Understanding with city workers granting union recognition and representation rights (collective bargaining for public employees is not covered by federal law and is illegal in Georgia and eleven other states).

The CLC then greatly augmented Campbell's field operations. We worked hard on union members: the state, county, and municipal workers union ran a fifty-instrument phone bank, calling every union member in the city three times. And every union member also got two mailings at home. But we went beyond just our own members. I went inside the campaign, becoming deputy campaign manager. Union volunteers leafletted churches every Sunday for two months. We walked working-class precincts every evening for two weeks, knocked on doors distributing leaflets. Members of the Pipefitters Union put up campaign signs. Other volunteers leafletted supermarkets and shopping centers every Saturday for two months. And on election day some union members drove voters to the polls while others gave out literature at the polls.

After the election, the CLC stayed focused on why it went to the trouble: hard bargaining, testimony before the city council, heart-to-heart reminders of his commitments, and the occasional demonstration produced the first Memorandum of Understand between AFSCME and a southern mayor since Dr. Martin Luther King Jr. was assassinated in Memphis in 1968, including a ban on privatization, no layoffs during a first-year fiscal crisis, and the afore-mentioned Olympic victory.

Mobilization, Militancy, Solidarity

For much too long the mobilization and the solidarity of too many labor councils were expressed by a labor council president in a business suit show-ing up at a picket line to chat or carry a picket sign for a half hour. That is not how power is built or exercised.

Marilyn Sneiderman, the new director of field services—now field mobi-lization—for the AFL-CIO, has said she would like to see CLCs move 1 per-cent of the members of their affiliates once a month and 10 percent once a year. That would exercise power.

If that goal is attainable and CLCs made a commitment to reaching it, CLCs would spark a mobilization of union members across America not seen since the CIO organizing and strikes of the 1930s and 1940s.

Effective solidarity is expressed locally. International unions and different locals express solidarity in important ways by sending donations to strikers or by participating in corporate campaigns; but the solidarity that most matters during a strike, that shows the most power, that can do the most to bring home the victory, is expressed locally. Plant gate rallies, mass picket lines, confronta-tions at shift change, media, picket-line prayer meetings—these are the kinds of things that do the most to encourage workers. And these are best organized by central labor councils.

When Local 254 struck the Red Cross in Atlanta, we had a weekly mass news conference on the picket line to announce the cancellation of yet another blood drive. That is what got those workers back on their jobs. When IBEW struck Lithonia Lighting in suburban Atlanta, Local 613 asked the labor coun-cil to help them organize a solidarity rally in the middle of their suburban town. Seven hundred union members from different unions and Congresswoman Cynthia McKinney showed up. The next week the strike was settled.

The demonstrations against Newt Gingrich that began in Atlanta and were carried on by unions and CLCs all over the county in 1995 directly con-tributed to his steep decline in popularity, the quickest descent in American history.

The kind of militant mobilization that can get the attention of the local power elite or move the movers and shakers cannot be organized from Washington, D.C. It can only be organized locally—and most effectively by a CLC committed to winning that understands power and knows that militancy, mobilization, and solidarity are tools for building it.

COALITIONS

The new administration of the AFL-CIO tried to jump-start coalition building and membership mobilization with a springtime campaign this year called America Needs a Raise (ANAR). Town hall meetings were held in twenty-five different cities. The town hall meetings were organized locally with much direction from Washington. They were hosted by one of the new principal officers and a local community leader.

The emphasis was on recruiting organizational allies to help build the crowd and to supply nonunion workers who along with union rank-and-filers testified about the effects of the economy and the decline/stagnation of wages on their lives and families. The new administration knows that without community allies and coalition partners it is much too easy for the other side to label us a special interest. In some cities we are much too susceptible to race-baiting. And, again, in most areas of America we no longer have enough members to win the really hard fights by ourselves.

So the ANAR campaign was designed to get the real issues of wages and job loss on the political radar screen but also to show that these issues are not just of concern to union members. And, finally, it was designed to help labor councils develop the capacity to work in coalition and to begin that process.

There just is not enough union diversity any more for us to win alone. Coalitions are crucial. Coalitions increase our power, thus allowing us to build more power.

CONCLUSION

One of the most important keys to labor victory is the central labor council. But the CLC can only be effective if its leadership understands power—how to build it, how to wield it. The best tools of power for CLCs are electoral action, solidarity, mobilization and militancy, and coalitions. We are in a climate today in which we have to fight to win. To fight effectively we must understand power, and where ours comes from.

8

DEFENDING WORKERS' RIGHTS IN THE GLOBAL ECONOMY: THE CWA EXPERIENCE

Larry Cohen and Steve Early

C apital in the 1990s is increasingly mobile and global, integrated and powerful. Organized labor tends to be fragmented and, in many countries, much weaker than in the past. At a time when workers of the world need to unite more than ever before to defend their interests, most unions still operate within the framework of a single nation state or, worse yet, one domestic industry, firm, or craft. To deal more effectively with common employers and similar antiunion strategies, union members in different countries must find ways to overcome the barriers of organizational bureaucracy, geography, nationalism, and language that separate them. Traditional forms of labor solidarity can be helpful, but they're hardly sufficient. International conferences, speech making, and resolution passing by high-ranking union officials are no substitute for cross-border activity that unites workers at the grass roots. The new labor internationalism that is needed to meet the challenges of organizing and bargaining in the next century must be built from the bottom up as well as the top down.

MOBILIZING BEGINS AT HOME

In this essay, we describe steps taken by the Communications Workers of America (CWA) to strengthen its ties to workers abroad in the face of sweeping changes in the telecommunications industry. CWA's cross-border work has involved labor organizations in North and South America, Europe, and Asia. It flows out of the more activist approach CWA has pursued at home in response to the 1984 breakup of the bell system and the union's ensuing difficulty dealing with multiple telephone companies in a competitive environment rather than a single regulated monopoly employing nearly 500,000 workers under one national contract. Since the "divestiture" of AT&T, CWA has faced the combined threats of deregulation, technological change, corporate restructuring, massive job losses, and the emergence of aggressive, antiunion competitors like MCI, Sprint, and Northern Telecom in telephone manufacturing and services.

CWA was established, as a national union, in 1947. Its predecessor organization, the National Federation of Telephone Workers, was a loose confederation of formerly independent telephone unions within AT&T. During the last fifteen years—when CWA has lost more than 100,000 jobs in its traditional jurisdiction—the union has undergone considerable diversification and amalgamation. While it remains the world's largest union of telecommunications workers, CWA now includes more than 80,000 health care and public employees, 45,000 newspaper and printing industry workers, and 15,000 workers in cable TV and broadcasting. Some of this growth has been the product of mergers with the remaining independent telephone unions or smaller AFL-CIO affiliates like the Newspaper Guild, International Typographical Union, and the National Association of Broadcast Engineers and Technicians. But much of it—particularly in health care and the public sector—has been the result of aggressive outreach to nonunion workers.

To overcome management resistance to unionization in the private sector and build strong new workplace organizations in any setting, CWA uses an organizing model based on several elements: "one-on-one" recruitment of activists; creation of "in-plant" committees; extensive training and leadership development; and encouragement of "direct action" on the job to give workers a sense of their own collective power. By the late 1980s, it was clear that this approach was needed not only in organizing campaigns, but also in long-established CWA bargaining units. Like employers throughout the country, telephone companies were seeking contract concessions and displaying a new willingness to use strikes to get them. The union's response was a program called CWA Mobilization. Employed in each round of telephone bargaining since 1989, mobilization seeks to strengthen and revitalize the union through systematic internal organizing and greater membership participation in the negotiating process. The program's goal is to make strikes, where necessary, more effective, and give CWA members the ability to pursue "in-plant" and corporate campaigns as an alternative or supplement to striking.

One of mobilization's earliest victories was a militant contract fight in 1989 with the "Baby Bell" that serves New York and New England. The four-month walkout over health care cost shifting at NYNEX united 60,000 members of CWA and the International Brotherhood of Electrical Workers (IBEW).

144

It became one of the largest, most successful anticoncessions strikes of the decade. The forty local unions involved in this struggle spent more than eighteen months preparing for it. They created a network of 4,000 stewards and workplace mobilization coordinators to distribute literature, organize displays of solidarity, and counter company propaganda about the need for increased employee payments for medical coverage. When negotiations deadlocked, the old contract expired, and work stopped, months of membership education and mobilization activity had already laid the groundwork for a high-impact strike. Strikers participated in mass and mobile picketing, civil disobedience, rallies of up to 15,000 people, and a sophisticated community-based campaign of political pressure on the company around its rates and relationships with regulatory agencies.

As impressive as this struggle was, firms like NYNEX are changing rapidly in ways that make them less vulnerable to strikes or other forms of workplace and community pressure in their traditional lines of business. A union postmortem on the 1989 walkout, for example, concluded, "that it takes at least two months to really begin to hurt the company" because of its high degree of automation and ability to maintain service using managers, retirees, and temps.

That was at a time when 90 percent of the firm's revenues were still derived from providing local telephone service. In the early 1990s, NYNEX became an increasingly diversified, multinational company, with ambitious plans to earn 25 percent of its income abroad by the year 2000. Its 1997 merger with Bell Atlantic created the second largest communications company in the United States. The $23 billion deal was necessary, management said, to meet "foreign competition" in the form of British Telecom (BT) and Deutsche Telekom (DT). "Our market isn't this country any more," explained Bell Atlantic chairman Ray Smith, "it's the world." According to BT chairman Iain Vallance, the industry's current merger trend will ultimately result in there being only "four or five global telecommunications companies."

In their foreign ventures, U.S.–based firms attempt wherever possible to operate nonunion (as NYNEX does with its multi-billion-dollar cable TV venture in Britain) or with the benefit of corrupt, company-union arrangements (as Lucent Technologies—formerly AT&T—does at its Mexican *maquiladora* plants). Meanwhile, the multinationals headquartered abroad that are expanding here—like Northern Telecom, the Canadian-based phone equipment manufacturer—concentrate their operations in "union-free" areas of the United States. The $3.7 billion capital infusion that CWA's bitter adversary, Sprint, recently received from DT and France Telecom has greatly strengthened its global position and ability to spread antiunionism abroad. The pending $20 billion marriage of MCI and several possible suitors, including BT, will likewise create another global giant with little affection for collective bargaining or respect for workers' rights.

THE GLOBAL TELECOMMUNICATIONS MARKET

Clearly, CWA's future bargaining or organizing involving multinational firms may not succeed unless the union has international alliances and joint ventures of its own that enable workers here to act in concert with their brothers and sisters abroad. CWA's pursuit of such relationships has followed in the footsteps of the companies themselves, as they've moved overseas in search of higher rates of profit. Foreign investment by U.S. telecommunications firms has expanded in two main areas: industrial economies, where state-owned telephone systems are being privatized and/or markets deregulated, and telecommunications services in developing countries.

Industrial Economies

In New Zealand, for example, two U.S. "Baby Bells" have played a key role in the sell-off and reorganization of Telecom New Zealand (TNZ). Bell Atlantic and Ameritech acquired a $2.5 billion stake in TNZ when it was privatized. After just five years under their management, the company's workforce has been reduced by 75 percent. Real wages have fallen, and pension coverage has been cut back. Aided by the antiunion legislation enacted by New Zealand's conservative government, worker organization has been thwarted at new, TNZ-related ventures. Within TNZ itself, management is insisting that separate union contracts be negotiated for each business unit, rather than a single companywide agreement—a strategy imported from the United States. The high purchase price of Bell Atlantic and Ameritech's TNZ ownership share requires these U.S. partners to squeeze as big a return as possible to justify the investment to their U.S. stockholders—regardless of the cost in jobs or service quality in New Zealand.

Deregulation in foreign countries also creates many opportunities in markets that American companies may still be awaiting regulatory approval to enter at home. The investment of American dollars in such ventures has—as at TNZ—been accompanied by the introduction of U.S.–style labor relations policies. For example, several other Baby Bells—including U.S. West and NYNEX—now compete directly with BT in the United Kingdom. There, they provide combined cable TV and local telephone services, which they cannot do yet in the United States. But their employment practices in these new cable systems are far below British standards and mimic the worst practices of cable TV operators in America. The UK cable subsidiaries of NYNEX and U.S. West turn over their entire network construction and maintenance to contractors who in turn employ workers as individual subcontractors. The latter are paid for each task they complete. Employees of these firms are thus not covered by workers' compensation when they are injured and have no right to collective bargaining since, in theory, they are self-employed.

Meanwhile, the still heavily unionized BT may soon be contributing to a similar undercutting of U.S. telephone labor standards via its possible acquisition of entirely nonunion MCI, the second-largest long-distance carrier here. MCI has relied heavily on a much-exploited contingent workforce in both operator services and customer support—and the kind of union-busting tactics that would be impermissible at BT itself inside the United Kingdom. While BT has been transforming itself into a big global player, however, it has eliminated more than 100,000 jobs at home in response to the lower labor cost competition from new cable TV and telco rivals. Union influence has been eroded as a result.

Telecommunications Services in Developing Countries

In the United States and other industrialized economies, telephone service is nearly universal. The potential for domestic growth is through the sale of additional information services such as video and electronic publishing and extra lines for fax and internet services. But in most developing countries, where less than 10 percent of the people currently have access to residential service, the big profit potential lies in extending basic telephone service to everyone else. U.S. investments in these countries assume a high rate of return—because the government typically guarantees a continued monopoly over basic telecommunications services for a fixed period of time—and are based on the expectation of low labor costs but high customer rates. Under such conditions, SBC Communications—formerly Southwestern Bell—has bought a stake and management role in Telmex, the former national telephone monopoly in Mexico (and also spent $1.26 billion for its 30 percent interest in Telekom South Africa as well). A multinational consortium led by GTE is currently operating the Venezuelan phone system. Telefonica de Espana of Spain has large stakes in the Chilean and Peruvian phone systems. France Telecom and STET, the Italian phone company, together own nearly 40 percent of Telecom Argentina.

In Mexico, the government's privatization of entities such as Telmex has been a quick source of cash for balancing federal budgets and improving currency valuations. But, all too often, the amount of money received in this fashion is based on quick calculations by private capital that its initial investment can be recouped soon through job cuts, price hikes, or market growth—or all three methods. SBC's purchase of 10 percent of Telmex in conjunction with France Telecom and other investors has, for example, generated a favorable rate of return despite the recent drastic devaluation of the peso. In addition to its ownership share, SBC is also paid to manage the company, providing an additional source of profits.

A Bottom Line That's Bad for Workers

One uniform result of all the international investment strategies described briefly above is the lowering of labor standards in an industry where, under private or public ownership, strong unions had previously been able to achieve good wages and benefits. The host country's workers are invariably made to pay for the new investment facilitated by privatization and/or deregulation through job losses or less favorable employment conditions. In many instances, these investments also represent a loss of social and local control. In exchange for promised modernization and cash, public entities around the world have readily surrendered their ownership or regulation of their nation's only telecommunications system and primary distribution channel for future information services. Globalization thus reduces the influence that any one nation has over the multinational enterprises operating within its boundaries. Where in the past, local, state, or national governments could set some operating standards, today's global telecommunications firms are increasingly well positioned to dictate their own terms of business.

THE UNION RESPONSE: MOBILIZING GLOBALLY

Efforts by these multinationals to boost their power and profits, often at the expense of workers, can only be challenged effectively through long-term, cross-border campaigns based on careful research and analysis, membership education and involvement, organizing, and international labor solidarity.

CWA and other communications unions are developing such campaigns through a Working Group on Multinationals that was organized in 1991 by the Postal, Telephone, and Telegraph International (PTTI). PTTI is a global coalition of postal and telecom unions with about five million members in more than one hundred countries. As information services including telecom, TV, and data have been privatized and sold off to multinationals, PTTI has promoted greater cooperation among its affiliates that deal with these firms. In particular, the Working Group has focused on the behavior of Sprint, AT&T, the "Baby Bells," Telefonica de Espana, France Telecom, British Telecom, and the U.K.-based Cable and Wireless.

In 1994, PTTI member organizations issued an international code of conduct for all firms operating internationally in the industry. The Working Group encourages all affiliates to make adoption of the code a goal in their individual negotiations with each multinational company. Unions are also trying to seek compliance with it through joint action. Violations by a particular firm elsewhere in the world have become a basis for workers and consumers opposing market entry by that firm in their country. Unions in a nation where an offending multinational is headquartered can play a particularly important role—if the firm is still heavily unionized at home—because they have leverage with management that can be used to defend worker organizing within overseas subsidiaries that are operating "union-free" and want to stay that way.

Under the code, telecommunications multinationals would be obliged to do the following:

1. Disclose, as soon as practical, their global activities, including forecasts of employment levels, possibilities for technological change, movement of work, and investment.

2. Meet, annually or whenever else necessary, with all organizations that represent their employees around the world. At such meetings, general information shall be exchanged on subjects including organizational rights, equal employment opportunities, safety and health, and education and training.

3. Abstain from interfering in worker organizing efforts in any country where they operate directly or through a subsidiary.

4. Recognize, on a voluntary basis, any union that presents them with evidence of an appropriate level of organizational support under the relevant standards for union recognition in the country involved.

5. Refrain from shifting production from one nation to another to avoid union recognition or to seek lower wages.

THE NORTHERN TELECOM CAMPAIGN:
A CASE STUDY IN INTERNATIONAL LABOR COOPERATION

Codes of conduct developed by international labor conferences have no more impact than passing a resolution or making a speech if there isn't serious follow-up work done to convert rhetoric into reality. One of the most extensive codes campaigns waged so far involves Northern Telecom (Nortel, or NT) and grows out of the international assistance that CWA received during a five-week strike against the company in 1989. Nortel is a Canadian-based telephone equipment producer with factories throughout North America, Western Europe, and the third world. It began as the manufacturing arm of Bell Canada but, in the 1980s, increased its worldwide workforce by 80 percent and its sales by 400 percent. Not surprisingly, the percentage of its workers belonging to unions declined by 50 percent during the same period.

In Canada, the company has ordered plant closings and layoffs in recent years but generally remains heavily organized; about 40 percent of its 22,000 Canadian employees are union-represented. South of the Canadian border, in a U.S. workforce about the same size, Nortel's unionization rate is less than 5 percent. While some equipment installation and maintenance technicians are organized, not a single one of the company's American manufacturing plants has a union contract. In 1982, Nortel's bad faith bargaining and other unfair labor practices drove CWA from the only factory where the union had ever been able to win a National Labor Relations Board (NLRB) election (after four unsuccessful attempts.) Following this victory in Nashville, Tennessee, the company extended its deunionization campaign to the smaller groups of workers around the country who install Nortel equipment. Between 1984 and 1989 alone, five out of seven CWA installer units were also decertified.

By the summer of 1989, CWA's largest remaining field technician unit consisted of about five hundred workers in eight northeastern states. The company was clearly preparing to press for concessions that would force a strike and set the stage for yet another union eviction drive. So the Nortel workers, who belong to CWA Local 1109 in Brooklyn New York, readied themselves for this struggle by creating an active mobilization network, issuing regular contract bulletins, and engaging in a variety of on-the-job actions before walking out three weeks after their contract expired. Almost immediately, management deployed replacement workers, who were confronted at key customer locations by teams of mobile pickets and their supporters from other CWA locals. The ensuing five-week strike was militant and well organized, but it almost certainly would have failed if CWA had not lined up international allies as well.

1989 Nortel Strike Support

Prior to Local 1109's bargaining, CWA had approached leaders of the company's two main unions at home, the Canadian Auto Workers (CAW) and the Communications Workers of Canada (now known as the Communications, Energy, and Paperworkers Union, or CEP). Soon after the U.S. installers struck, both the CAW and CEP intervened in the dispute. Letters of protest were sent by CAW president Bob White and CEP president Fred Pomeroy to Nortel's chief executive officer. Copies of this correspondence were then widely distributed among members of all three unions to inform them about the emerging cross-border solidarity campaign. The Canadian unions immediately launched their own grassroots mobilization in support of the strike. Leaflets distributed in CAW and CEP workplaces throughout Canada recounted Nortel's history of "anti-worker, anti-union activities in the United States" and linked this to the export of jobs from Canada to the United States. Strikers from Local 1109 were dispatched to Canada to meet with Nortel workers there.

The unions also conducted a coordinated public information and press campaign that proved to be very embarrassing to a firm widely regarded as the crown jewel of Canadian high-tech manufacturing. Pomeroy personally joined CWA's negotiations with the company in New York to deliver the message that Canadians would not stand by and watch one of their major employers abuse the rights of its U.S. workers. "Northern Telecom has to understand that it cannot pretend to be a good corporate citizen in Canada while it denies basic rights to its employees in other parts of the world," Pomeroy said. "We intend to do all in our power to help Northern Telecom workers—wherever they live in the world—improve their working conditions." As a direct result of Canadian labor's solidarity work and intervention in the strike, Local 1109 was finally able to settle the dispute without concessions or the loss of any striker's job.

The three-way union partnership forged in 1989 achieved its next victory one year later. In the course of a lawsuit against Nortel, CWA uncovered dramatic evidence of the company's systematic and illegal invasion of workers' privacy during the long campaign to prevent unionization of its Nashville plant in the early 1980s. Copies of tape-recorded telephone conversations, wire-tapped from pay phones in the employee cafeteria, were provided to the union by a former security officer in the plant. Additional tapes had been made from listening devices in the sprinkler system. The surveillance had occurred over a number of years in which workers had been trying to form a CWA local and negotiate a union contract.

White and Pomeroy called a press conference in Toronto, Nortel's world headquarters, to publicize these disclosures and again denounce the company's conduct. The matter received wide coverage in Canadian TV, radio, and newspaper reports and also prompted calls for a parliamentary inquiry into the company's behavior. The combination of the wiretapping revelations and related legal pressure helped bring about a settlement of CWA's lawsuit against the company. As part of this settlement, NT agreed to become the first telecommunications firm in the United States to ban all secret monitoring of employees, including unannounced eavesdropping on their work-related phone calls (which is not illegal in the United States).

151

Expanding the Union Coalition

In October 1991, the North American labor coalition within the company sponsored a conference in Toronto for Nortel unionists from around the world. More than 150 workers and union officials attended, including delegates from Ireland, England, Germany, Turkey, Malaysia, and Japan. The participants developed an "Education and Action Plan" that called for coordinated rank-and-file activity in defense of workers' rights to organize and bargain at Nortel. As part of this plan, a campaign brochure was produced in eight languages. It described the company's global expansion strategy and exposed its record of labor law violations and union busting in places like Malaysia (where Nortel secured an agreement with the government barring unionization of its plant for at least five years after it opened). All the conference participants committed to return home and in early 1992 began a petition-signing drive aimed at building worker support for the group's central demands—management neutrality and noninterference in all organizing drives and negotiations with a multinational union committee on a global code of conduct. Many participating unions also organized local press conferences, rallies, picketing, or solidarity button-wearing in Nortel workplaces.

On July 19, 1993, after thousands of workers around the world had signed the petitions, a joint delegation from CWA, CAW, and CEP presented them to the company's vice president for global labor relations. Nortel subsequently agreed to exchange some information on its business plans and discuss its labor relations practices with this joint union group. Management continues to reject the unions' demand that it remain neutral when workers are organizing or recognize new union bargaining units on the basis of card-check procedures. However, since the unions' ongoing campaign was launched, Nortel has appointed a new vice president and North American director more respectful of collective bargaining.

The company's U.S.–based human resources director also pledged, in an exchange of letters with CWA president Morton Bahr, that "respect, trust, and mutuality of interest" would be the basis for future company dealings with CWA. Since then, workers and local union officials have both reported some improvement in labor-management relations. Technicians like John Viverito from New Jersey—who struck Nortel in 1989 and attended the Toronto conference two years later—know how this change came about. "We realize now that working for an international firm requires contact, information exchanges, and solidarity between all our unions in different countries," Viverito says. "We need their support and must be willing to help them in return, in whatever way we can."

CASE STUDY #2: CWA'S ALLIANCE SOUTH OF THE BORDER WITH STRM

CWA's ongoing relationship with Mexican telephone workers provides another important example of how international solidarity can and must be a two-way street. The 1990 privatization of Telmex, SBC's management role with the company since then, and the creation of "free-trade" links between Canada, the United States, and Mexico have led telephone worker unions from all three nations into a joint venture of their own. This alliance was formalized in an agreement signed by CWA's Bahr, CEP's Pomeroy, and Francisco Hernandez Juarez, general secretary of Sindicato de Telefonistas de la Republica Mexicana (STRM). It commits their organizations "to defend union and workers' rights" through "joint mobilization" of members in Mexico and throughout North America.

High-level representatives of CWA and STRM have since conducted periodic meetings with SBC to discuss mutual concerns about new technology, downsizing, deregulation in Mexico, and the company's stance toward organizing efforts at its new cellular phone subsidiary in the United States. But, as in the case of its cross-border work within Northern Telecom, CWA has tried to cement its relationship with STRM through direct worker-to-worker contacts. In September 1995, fifteen CWA organizers and eighteen from STRM spent three days together in Laredo, Texas, at a training and strategy session. The U.S. participants came from local unions in Texas, California, and New Jersey. All were bilingual and had experience organizing immigrant workers from Mexico and Central and South America. The STRM activists were eager to learn about CWA's organizing work, including its efforts to unionize firms that have entered the telecommunications field since deregulation in the United States. As a follow-up to the exchange in Texas, two STRM organizers spent a week working on a CWA campaign in Los Angeles among five thousand Spanish-speaking truckers who transport freight from the city's harbor.

STRM still represents fifty thousand workers at Telmex. But other Mexican companies have recently been allowed to provide local phone service, cellular phone service, and cable TV access in competition with the former state-owned monopoly. Its hold on long-distance customers is also being challenged by new competitors from north of the border like AT&T and MCI. The problem for STRM is that many of these firms don't want to deal with the independent telephone workers' union, preferring instead to install company unions or arrange cozy deals with affiliates of the three-million-member Confederation of Mexican Workers (CTM), the government-dominated labor federation. In 1991, for example, CWA visitors to an AT&T (now Lucent) manufacturing plant in Matamoros found that its CTM–represented employees were being paid wages low even by Mexican standards. The company had granted immediate recognition and automatic dues deduction to the CTM, which was providing little or no protection to the workers in return. Furthermore, CTM leaders were not at all interested in developing joint strategies with CWA for dealing with AT&T at any of its runaway Mexican plants.

STRM, on the other hand, is a different kind of union—as demonstrated by the enthusiasm and commitment of its organizers at the Laredo meeting. It is part of the Forum, a grouping of more than twenty Mexican labor organizations that are campaigning for greater internal democracy and political independence. STRM is also trying to give workers in the expanding Mexican telephone sector a real voice on the job. Now facing some of the same employers that CWA has bargained with or tried to organize over the years, STRM understands the importance of developing a united front, north and south of the border. Since 1995, STRM has thus played a key role in CWA's ongoing solidarity campaign on behalf of workers fired by Sprint, which operates as America's third largest long-distance carrier on an entirely nonunion basis. CWA in turn has taken up the cause of Mexican workers also victimized by union busting.

Union Busting At Sprint

Everywhere that groups have tried to organize in the United States as part of a CWA–backed Sprint Employees Network, they have been threatened, harassed, spied on, or dismissed. At La Conexion Familiar (LCF) in San Francisco, the company staffed an entire facility with Latinos to help target Spanish-speaking customers. With support from CWA Local 9410, a strong majority of the seven-dollar-an-hour LCF service reps and telemarketers signed up for the union and petitioned for an NLRB election. On July 14, 1994, one week before the scheduled vote, Sprint topped off a brutal antiunion campaign by closing the entire office. Cornell University researcher Kate Bronfenbrenner described the scene as follows:

> [After] securing the building with extra security guards, the president of Sprint's Hispanic marketing division announced over the loudspeaker that Sprint had decided to shut down LCF. With no advance notice, employees were told to collect their belongings, undergo a search by security guards, and immediately vacate the premises. All Latino and mostly women, many of the LCF workers were single parents with no other source of support. Still others were legal immigrants from countries such as Chile and El Salvador, worried that without a job they would be forced to return to an uncertain future at home. Shocked and dis-

traught at the sudden shutdown, many workers wept openly. One woman fainted and paramedics had to be brought in.

This mass firing of 177 workers, plus many other illegal management activities, led the regional director of the NLRB to cite Sprint for forty-eight separate violations of federal labor law. The region then tried to get a federal court order reinstating the workers immediately, but the request was denied. An administrative law judge (ALJ) who heard the case thirteen months later found Sprint guilty of almost every allegation of illegal conduct but nevertheless concluded that LCF was shut down because it was losing money, not because the office was unionizing. The ALJ proposed, as a remedy, that Sprint send a letter to all former LCF employees admitting its violations! The ALJ's ruling was then reviewed by a three-member NLRB panel in Washington, D.C. Their decision on December 27, 1996—two and one-half years after the vote—was a much stronger vindication of the workers' position. (See NLRB decision and order in *LCF, Inc. d/b/a La Conexion Familiar and Sprint Corporation and Communications Workers of America, District Nine and Local 9410, AFL-CIO.* Case 20-CA-26203.)

The panel, which included NLRB chairman William Gould, cited the falsification of documents by a Sprint vice president at corporate headquarters in Kansas City who tried to create a "paper trail" indicating that management was more concerned about LCF's financial performance than it really was. Just prior to the July 1994 office closing, the NLRB noted, Sprint had hired a new manager for LCF and was making other long-term plans for this unique Spanish-language marketing center. The decision by Gould and his fellow board members requires Sprint to rehire all LCF workers into "substantially equivalent" jobs elsewhere in the company, provide moving expenses, if necessary, for them to relocate, and pay the group more than $15 million in back wages and benefits. In addition, because of the company's "widespread misconduct demonstrating a general disregard for the employee's fundamental rights," the NLRB issued a broad order that Sprint "cease and desist from threatening employees with the closure of any of its facilities if the union comes in" and that it stop engaging in other illegal acts of coercion.

Unfortunately, NLRB orders are not self-enforcing. When employers disagree with them, they can be appealed to federal court. Sprint immediately challenged the ruling in the U.S. Court of Appeals in Washington, D.C., guaranteeing that there will be many more months in which justice for the LCF workers is delayed by the slow-moving machinery of American labor law. That's why, from the very beginning of this struggle, CWA responded not just with the usual legal countermeasures but with a wide-ranging protest campaign aimed at making the LCF workers a labor cause célèbre at home and abroad. Within weeks of their firing, for example, eighty of the LCFers marched on a meeting of the San Francisco Board of Supervisors and secured a resolution censuring Sprint and demanding full reinstatement. The fired workers conducted a round-the-clock vigil in front of Sprint's downtown office building. They set up tents on the sidewalk, gave press interviews, and hosted visiting delegations from churches and other unions. In the city's "Mission District," LCF workers and their families went door-to-door to persuade Latino-owned businesses to display signs supporting the solidarity campaign. Dozens of U.S. congressmen signed a joint letter to Sprint's chief executive officer, William Esrey, condemning management's behavior. San Francisco Bay Area community groups were also enlisted to bombard the company with angry mail. Trade unionists active in Jobs with Justice coalitions joined the fray by picketing Sprint locations throughout the country. CWA also asked telephone worker unions in Mexico, Canada, Brazil, and Nicaragua to raise, in their own countries, the issue of Sprint's union busting. On July 14, 1997—the third anniversary of the LCF firings—CWA locals and their allies in other unions and community organizations held protests at Sprint facilities in sixteen American cities, as well as in Ireland and Puerto Rico.

The STRM Response

STRM went further than any other LCF supporters abroad when it filed the first formal complaint ever made by a Mexican union under the NAFTA labor side agreement (known formally as the North American Agreement on Labor Cooperation, or NAALC). This move attracted considerable publicity on both sides of the border in 1995. It had previously been assumed that NAALC's complaint procedures—a sop to NAFTA foes in the United States—would mainly be used by American unions complaining about workers' rights violations in Mexico that help keep unions weak, wages low, and working conditions poor in the runaway shops of U.S. multinationals.

However, as STRM's Francisco Hernandez Juarez pointed out, his union has good reason to mount its own legal challenge to Sprint's violation of the "basic norms of labor rights" in the United States—namely the company's entry into the long-distance market in Mexico as part of a joint venture with Telmex. "We don't want the mass firing of workers to happen here," Hernandez Juarez said. STRM's complaint demanded that the National Administrative Office (NAO) established in Mexico under NAFTA, bar Sprint from operating in the country until it reinstates all the fired LCF workers and agrees to recognize unions on either side of the border whenever a majority of them choose to be

156

represented. The Mexican union charged that the absence of any prompt remedy for the denial of LCF workers' rights demonstrates "the ineffectiveness of U.S. law to comply with the principles contained in [the NAALC] to which the U.S. is now obligated."

In June 1995, the Mexican NAO issued an eighteen-page report upholding the STRM complaint. In it, NAO secretary Miguel Angel Orozco expressed concern about the adequacy of U.S. labor law enforcement and called for ministerial consultations between the labor secretaries of Mexico and the United States about the disposition of the LCF unfair labor practice case. STRM reiterated its demand that the NAO develop clear "standards, guidelines, and remedies to address violations of Mexican workers' rights while they are employed in the United States" and to insure that all "companies seeking to conduct business in Mexico" who employ such workers abide by these standards as well.

In February 1996, labor ministry representatives from Mexico, Canada, and the United States convened a widely publicized one-day hearing in San Francisco on the STRM complaint. Sprint boycotted the event. But testimony from STRM, CWA, the PTTI, sympathetic elected officials and academics, and—most effectively—the fired Sprint workers themselves demonstrated the need for stronger action against international labor law violators. Following the San Francisco hearing, the labor ministers asked the Commission for Labor Cooperation (CLC), another trinational body spawned by the NAALC, to conduct "a study of the effects of plant closings on the principle of freedom of association and right to organize" in the three countries involved.

The purpose of the inquiry was presumably to determine whether Sprint's actions at LCF were an aberration or reflected a pervasive pattern of employer behavior in the 1990s. Among the academic researchers retained to explore this question was Kate Bronfenbrenner of Cornell. After collecting and analyzing data on hundreds of U.S. union organizing efforts in recent years, Bronfenbrenner concluded "that plant closing threats and plant closings have become an integral part of employer anti-union campaigns." She found that the rate of plant closings after NLRB elections "has more than doubled in the years since NAFTA was ratified," indicating "that NAFTA has both amplified the credibility and effectiveness of the plant closing threat for employers and emboldened increasing numbers of employers to act on that threat."

These were not the kind of findings that the U.S. Department of Labor was eager to release right before the Clinton administration sought congressional approval for "fast track" expansion of NAFTA to include Chile and other Latin American countries. The DOL delayed release of the CLC report for many months. When it was finally issued in June 1997, Bronfenbrenner's findings were buried or otherwise watered down in a bland 191-page document that failed to single out Sprint for any criticism whatsoever. As a CWA press statement noted at the time, the report was "a huge disappointment." The recommendations it made only "addressed bureaucratic issues, not the real needs of fired workers." Nevertheless, the LCF complaint initiated by STRM did expose the glaring limitations of labor side agreements in general by showing that they don't provide aggrieved workers with any effective international recourse. Labor opponents were able to use this experience under the NAALC in their late 1997 lobbying against NAFTA extension.

CWA Returns the Favor at Maxi-Switch

CWA and STRM have had more success working together on a NAFTA labor side agreement complaint involving Maxi-Switch, a U.S.–based subsidiary of a Taiwanese company called Silitek. Maxi-Switch is a manufacturer of high-technology keyboards, including Gameboys and various Nintendo game products. To comply with *maquiladora* zone rules, Maxi-Switch maintains a "bag-and-ship" operation in Arizona—160 miles from its assembly plant in Cananea in the state of Sonora. Products are made in Mexico by workers earning three dollars a day and then shipped across the border to Tucson, where a smaller number of higher-paid employees operate a U.S. distribution center.

The Tucson connection became the basis for direct rank-and-file participation, on the CWA side, in the effort to support Maxi-Switch organizing. The workers in Senora were led by Alicia Perez Garcia, a nineteen-year-old woman who spent two years quietly building support for "the Union of Workers of Maxi-Switch," an affiliate (like STRM) of the Federation of Unions of Goods and Services Companies (FESEBS). When 70 percent of Perez Garcia's six hundred coworkers had signed up, she and other in-plant leaders of the drive petitioned the government for official recognition of their new union's majority status. The very next day, she was punched and shaken up so badly by a supervisor that she had to be taken to a hospital. All of the leaders of the union were fired or forced to resign. To emphasize further its opposition to unionization, Maxi-Switch also dismissed other workers and implemented a pay cut—even though wages in the plant were already low and their benefits barely met minimum legal requirements in Mexico. Later, the workers learned that the assault on their leader—for which the supervisor was later fined—and the retaliatory firings had both been triggered by a government official tipping off the company about the recognition petition. FESEBS supporters were, in turn, notified that their petition was invalid because Maxi-Switch already had a CTM–affiliated "phantom union"—that none of the workers knew about. When they asked to see a copy of their *contrato fantasmas*—or "ghost contract"—they were denied access to it.

Members of CWA Local 7026 in Tucson learned of this situation and brought a letter of support for the Maxi-Switch workers to a cross-border meeting in Hermosillo that was sponsored by STRM and other unions involved in the Forum.

According to President Michael McGrath, a worker at U.S. West, "Thirty-five percent of the local's membership has family or roots in Mexico." Among them are chief steward and organizer Estella Valencia, whose father emigrated after the 1919 revolution. Led by 7026 vice president Randy Clarke, the CWA delegation met with Perez Garcia and gathered information about conditions in her factory, which included fire hazards and child labor involving workers as young as age thirteen. Based on their report and information supplied by STRM, CWA went to its own NAO and filed an October 1996 complaint alleging that a NAFTA signatory—the Mexican government—was failing to protect workers' right to organize. CWA argued that "Maxi-Switch, in collusion with government officials, representatives of the CTM, and the Conciliation and Arbitration Board of the State of Sonora, had consistently violated the law to prevent workers from joining a union of their own choosing."

As CWA president Bahr pointed out, this was not the first time that "the Mexican government has failed to enforce its own Federal Labor Code and the international treaties to which it is bound" in a "freedom of association" case involving a multinational firm. However, three earlier complaints filed by American unions with the U.S. NAO to challenge mistreatment of Mexican labor organizers at Honeywell, GE, and Sony only resulted in hearings being held. There was no effective redress for the fired workers involved—and sometimes not even nonbinding rulings in their favor. The NAO—which is part of the U.S. Labor Department's Bureau of International Affairs—finally scheduled a public hearing on the Maxi-Switch case in April 1997. Four days before it opened, however, the Mexican government agreed to issue a legal registration of the independent union at Maxi-Switch in Sonora and hear the reinstatement appeals of its fired workers. The union's now-official status has allowed it to continue organizing within the plant to achieve the goal of a first contract. This is the first time that a participant in a NAFTA labor side agreement proceeding has capitulated and agreed to follow its own laws, although STRM, CWA, and the PTTI are all monitoring the situation closely to insure full compliance. As part of this process, the respective affiliates of STRM in Cananea and CWA in Tucson have maintained their cross-border contacts and sent representatives to each others' membership meetings on a regular basis.

EUROPEAN CONNECTIONS:
CHALLENGING SPRINT AND BUILDING A HIGH-TECH WORKERS NETWORK

STRM's challenge to Sprint has pointed the way for other PTTI affiliates to join the fight against an adversary now partly owned by the national telephone companies of France and Germany, which are currently being privatized. France Telecom, Deustche Telekom, and Sprint have united to create a "world class super-carrier" called Global One to serve the business communication needs of multinationals operating in western Europe and elsewhere. At CWA's behest, trade unionists in France and Germany have written directly to Sprint CEO William Esrey warning him that the company's antiunion activity in the United States has aroused serious concerns about the likely direction of labor-management relations at Global One. In addition, representatives of Deutsche Postgewerkschaft (DPG)—the postal and telephone workers union—who serve as DT directors have gotten its board to adopt a set of "principles of conduct" for the firm in its "global telecommunications partnerships." This resolution commits management to "ensuring that employer-employee relations customary in Germany are recognized and complied with in all business sectors and organizational units in which Deutsche Telekom AG operates jointly with its global partners and their enterprises in Germany." Several follow-up letters from DPG president Kurt van Haaren to Esrey have reminded him that what is customary in Germany is "elected employees' representation" through unions. As for Sprint's conduct in the United States, van Haaren warned Esrey that "we will make our assessment of Sprint dependent on how your enterprise respects our partner organization, CWA, as the rightful representative of employees" at LCF.

In response, Sprint has continued to blast the NLRB's LCF case handling as the work of a "biased, pro-labor panel" and refused to settle with the fired workers. The firm has insisted that its eighteen thousand long-distance and wireless employees are treated well and paid no less than workers at any other telephone company. In April 1997, DPG leader Veronika Altmeyer, vice chairwoman of the supervisory board of Deutsche Telekom, traveled to Kansas City for a top-level meeting with Sprint about these and other labor issues. (Altmeyer had previously visited the United States on behalf of the LCF workers in February 1996 to testify at the trinational labor secretariat hearing in San Francisco.) She pressed Sprint management to abide by the latest NLRB decision in the LCF case and provide the job offers, back pay and benefits, and notice-posting required by the board. She also urged the company to open discussions with CWA about an agreement to recognize the union any time in the future that it can demonstrate majority support through an authorization card check.

160

The DPG's fellow union, IG Metall, has—like STRM, CWC, and CAW—developed a formal mutual aid pact with CWA. The big German metalworker's federation represents workers at multinational firms, such as IBM and Digital Equipment Corporation (DEC), that have created total "union-free environments" in the United States. As the CWA-IG Metall agreement notes, even in Europe, with its much stronger protective labor legislation, these high-tech firms "try to avoid any trade union involvement and go to great lengths to obstruct unions' attempts at organizing the workforce. During collective bargaining conflicts, they often prove to be the hard-liners among employers' associations." IG Metall members and works council leaders within DEC in Germany have, for example, had great difficulty getting the company to recognize a Pan-European Works Council that includes delegates from Digital facilities in France, Italy, Austria, and Belgium. In 1994, 1995, and 1996, DEC Works Council leaders came to Boston to attend the company's annual meeting and confront top management over its refusal to meet with them. They also protested the DEC's job elimination and corporate restructuring schemes in Europe. Their shareholder meeting interventions have been coordinated with and supported by CWA–backed Massachusetts Jobs with Justice, a coalition of forty labor and community groups. JWJ activists have helped generate press coverage about the Digital workers' visits, joined them in picketing the annual meetings, and aided their search for sympathetic Americans employed at DEC, the third-largest computer maker in the country. In conjunction with its European allies, CWA used its pension fund holdings of Digital stock to initiate a shareholder proposal for the 1997 annual meeting that sought to make the company's chairman and CEO—currently one person—more accountable to DEC's board, shareholders, and employees.

Joining Forces in New Zealand and England: CWA, CEWU, CWU, and STE

The increasingly close ties between CWA and telephone workers in New Zealand and the United Kingdom are also a product of adversity. For the latter, adversity is manifest in the Americanization of telephone industry labor relations. In New Zealand, conditions under deregulation have been steadily deteriorating. Ameritech and Bell Atlantic acquired 49 percent of TNZ and took over its day-to-day management. As noted previously, the Thatcher government's sell-off of British Telecom and its subsequent downsizing posed a similar challenge to England's 300,000-member Communications Workers Union (CWU) and the smaller 27,000-strong Society of Telecom Executives (STE). Like STRM in Mexico, the CWU and STE now face the difficult task of recruiting new members at the growing array of cable TV and telecom companies

161

competing with the former monopoly firm in their country. Learning more about CWA's recent organizing and bargaining experiences—both positive and negative—has been helpful to architects of union survival in the United Kingdom and New Zealand in both postmonopoly situations.

Prior to Communications and Energy Workers' Union (CEWU) 1994 contract talks with TNZ, CWA organizers were invited to New Zealand to conduct training sessions on membership mobilization techniques. CEWU knew, going into bargaining, that the company was "likely to take an aggressive stance in order to maximize its opportunities under the anti-union Employment Contracts Act and because management's attitude had changed markedly now that it was controlled by the two U.S. multi-nationals." According to sector industrial officer Neil Anderson, the union "recognized that we had made some errors in how we had organized at the work site level." CEWU's large membership losses because of privatization and job cuts had left it in a "serious financial position" with a "small, rapidly dwindling funding base" and no strike fund. In order to address this situation, Anderson recalls, "we looked around the world at other telecom union operations. In CWA's mobilization program, we saw what we believed was the basis for the correct future direction for CEWU."

A key element of CEWU's 1994 contract struggle was solidarity activity between unionists at Bell Atlantic in the United States and TNZ in New Zealand—coordinated through the use of conference-calling, which enabled dozens of union activists in both countries to participate. Simultaneous and widely publicized demonstrations were held in seven New Zealand and American cities to support CEWU bargaining and, says Anderson, "to motivate our members so they did not feel so isolated and alone fighting these huge new employers." A "solidarity day news" was produced and distributed throughout TNZ to assist the union's workplace mobilization. This initial collaboration was, according to the CEWU, "an outstanding success." "There is no doubt in the minds of CEWU negotiators," says Anderson, "that the solidarity campaign had a significant impact on a company which was trying to smash the union. They were ultimately reluctant—or unable—to deliver what might have been a death blow to our organization because of the obvious cooperation with CWA that was taking place. The settlement achieved was a direct result of the assistance from our fellow workers at Bell Atlantic in the United States."

One year later, it was CEWU's turn to come to the aid of U.S. workers victimized by Bell Atlantic's union busting back home. In March 1995, Bell Atlantic fired five CWA supporters at National Telephone Directory (NTD), a subsidiary that sells directory ads in New Jersey. A crowd of nearly three hundred CWA members and other trade unionists gathered outside Bell Atlantic's headquarters in Newark for a noontime rally denouncing the illegal dismissals.

Meanwhile, on the same day—ten thousand miles and many time zones away—a high-level delegation from the CEW delivered letters of protest to Bell Atlantic CEO Ray Smith via TNZ's chief executive in Wellington. "We stand by our work mates at NTD," declared CEW president Dave Udy. "We urge you to reinstate these fellow Bell Atlantic employees and respect their wishes to bargain a fair and equitable contract." Udy also urged Bell Atlantic, Ameritech, and TNZ to respect workers' rights at all their subsidiaries, at home and abroad, in accordance with PTTI's corporate code of conduct. (Unlike the LCF workers at Sprint, who were still awaiting justice in late 1997, the fired NTD organizers did ultimately receive back pay totaling almost half a million dollars. However, reinstatement was not part of the settlement of their unfair labor practice case before the NLRB. Bell Atlantic continues to operate new subsidiaries like NTD— including its fast-growing cellular phone operations—on a nonunion basis.)

CWA's "Atlantic Alliance" with CWU and STE began in similar fashion with an exchange of information about the problems of organizing new members in a privatized, deregulated market environment. These contacts accelerated after British Telecom made a bid to acquire the remaining 75 percent of MCI that it did not already own. The cooperation agreement between CWA, CWU, and STE states that, whenever members of the three unions are bargaining with a common multinational employer, they will establish some form of direct "communication and joint education." In addition, "a contract mobilization timeline" will be developed, and the resulting "joint action will be more an expression of basic union strategy in negotiations and less an exceptional example of international solidarity."

The agreement declares that "joint organizing strategies" will be developed for key information sector firms such as "BT- MCI, News Corp., C & W, AT&T, Bell Atlantic (NYNEX Cablecom) and US West (Telewest)." Per this provision, the unions have begun "cross-training of organizers" who may be involved in recruitment drives "involving similar firms and industries." In 1997, three CWA organizers with experience in telephone and cable TV campaigns spent four months in Britain working with their counterparts in the CWU. They lived with CWU members and their families and assisted organizing at Cable and Wireless. Plans are being made to have CWU members work in the United States on future CWA drives involving U.K.–based firms.

Conclusion

In the mid-1980s, CWA was the first among its global colleagues to face deregulation, corporate restructuring, job cuts, and new, antiunion start-up firms. It had to find ways to increase its bargaining and organizing leverage by engaging tens of thousands of rank-and-file members in activity that had previously been left to local or national officers, stewards, and staff. Reaching out to telephone workers and their organizations abroad was a natural extension of this strategy—given the globalization of telecommunications services. Working together in a variety of campaigns—some of which are ongoing— CWA and its international union allies found that their partnerships were mutually beneficial. By joining forces, they clearly increased their ability to maintain or increase membership strength, defend wage and benefit standards, and have an impact on public policy making.

Progress has not always been easy, but it is being made. In early 1997, for example, SBC—a focus of much CWA international work—agreed to recognize the union at its nonunion subsidiaries in the southwestern United States on the basis of signed authorization cards demonstrating majority support. (This card-check deal has since been extended to PacTel, which is being acquired by SBC.) It took seven years of membership mobilization and ten mobile phone organizing drives to achieve this representation mechanism within the company. The issue was raised in CWA-SBC bargaining, in joint CWA-STRM meetings with the company, and in CWA's contacts with South Africans concerned about the SBC's big investment in their country. Card check enables CWA to bypass the frustrating, time-consuming processes of the NLRB and give hundreds of U.S. telephone workers the ability to organize on the same level playing field as workers in Canada, where this procedure is often available as a matter of provincial law. This victory at SBC could not have been achieved without membership education and organizing, continuous bargaining, political pressure in the regulatory arena, and solidarity work abroad.

A decade ago, rank-and-file members had few opportunities to be involved in CWA's cross-border organizing. Since that time, however, CWA's international efforts have moved from a series of high-level meetings and conferences to much deeper participation by local officers and activists. Aided by the new technology of the information age—communications tools like E-mail and the World Wide Web—some CWA members are networking with trade unionists overseas just as if they belonged to another local union in this country. A growing number have had the chance to meet and talk face-to-face with their counterparts abroad: fired organizers in Mexico, factory workers in Canada, telephone operators from the United Kingdom and New Zealand, computer technicians from Germany. Together, they are discovering that the workers of the world do need to unite. Otherwise, the telecommunications revolution could end up forging what, for them, will be a new set of chains.

IV

INTERNAL TRANSFORMATION

9

RECENT INNOVATIONS IN THE BUILDING TRADES

Jeff Grabelsky and Mark Erlich

This isn't the same business I came into thirty years ago," says Leroy MacPhail, a sixty-four-year old Boston carpenter. That perception, common to veteran building trades insiders, runs counter to the conventional wisdom of outside observers who are often perplexed by an industry with a seemingly slow, evolutionary pace of change.

In fact, construction has undergone a transformation with a profound and unmistakable impact on building trades unions and their members over the course of a single generation. Once the bastion of strength and stability in the labor movement, construction unions have suffered a severe loss of membership and market share. The decline has shaken the building trades' wing of the House of Labor to its foundations and prompted a searching reexamination of fundamental beliefs. While some unions may have been irrevocably weakened by an erosion of bargaining power and political influence, others are now responding with renewed spirit and determination.

Construction is a pivotal industry in the United States, the single largest goods-producing sector of the economy. Despite the inevitable cyclical swings, construction has expanded steadily since World War II. Today, over half a trillion dollars' worth of construction activity is performed on an annual basis by more than a half million firms employing nearly four million construction workers. The industry's size and sensitivity to economic trends make it a useful barometer of the nation's well-being.

The unchanging rhythms of construction—the booms and the busts, the seasonal nature, the persistence of small employers—appear to contradict the reality of wrenching change. Tradesmen and women arrive at the job site at 7 A.M. ready to pick up hammers, pliers, paintbrushes, levels, and other time-tested hand tools wielded by generations of craftsmen. Construction involves the largest number of skilled craft workers in any industry. For all the new technology and prefabrication, buildings are still erected with the trade knowledge, strength, and ingenuity of groups of individual craft workers. Automation and outsourcing to cheap labor markets have not yet overrun onsite building trades workers. A skyscraper in Chicago cannot yet be assembled by robots in a South Carolina plant or by low-waged workers in third world countries and shipped to the shores of Lake Michigan. The temporary work sites, local markets, and transient workforce still define the backdrop of labor relations in the industry.

MacPhail's comment speaks to a different set of issues. While the daily tasks of a construction worker have changed less than those in most other occupations, the context in which they are carried out has changed dramatically. When MacPhail joined the Carpenters Union in the 1960s, he entered a work environment with a stable set of assumptions and a powerful internal culture. It was an all-male, virtually all-white world, often passed from father to son. The building trades represented an opportunity for bright and ambitious young men who did not want to pursue a college education and the white-collar job track. It was a dangerous vocation with uncertain employment, but the wages and benefits were higher than those offered in other blue-collar jobs. More important, construction operated under a strong union umbrella. Careers often began with union apprenticeships and ended with union pensions.

Unionism in construction in its present form dates back to the 1880s. The strength of the building trades unions derived from their organization of the skilled workers that the industry needed. Despite several extended and intense open shop drives, employers generally accepted union recognition and higher wages in exchange for labor peace and industrial stability by the early part of the twentieth century. Often former tradesmen themselves, construction employers had neither the financial resources nor the burning desire to crush trade organizations. Small firms operating on tight schedules tolerated unionism as an unavoidable and even acceptable business cost. Unions emerged from the early years of labor strife as the glue that held the industry together. Union-initiated apprenticeship programs replenished the industry's human capital. Union-run referral halls maintained the labor pool to meet the industry's variable demand for skilled workers. Perhaps most important, union-negotiated wages, benefits, and conditions stabilized the industry with a uniform level playing field that allowed contractors to compete based on managerial efficiency and business acumen rather than cutthroat wage competition.

The uneasy consensus that defined labor relations in construction for the first seven decades of the twentieth century has vanished. While statistical information in construction is notoriously unreliable, there is no question that the industry has undergone wholesale changes. Most observers agree that as late as 1970, nearly 80 percent of total construction dollar volume in the United States was performed under union contract. Today that figure is probably closer to 30 percent or less. Regional variations are significant. Union members are few and far between south of the Mason-Dixon line. Large commercial and industrial projects in the urban centers of the Northeast, Midwest, and West Coast are still largely union built. But even in the suburban and rural communities of those regions, union labor can often be found only on megaprojects. Many buildings are now erected on an open shop basis, that is, with a mix of union and nonunion subcontractors and workers, a circumstance that would have been unthinkable in earlier years of building trades' union strength and mutual solidarity.

A Wharton School of Business study estimated that total open shop construction overtook union building by the middle of the 1980s (Northrup and Foster 1984). While that study was unsympathetic to the union perspective, other researchers have reached similar conclusions. The percentage of workers in the industry represented by unions has dropped by 50 percent since 1970. Today fewer than one in four, or about one million construction workers, are union members (*Construction Labor Report,* 2/15/95; Allen 1994; Belman 1997).

The roots of this shift date back to the spiraling construction costs of the 1960s, a result of the climbing prices of building materials, a booming demand for new construction, and a labor shortage exacerbated by the drain of young male workers to the Vietnam War. Building trades unions, with a near monopoly on the labor force, demanded and won sharp wage and benefit increases. With profits calculated as a percentage of total price, employers had little incentive to resist union demands. On the contrary, they often preferred to pass on the escalating cost of labor to the customer.

Large corporations and other construction users who were footing the bills launched a campaign to contain costs. In 1969, two hundred of the nation's major chief executive officers formed the Construction Users Anti-Inflation Roundtable (renamed the Business Roundtable three years later) with the expressed goal of restoring order to an industry that they perceived to be out of control. The onset of economic stagnation and the 1973 oil embargo fueled corporate resolve. The roundtable laid out a blueprint for change that helped frame the ideological attack on unions, first in construction and then across the industrial landscape.

169

Executives representing General Motors, General Electric, Exxon, U.S. Steel, DuPont, and other giant firms issued twenty-three booklets with a series of recommendations aimed at transforming the construction industry. The roundtable reports sharply criticized construction employers for their informal alliance with building trades unions and the resulting inability to "restore the control that employers traditionally exercise." They argued that contractors' feeble gestures of authority reduced collective bargaining to a mockery. In this view, contractors' willingness to cede control over wage levels, job referrals, and training programs allowed unions to "usurp the employer role normally reserved to management in other industries" ("More Construction for the Money" 1983).

The severe construction recession of 1974–75 provided an opportunity for construction users already poised to subvert the unionized sector. As the recession hit and the number of available projects dwindled, nonunion companies extended their share of the shrinking market. They were able to submit substantially lower bids based on minimal labor costs while unionized employers were saddled by the sizable union wage gains of the late 1960s. According to one study, the always present gap between union and nonunion building trades workers widened between 1967 and 1973 (Allen 1986, 33). The competitive dynamics of the recession dovetailed with the roundtable's aggressive approach. DuPont, Dow Chemical, and other corporations consciously excluded union contractors from bidding on their capital projects as a matter of policy in order to subsidize and nurture fledgling nonunion alternatives.

The rise of the open shop sector was accompanied by a new political prominence. The Associated Builders and Contractors (ABC), once an obscure organization of small commercial and residential builders, soon rivaled its union employer counterparts, topping nine thousand members by 1975. The active young organization threw its resources into the political fray, advocating a consistently antiunion legislative agenda and emerging as an important element in the New Right coalition that swept Ronald Reagan into office in 1980.

Since 1979, the centerpiece of the ABC's national program has been the repeal of the Davis-Bacon Act, a 1931 law that sets wage standards on all federally funded construction projects in order to prevent the government from depressing local wages in the competitive bidding process. In labor strongholds the established prevailing wage is often the same or close to the union scale. Advocates of repeal have long argued that prevailing wage laws artificially inflate the costs of public construction and unfairly strengthen labor's position in a given market. Their goal is to diminish the impact of collective bargaining on public and, ultimately, on private construction.

As the conservative pole within the American labor movement, the building trades have historically enjoyed broad bipartisan political support. Until very recently, Davis-Bacon was a sacred cow, untouchable by congressional critics and ABC lobbyists. President Reagan declined to tackle the issue head-on, preferring to allow his secretaries of labor to institute administrative changes designed to weaken wage determinations and enforcement. Thwarted in Congress, the ABC turned its guns on the mini-Davis-Bacon laws, statutes that regulate wages on state-funded construction projects. Between 1979 and 1988, ABC officials and their allies managed to repeal the law in nine of the forty-one states that had enacted prevailing wage provisions. The legislative action in each state was followed by a minimal reduction in short-term construction costs and a severe decline in wages, training, union density, and supply of skilled labor. A study from the University of Utah calculated that real annual construction worker earnings dropped 7.5 percent immediately in the nine states that witnessed repeal of the prevailing wage law (Mangum et al. 1995, 16).

The courts and the National Labor Relations Board, always responsive to shifts in the political winds, provided legal bulwarks for the open shop as it gained strength. The unique dynamics of construction—the mobile workforce, the large number of employers on a single site, and the brief duration of individual projects—have produced a branch of labor law exclusively germane to the building industry. Section 8(f) of the National Labor Relations Act recognized the impractical application of NLRB elections to construction's temporary work sites and transient workforce by formally authorizing the long customary use of prehire agreements between contractors and unions without certification of majority status.

However, a series of decisions in the last twenty years simultaneously unshackled employers from the constraints of prehire agreements and tied the hands of union officials. In *Kiewit* (1977), the board sanctioned "double-breasting," a practice in which union employers establish a nonunion subsidiary in order to escape contractual obligations. While the ruling called for a "maximum separation of operations" between the entities, in reality, two separate mailing addresses and phone numbers have provided adequate legal cover. By 1984, eight of the nation's top ten contractors were double-breasted. *Deklewa* (1987) freed prehire signatories from 8(d) requirements to bargain successor agreements, thus allowing far greater latitude for employers to walk away from 8(f) labor contracts.

Construction unions have been hamstrung by laws restricting potential targets of organizing campaigns. The presence of multiple unions and contractors on any given project confuses labor relations. The actual decision-making power regarding the presence of union or nonunion workers rests with the general contractor and, ultimately, the project owner. Yet the laws defining "neutral" employers and secondary boycotts limit an individual union's potential activities to one target, its trade's employer (that is, a Bricklayers local can only focus on a masonry subcontractor). The real decision makers are shielded from union pressure by nonsensical rules governing picket sign language and picket locations. Campaigns against individual subcontractors mock the true power dynamics in the industry.

For years, building trades unions had sought to enact a common situs picketing bill that would have allowed picketing of entire construction sites without arbitrary entrance gate restrictions. As late as 1976, the trades had sufficient clout to win congressional passage, but President Gerald Ford's veto ended any chance to restore a dose of reality to construction site picketing. In another blow to organizing programs, the *Lechmere* ruling of 1992 limited union access to workers on private construction sites.

By the early 1980s, the industry had been transformed by a combination of economic, political, organizational, and legal factors. In the 1980s an ABC advertising supplement featured Charles Brown, CEO of DuPont Chemical and a leader of the Business Roundtable. "The construction industry was monopolized by the union segment with no apparent alternative in sight," Brown wrote. "Fortunately for all of us, the capitalistic system worked again. 'Free market' forces prevailed" (Associated Builders and Contractors 1982).

Certainly, the industry is now "competitive" in the fashion that free market advocates celebrate. While their rhetoric was always overblown, construction users can no longer claim to be the powerless victims of contractor/union collusion. On the contrary, they are in the driver's seat, dictating project price tags by playing union and nonunion firms against each other. But as a growing number of construction markets have been deunionized, a fierce and destructive competition has been unleashed on the industry. Without the regulatory infrastructure of collective bargaining, industrywide investments in training have diminished, wages and conditions have eroded, and skilled workers have been driven out. A 1996 report commissioned by three nonunion construction giants analyzes severe craft pool shortages in the Gulf Coast region and notes that "all parties understand that the problem exists nationwide." Recent developments have shifted "the intensity of the problem [of attracting and retaining skilled workers] from a nagging nature to mission critical." Overall, real wages in construction have declined 25 percent since the 1970s and average construction earnings have fallen below those in manufacturing ("Gulf Coast Staffing/Retention" 1996, 2; Center to Protect Worker Rights 1997, 19).

172

Nonunion firms have brought the underground economy from the margins to the mainstream of the industry. They rarely provide health insurance, pension benefits, or training programs for employees. Furthermore, in a growing trend in the industry, many nonunion companies flaunt legal as well as social obligations. A 1992 congressional report entitled "Contractor Games" described the practice of willfully misclassifying employees as "independent contractors" as a "pervasive and serious problem." Employers compensate workers in cash and are thus relieved of expenses such as Social Security and Medicare taxes, unemployment insurance, and costly workers' compensation insurance premiums. According to the House report, "the combination of mandated and optional or negotiated benefits has been reported as costing up to 37 percent of wages" ("Contractor Games" 1992, 7).

Nonunion contractors have altered the industry beyond the straightforward degradation of wage and benefit standards. The open shop reorganization of construction work has brought growing specialization and deskilling of many tasks. For example, the once highly prized all-around carpenter is now a liability because he or she cannot compete successfully with carpenters who function exclusively as either concrete form, framing, drywall, ceiling, finish, or hardware installers. The union tradition of teams of competent journeymen working their way through a building has been supplanted by the open shop model of a small number of experienced and relatively well-paid craftsmen supervising a large number of semiskilled, specialized, poorly paid, replaceable young workers.

Union firms have mimicked the open shop organization of tasks and work style in order to stay in business. While wage compensation in the union sector continues to run up to 30 percent ahead of nonunion pay (Allen 1994), work practices are increasingly similar. Smaller numbers of tradesmen are producing more. The introduction of new tools, equipment, technology, and prefabricated components explains some of the reasons for reduced crew sizes, but old-fashioned speedup is also a major factor. Union contractors continually exhort employees to work harder and faster in order to stave off the ever-present nonunion threat.

A cultural gulf increasingly separates labor from management in an industry once noted for its fluid upward (and downward) mobility. In the past, construction employers that ascended from the ranks wore their calluses proudly. The white collars of today's executives, project managers, and estimators, however, were seldom ever blue. They are more often graduates of business administration or civil engineering programs than the muck of a construction site. These professionals work for the new breed of general contractor or, in the current lingo, construction manager. These firms are brokers that execute contracts and manage groups of subcontractors who, in turn, employ the workers in the field. The sense of commonality that blurred class distinctions has been weakened. Subcontractors and workers operate in the field while the general contractors' staff has little understanding of or sympathy for the daily travails of craftsmen and their need for unions.

Open shop contractors may have shaped a new environment and dislodged the unions from their position of monopoly control, but the costs have been substantial. In a remarkable 1992 speech, Ted Kennedy, president of the fiercely antiunion BE & K and a longtime leader in the ABC, decried the "shortsightedness" and "corporate folly" characterizing the contemporary construction scene. He mourned the "devaluing of our profession . . . a constant pressure on price, price as opposed to qualifications and total project value."

Owners, said Kennedy, "reveled in the competitive world of union and merit shop contractor fighting it out for market share. You've sat back and watched with glee as we beat each other down . . . And as the wages fall, the benefits disappear and more and more leave the industry, you take refuge by saying, `It's the American way, the competitive market place at work, the free enterprise system in motion.'"

Kennedy's speech was delivered to a group of construction users, and he minced few words in assigning the blame: "We constantly sell our talent just as a prostitute sells her body . . . We sacrifice our futures. We cut our R&D. We neglect education. We change from entrepreneurial to one of avoiding risk . . . And if we contractors and engineers are the biggest prostitutes, you owners are the pimps and procurers" (Kennedy 1992, 3, 4, and 6).

The wheel has nearly come full circle. An alliance of construction users and nonunion contractors successfully broke the union monopoly on skilled labor, but the very integrity of the industry may be the price of their success. The impact has been gradual but unmistakable. As opportunities for employment in the union sector diminished, union members either put their "ticket in their shoes" and staffed nonunion jobs, traveled to union strongholds, left the industry altogether, or retired. They have not been replaced. In the brave new world of open shop construction, the labor supply is often exploited but rarely replenished.

Participants in a 1994 meeting of the Associated General Contractors repeatedly complained about skilled labor shortages in regions of the country that had become predominantly nonunion. They noted that they had been unable to create recruiting alternatives to union training programs. And they even acknowledged that their victories in driving down wage rates had priced skilled labor so low that interest in construction as a career is on the wane (*Construction Labor Report,* 10/12/94). As Ted Kennedy asked in his 1993 speech, "How in the world do we attract bright, energetic, young people into a business where . . . they can't expect to work a full year . . . and benefits are virtually nonexistent?"

The 1996 Gulf Coast report paints a devastating portrait of an industry in which "clients have created a 'playing field' which forces contractors to under-cut one another to obtain work . . . [and] craftsmen are treated as expendable commodities" ("Gulf Coast" 1996, 3). Articles in *Engineering News Record* regularly report severe labor shortages in those regions of the country in which building trades local unions have been reduced to little more than empty shells. An Orlando-based contractor claimed that those few workers who were available lacked "a fundamental understanding of their trade, such as carpenters who can't saw" (Korman and Kohn 1995; Krizan 1995; Krizan 1996). Yet these same articles often report ample supplies of skilled workers in unionized markets in the Northeast, Midwest, and Far West. A *Construction Labor Report* survey of labor shortages confirmed the problem. "What emerges is a picture of an industry with relatively low wages in which workers no longer compete to get into what had been coveted union apprentice programs" (*Construction Labor Report,* 12/21/94).

The conclusion is crystal clear. In union markets, employers offer decent wages, secure job site conditions, training opportunities, and, as a result, continue to attract qualified craft workers. In nonunion areas, compensation for dangerous and skilled construction occupations is on a par with wages in the fast food and retail sectors. "We're paying less than Wal-Mart," acknowledges Jeff Masters, executive director of ABC's Alabama chapter (Powers 1996). There is little incentive to risk serious injury, face exposure to the elements, and devote years to learning a craft when a McDonald's or a Gap offers comparable rewards. In many parts of the country, the magnet of the promising career that brought Leroy MacPhail and millions of other talented young men to construction has disappeared.

The rise of the open shop altered the world of construction workers and challenged the operating assumptions of union leaders. Some unionists remained complacent, seduced by a false sense of security after decades of labor dominance. They clung to policies that no longer reflected the changed circumstances of the industry. Others reacted to the nonunion assault by escalating traditional activities that had sustained union markets in the past. They continued to try to convince open shop contractors to sign union agreements through "top-down" organizing. They initiated strategies to sharpen the competitive edge of unionized employers. They applied pressure tactics during the development process to secure construction projects for signatory employers.

175

They engaged in political action to protect and preserve union conditions. In the end, none of these were sufficient to stem the open shop tide.

In retrospect, some leaders are now struck by the apathy that paralyzed their ranks. "We refused to accept that the world was changing and continued doing what we had done for decades," says Tim Nichols, director of external relations for the AFL-CIO's Building and Construction Trades Department. "We hoped against hope that the nonunion problem would just go away" (Nichols interview 1997; Nichols was the secretary-treasurer of the Michigan State Building and Construction Trades Council before joining the Building Trades Department).

Stubborn adherence to restrictive membership policies revealed the enormous difficulty building trades unions had in recognizing and adjusting to change. Before the rise of the open shop, nonunion contractors signed prehire agreements because unions controlled the supply of skilled labor. As the nonunion workforce grew with an expanding industry, the union's loose labor monopoly unraveled. For example, the electrical construction workforce grew from 200,000 to 550,000 from 1965 to 1990. But during those twenty-five years, International Brotherhood of Electrical Workers (IBEW) construction membership remained virtually static at 140,000. Traditional top-down organizing became an exercise in futility in many areas as open shop contractors were able to draw on more than 400,000 available electricians (International Brotherhood of Electrical Workers 1991).

In those areas with an abundance of union work, local unions invited "travelers" from other areas to staff their jobs rather than recruit new members into their ranks. In many cases, unions issued temporary permits to nonunion workers for the same purpose. "We gave them union jobs and a chance to acquire new skills, but we foolishly refused to give them membership in our unions," explains Jim Rudicil, director of the Building Trades Organizing Project in Las Vegas and former IBEW construction organizing director. "Then, when work slowed down we turned them out on the street. Of course, they didn't just disappear. They continued working at the trade for substantially lower wages. In effect, we helped create an alternative nonunion labor supply that was understandably resentful of our restrictive membership policies" (Rudicil interview 1997).

Unions picketed nonunion job sites, declaring that these employers ignored "community labor standards," but the effect of these efforts diminished in the increasingly antiunion climate of the late 1970s and early 1980s. The unyielding defense of well-established but nonproductive practices on union job sites added to the problem. Contracts retained archaic work rules even though they were costly and compromised the competitiveness of signatory contractors. In some areas, collective bargaining continued to deliver rising wages at the same time that unionized employers lost market share to nonunion competition.

Many building trades leaders concluded that union contractors could survive only by becoming more competitive. Initial efforts focused on providing signatory companies with some relief, first with simple concessions and later with more elaborate cost savings. During the early stages of the decline, the unionized sector of the industry rarely explored routes to enhanced competitiveness other than concessionary remedies.

Give-backs first appeared in the mid-1970s, often driven by developments at the national level. The national Building and Construction Trades Department had once negotiated terms and conditions on megaprojects, like the huge powerhouses and refineries built in the 1960s and early 1970s, that exceeded those prevailing in local markets in order to attract a sufficient supply of skilled workers. These project agreements took on a different character in the face of rising nonunion competition and dwindling union market share. National industry leaders argued that local contracts were too lavish and prevented unionized employers from successfully bidding on these plums. For example, the General Motors Saturn plant was built in the overwhelmingly nonunion state of Tennessee using all union labor at 90 percent of the local scale. These kinds of agreements enabled the building trades to secure big projects but were often resented by local union leaders and members (Erlich and Grabelsky 1988).

Local collective bargaining patterns also contributed to the concessionary wave. Wages were frozen, and in some jurisdictions even slashed by several dollars an hour. In 1984, for example, freezes and rollbacks actually outnumbered increases in union contracts ("Wage Hikes Hit Rock Bottom" 1985). Nonunion employers quickly responded to these cuts by reducing their wage rates. Instead of revitalizing unionized construction, these concessions contributed to a downward spiral in industry standards. "As unions' market share dwindled," observed the *Wall Street Journal*, "cutthroat competition among [nonunion] firms drove down wages" (Tomsho 1994). A Salt Lake City union plumber working on a job with nonunion electricians described the trend. "The day after the union electricians took that [$3 an hour] cut, the contractor came on the job and told these non-union guys they would have to take a $3 cut too . . . Our union held off two years before we had to do the same thing the electricians did, and when we took our cut the non-union plumbers' wages fell right along with ours" (Magnum et. al. 1995, 16).

Some leaders came to believe that across-the-board concessions were ineffectual and began to promote more complex market recovery plans. The Los

Angeles District Council of Carpenters introduced greater flexibility into its contracts to conform with the differing realities of various segments of the industry. Doug McCarron (then president of the council and now general president of the United Brotherhood of Carpenters and Joiners of America [UBCJA]) explained: "One [problem] was we negotiated one contract and really didn't address the nuances of the framing industry or the drywall industry . . . We figured this is what we want, here it is, you contractors sign it or . . . we'll shut you down" ("One Union—One Voice" 1990). That monolithic approach did not address the diversified commercial and residential markets in which average wages were a fraction of the union scale.

Beleaguered union contractors in Los Angeles welcomed the council's strategy of seeking to negotiate more competitive contracts in specific markets by establishing lower "market recovery" rates in industry segments dominated by nonunion standards. "Had they had this spirit of cooperation in the seventies," suggests one contractor, "we wouldn't have had so many nonunion employe[r]s in the eighties." In other areas, however, these "market recovery" rates were a classic case of too little too late.

Some union officials preferred the concept of selective wage concessions at targeted construction projects within their jurisdictions to help a signatory contractor secure the work, that is, a project agreement for a single trade. In order to avoid dissension within local unions over dual wage rates, unions began subsidizing these target programs through a per capita contribution from each member into a fund. In the "Kansas City" Plan, the target fund was used to augment the wages of individual members working below scale on targeted jobs, spreading the "pain" of market recovery across the entire local union. The "Elgin Plan" directed job target funds to contractors who won bids on targeted projects and agreed to remain or become union signatories. "Elgin II" target funds were used to offer "rebates" to construction users who awarded bids to union contractors. As clever as these market recovery programs were, they remained, at their core, concessions that tended to drive down wages in the local union market.

Competitiveness strategies were not confined exclusively to concessions. A few programs sought ways to enhance competitiveness by promoting greater labor-management cooperation and tapping the ingenuity of the workers on the job site. Management and Organized Labor Striving Together (Operation MOST), established in Ohio in 1976, involved twenty building trades unions and ten contractors' associations, and focused primarily on large commercial and industrial projects. MOST unions agreed to reduce inefficient work practices and resolve contract and jurisdictional disputes without work stoppages while MOST contractors agreed to employ only union labor. The dollar volume of MOST projects climbed from $263 million in 1978 to over $1 billion in 1985 (Schneirov 1993, 120).

Stone and Webster and Maine building trades unions set up Project Equity Account Trust (PEAT) in 1995, an escrow fund designed to cover the costs of project delays directly attributable to poor labor-management performance (*Construction Labor Report*, 6/1/95, 7). In the Chicago area, several thousand signatory contractors joined with building trades unions in the Construction Industry Service Corporation (CISCO) to advance common interests. While many of these cooperative efforts have secured work for signatory contractors, there is no way to measure how much of that work would have been built union in any case.

A number of unions argued for a more aggressive response to the open shop, one that could influence the decision making of construction users. The United Brotherhood of Carpenters and Joiners of America established a Special Projects Department to conduct sophisticated corporate campaigns against construction users, like American Express, that built projects with nonunion labor. In 1986, the national Building Trades Department initiated a corporate campaign to prod Toyota at its projected $800 million Kentucky factory. Lobbying in Kentucky and Washington, D.C., supported by mass demonstrations of solidarity across the country, convinced Toyota to build with union labor. These kinds of campaigns occasionally produced victories on individual construction projects, but they rarely turned around entire markets that had been overtaken by the open shop.

In the 1970s, union leaders began to recognize that strategic use of union pension funds offered enormous potential economic leverage. Over the last twenty years, some union trustees have sought to invest workers' deferred wages in union-built projects in order to generate returns and create jobs. The sheer volume of pension fund assets—over $60 billion in the building trades alone—has created a political and legal tug-of-war between unions, employers, and governmental regulatory agencies. Nonetheless, there have been countless examples of solid investments on the national level by the AFL-CIO Housing Trust and the J for Jobs program as well as innovative projects on the local and regional levels (Erlich and Grabelsky 1988).

Union officials have always understood that participation in the local city or town permitting process can impact construction decision makers. Vigilant unions established systematic tracking mechanisms to encourage prounion decisions at every stage of the development process, such as with the Chicagoland/Carpenters program. Unions have helped enact local ordinances in some cities and towns in an effort to bar irresponsible contractors from getting jobs in the first place rather than relying on lackadaisical public agencies to chase violators after the completion of the project.

In recent years construction unions have started to reverse the string of political setbacks. In 1988, the building trades in Massachusetts led a broad coalition of labor and community groups to defeat an ABC–sponsored ballot referendum that would have repealed the state's prevailing wage law. Six years later, Oregon unionists won a similar contest. In 1995, the California Building Trades produced a widely circulated videotape called "Unnatural Disaster" to defend that state's prevailing wage and to stall the open shop offensive against union standards on the West Coast. Despite these victories, the future of the federal Davis-Bacon and state prevailing wage laws remains in jeopardy, particularly with the ascendance of Republican majorities in both branches of Congress (Erlich 1990; "Unnatural Disaster" 1995 was produced by the California Building and Construction Trades Council).

The building trades have also attempted to revitalize the regulatory machinery that has traditionally governed the industry. Unions have pressured government agencies to become more vigilant in the face of ever more blatant legal violations. In Massachusetts, for example, unions lobbied to transfer prevailing wage compliance from the ineffective Department of Labor and Industries to the somewhat more aggressive state attorney general's office, thus making violators subject to criminal prosecution as well as debarment from state projects. As public funds disappear, however, unions and contractors have been forced to establish their own watchdog groups, like the California Center for Contract Compliance, to encourage greater adherence to existing protective legislation (Dart interview 1997; Balgenorth interview 1997).

Building trades unions have negotiated a series of project labor agreements, or PLAs, with government bodies on large public works projects. PLAs stipulate common terms and conditions for all trades, forbid work stoppages, and commit all successful bidders to hire union labor. While PLAs are routinely challenged by open shop contractor associations, the Supreme Court found them legal in the *Boston Harbor* case in 1993. On June 5, 1995, President Clinton issued a Memorandum of Understanding encouraging federal agencies to pursue PLAs when appropriate. While ABC executive vice president Charles E. Hawkins has declared his organization's readiness to "challenge this and any other back door attempts to pay off unions," PLAs appear to be another tool that building trades unions are wielding effectively (Cockshaw 1997, 8).

In the final analysis, efforts to influence contracting decisions on public construction, through attempts to "level the playing field" by reinforcing the regulatory infrastructure, reducing union costs, or enhancing union competitiveness, have not adequately addressed the underlying economic context of a vast, unorganized labor market of three to four million workers. Union leaders have been forced to acknowledge that the only long-term way to "level the playing field" is to organize that unrepresented workforce and elevate its substandard wages and conditions.

In the early 1980s, few building trades leaders were prepared to face that challenge. "We tried everything else but organizing workers," argues Martin Maddaloni, president of the United Association. Maddaloni reasons: "Employers sign agreements primarily because we have something they want and need: a pool of qualified workers. When we open our doors to the millions of unorganized workers in our industry and regain control of the labor supply, we will once again sign contractors, recapture market share and rebuild our bargaining strength" (Maddaloni interview 1997).

A few unions began to implement organizing programs to recapture the market share that had slipped from their grasp. The Boilermakers inaugurated its "Fight Back" program, targeting large open shop contractors for unionization. The Sheet Metal Workers established a "Youth-to-Youth" program, utilizing apprentices as "missionaries" who sought to recruit unrepresented workers into the union. The Electricians launched "bottom up" campaigns, "salting" nonunion contractors with activists seeking to unionize employers by organizing their workers. The Carpenters embraced "workforce organizing," exploring ways to organize workers independent of their immediate employers.

Unionists quickly discovered that construction organizing is an arduous undertaking. The transient workforce makes contact and communication with unrepresented workers difficult. Mobile and multiemployer work sites make ongoing access to employees problematic. Perishable bargaining units and transitory targets make the NLRB certification process cumbersome, if not irrelevant. And the local nature of the industry makes organizing essentially a local responsibility.

But those who undertook the challenge soon confronted another obstacle capable of derailing even the best-conceived organizing plans. Local members and leaders often resisted the idea of recruiting nonunion workers into their organizations. They had internalized the exclusionary philosophy that had informed union affairs for the entire postwar era. They believed that restricting membership elevated their own worth and that organizing new members would inevitably add to a local union's unemployment. As a result, at election time members occasionally punished local union officers who championed organizing and discouraged others from picking up the banner.

In the late 1980s, some national building trades leaders sought to address this political problem by developing an internal education program called COMET (Construction Organizing Membership Education Training). Designed to explain to members why local unions must organize unrepresented construction workers in order to regain control of the skilled labor supply, recapture market share, and rebuild bargaining strength, the four-hour COMET program is delivered by trained union instructors. (For a full discussion of COMET see Grabelsky 1995). First implemented by the International Brotherhood of Electrical Workers, COMET has been adopted by the Building and Construction Trades Department, AFL-CIO, and endorsed by each of the department's fifteen affiliates.

COMET emerged as the chief instrument to transform the internal political culture of building trades unions that had been indifferent, if not hostile, to calls for external organizing. (See Grabelsky and Hurd 1994.) By 1995, more than 100,000 members had been trained through COMET and leaders began to exhibit a renewed spirit of hope about revitalizing unionized construction. "COMET is the spark that has regenerated our union fervor," exclaimed IBEW international president Jack Barry, "If there is increased power and energy flowing through [our] ranks . . . these days, it is because we tapped our greatest strength: our members. The introduction of COMET entailed nothing less than remaking our own culture" (Barry 1994).

COMET has generated the kind of membership support at the local union level necessary to launch and sustain external organizing campaigns. "COMET lifted us from despair to hope to success," says IBEW 611 organizer Tom Davis. The local has recruited more than three hundred new members, organized fifteen electrical contractors, including the largest former open shop employer in New Mexico, and reestablished the union as a dominant force in the market. (For a full discussion of IBEW 611's experience, see Condit et al. 1998.) Even in traditionally strong union areas COMET has galvanized support for organizing. In Chicago, for example, U.A. Local 130 has built an organizing committee of more than seventy-five COMET activists to unionize unrepresented plumbers (Sullivan interview 1996).

Though leaders applaud COMET as a fresh and innovative program, it is, in fact, a return to union roots. A century ago, craft unionism in the building trades was the fruit of unrelenting recruitment of all qualified tradesmen in the field. "In the spirit of our traditions," explained Building Trades Department president Robert Georgine, "we have begun a new, yet time proven initiative. . . . [W]e are building on COMET to organize nonunion workers on the job—the way it once was done" (Cockshaw 1994, 3).

The Electricians and others have used the COMET program to train members in "salting," a tactic in which union activists are sent to apply for jobs with nonunion contractors. If those employers unlawfully discriminate against legitimate job applicants because of their union affiliation, unfair labor practice charges are filed with the National Labor Relations Board. The adjudication of those charges can be very costly for lawbreaking employers: in one case the settlement exceeded $2 million and more than one hundred IBEW members received back-pay awards of more than $5,000 each. If employers obey the law and hire these "salts," the activists simultaneously work for the contractor and attempt to organize the workforce. The potential costs of the legal procedures associated with unlawful employer conduct have become a powerful tool in unionizing open shop contractors. For example, after a multiyear campaign, the Boilermakers signed Sunland Construction to a national agreement in 1995. As part of the settlement, Sunland was required to pay over $1 million in back-pay awards to union members against whom it had illegally discriminated and $500,000 to the international union for organizing and other costs (Pleasure and Cohen 1997, 45)!

Salting has been challenged, unsuccessfully to date, in the courts. In 1995, the Supreme Court ruled in the *Town and Country* case that union members as well as full-time, paid organizers are employees under the meaning of the act and must be afforded the same rights as any other job applicant or employee. Having failed in the legal arena, open shop employers have turned to their allies in the congressional leadership to file the "Truth in Employment Act," a bill that would amend the National Labor Relations Act (NLRA) to overturn *Town and Country.* The Senate version of the bill, introduced by U.S. senator Tim Hutchinson (Republican-Arkansas), specifies that a contractor not be required "to employ any person seeking employment for the primary purpose of furthering the objectives of an organization [i.e., a union] other than the employer." Senator Ted Kennedy (Democrat-Massachusetts) warned that the proposed change would institutionalize the blacklist and legalize "mind-reading" by employers to screen applicants who might wish to engage in union organizing (*Town and Country* 1995; on the "Truth in Employment Act," see *Construction Labor Report* 6/18/97, 387).

One of the most significant labor struggles of the early 1990s involved an organizational effort to reunionize the residential drywall industry in Southern California. During the recession of the early 1980s, developers broke the unions in the residential market. In 1992, after years of wage and benefits cuts and an erosion of job site conditions, four thousand drywallers, primarily Mexican immigrants, walked off their jobs. The strike, which spread from San Diego to San Bernadino to Los Angeles, captured the attention of the Latino community, social activists, and the entire labor movement. Donations of food and money and acts of solidarity helped sustain the strikers through a bitter six-month battle. In the end, contractors negotiated an agreement with the Carpenters Union that provided a substantial pay raise, a health care plan, and provisions to adjust wages to conform to prevailing standards determined by changing union density (Pleasure and Cohen 1997, 47).

The Southern California drywall strike exposed the limits of a "one-unit-at-a-time" organizing strategy in a highly competitive market dominated by open shop contractors. No single employer would sign a union agreement that provided substantial wage and benefit increases if his competitors remained outside the union fold. The strike helped the Carpenters and other building trades unions crystallize a "whole market" approach to organizing, which has been applied to other campaigns. For example, the Laborers Union (LIUNA) conducted two highly successful marketwide campaigns in New York City in 1996. Their asbestos abatement and demolition campaigns yielded several thousand new members in a matter of months and unionized significant portions of these two industry sectors (Furman interview 1996; Kieffer interview 1996).

In 1996, the fifteen affiliates of the AFL-CIO's Building and Construction Trades Department (BCTD) agreed to launch an ambitious campaign to test the principles of a multitrade, marketwide, workforce organizing. The multitrade strategy is based on the premise that the open shop neither reflects nor respects the traditional jurisdictional distinctions locked in the union sector and that no individual trade union can successfully organize an industry composed of diverse crafts. Marketwide organizing recognizes the interdependence of all the players in the industry and the futility of unionizing individual contractors without simultaneously targeting their chief competitors. Workforce organizing presumes that the building trades cannot enjoy a significant share of the market without organizing a significant majority of the workforce.

After surveying more than 270 potential markets, the BCTD selected Las Vegas as the target for a pilot campaign designed to train hundreds of construction organizers from across the country and develop an organizing model for the industry. Las Vegas is an attractive target, with a hot construction market and a strong existing union base. In addition, the powerful culinary union Hotel Employees Restaurant Employees (HERE) and the Service Employees (SEIU) are planning major organizing efforts in the city, and the building trades recognized the potential synergy among these three campaigns. The six-million-dollar, multiyear Building Trades Organizing Project (BTOP) is supported by the national AFL-CIO, the national Building and Construction Trades Department and its fifteen international affiliates, and the local unions and councils in Las Vegas. With more than seventy organizers on the ground, the Las Vegas initiative represents one of the largest joint organizing efforts undertaken by the labor movement in recent memory. Local unions in Las Vegas have reported an increase of 2,500 new members since the BTOP campaign was launched (Winston 1997, 1).

The momentum for open shop supremacy in construction appears to have been stalled. Contradictions within the nonunion sector have contributed to the open shop's predicament. The 1996 Gulf Coast report charges that owners and contractors are in a "state of denial" and concludes that clients and consumers will pay a high price for "the industry's inability/unwillingness" to address the degraded conditions on the site ("Gulf Coast" 1996, 3, 5).

Contractors complain about labor shortages, but it is nonunion standards that have driven wages down and skilled workers out of the industry. They plead for qualified workers but lack the resources or will to invest in training to replenish the pool of skilled labor. At one open shop gathering, a frustrated employer conceded that a funding mechanism is needed "that forces us to pay for training" (*Construction Labor Report,* 10/12/94, 768). Nonunion employers are battered by their own cutthroat competition but are unable to impose any discipline or stability in the open shop. "If you dropped two contractors off a bridge," remarked one nonunion employer, "we would scratch and bite each other all the way down to impact" (Tomsho 1994).

The open shop's growth has also been stymied by the resurgence of activism among building trades unions. Union progress has demanded the reevaluation of contradictions internal to the union sector. The revitalization of some union markets and the rebirth of organizing could not have occurred without first confronting inflexible bargaining models, nonproductive work rules, and restrictive membership policies. But continued progress will require rooting out other persistent contradictions that threaten the integrity of the building trades. The problems of racial discrimination are industry-wide, but the commitment of construction unions to integrate the trades varies substantially. Union efforts to recruit and retain tradeswomen have been similarly problematic. Nowhere have the issues of race and gender been completely resolved, and, in some areas of the country, racial barriers represent the primary obstacle to organizing an increasingly diverse workforce successfully.

Outdated structures, jurisdictional disputes, and allegations of corruption also haunt the unionized sector. In a series of sweeping and controversial initiatives, new UBCJA general president Doug McCarron has upset the century-old applecart of the Carpenters Union by replacing decentralized local union autonomy with regional councils based on uniform policies, streamlined administration, and a shift in financial resources from servicing to organizing. While autonomous local unions have long been the source of the building trades' community-based grassroots presence, McCarron argues that the local fiefdoms all too common in the highly politicized union environment are impediments to organizing labor markets that are regional in nature.

In recent years the building trades have demonstrated the ability to break out of old patterns of behavior and embrace new approaches. None of the tools being used—political action, top-down tactics, bottom-up workforce organizing, corporate campaigns—are sufficient in and of themselves. All of them may be crucial pieces of an overall strategy for union renewal. Given the regional nature of the industry, unions must assess the particular circumstances they face in terms of market share, labor supply, and construction activity and then determine which combination of tools in their toolbox is most appropriate. Like any skilled craftsman, a building trades leader must have all the tools to get the job done; the mark of a good craftsman, or leader, is to know which tools are required for which tasks and to use them in a way that complements the efforts of their fellow craftsmen, or unionists. For decades craftsmen have constructed countless impressive buildings in that way. Now the question is whether unionists can show the same talent in rebuilding a unionized industry.

The future of the building trades and construction itself may depend on the answer to that question. The industry is inherently chaotic. It requires a center to tame its centrifugal forces and maintain stability, professionalism, and standards. Without a center, construction's wages, benefits, and quality of work fall victim to the anarchy of the market. Unions have historically been that center. Regardless of what the ABC may claim, no other force has been able to fill that void. Thus, the role of the building trades unions is not only to serve construction workers but, in ways that employers rarely admit and users never recognize, to serve the entire industry as well.

Construction is a dynamic business. Without unions, the natural tendency of the open shop is to establish a playing field by leveling down. With unions, the playing field is leveled up so that contractors are rewarded for managerial competence and a stable supply of skilled workers is assured. Without unions, the industry is gripped by the crisis of falling wages, labor shortages, and cutthroat competition. With unions, users buy quality, contractors enjoy stability, and workers win the promise of dignity and fair compensation for a difficult job.

BIBLIOGRAPHY

Allen, Steven. 1986. "Declining Unionization in Construction: The Facts and the Reasons." Working Papers Series. Cambridge, Mass.: National Bureau of Economic Research.

———. 1994. "Developments in Collective Bargaining in Construction in the 1980s and 1990s." Working Papers Series. Cambridge, Mass.: National Bureau of Economic Research.

Associated Builders and Contractors advertising supplement. 1982. *Engineering News-Record* 209, no. 25 (December 16): 132.

Barry, J. J. 1994. Construction conference speech, International Brotherhood of Electrical Workers. Washington, D.C. April 2.

Belman, Dale. 1997. "An Analysis of the Labor Force of the Construction Industry, 1979–1995: Demographics, Union Membership, Wages and Benefits." Unpublished report, University of Wisconsin, Milwaukee.

Center to Protect Workers' Rights. 1997. *Construction Industry Chart Book: The U.S. Construction Industry and Its Workers.* Washington, D.C. February.

Cockshaw, Peter. 1994. "Labor Leader Responds to ABC's Attack: Georgia Defends Union Tactics and Criticize Merit Shop." Newton Square, Penn. *Cockshaw's-Construction Labor News & Opinion.* March, 3.

———. 1997. "Project Labor Pacts Too Hot to Handle: Intense Political Pressure Forces Clinton to Back Down." Newton Square, Penn. *Cockshaw's-Construction Labor News & Opinion.* June, 8.

Condit, Brian, et al. 1998. "Construction Organizing: A Case Study in Success." Pp. 309–19 in *Organizing to Win,* ed. Kate Bronfenbrenner, Sheldon Friedman, Richard Hurd, Rudolph Oswald, and Ronald Seeber. Ithaca, N.Y.: Cornell University Press.

Construction Labor Report: Employment Developments in the Construction Industry. Serial publication. Washington, D.C.: Bureau of National Affairs. October 12, 1994; December 21, 1994; February 15, 1995; June 1, 1995; June 18, 1997.

"Contractor Games: Misclassifying Employees as Independent Contractors." 1992. Twenty-ninth Report by the Committee on Government Operations, U.S. Government Printing Office, Washington, D.C.

Erlich, Mark. 1990. *Labor at the Ballot Box: The Massachusetts Prevailing Wage Campaign of 1988.* Philadelphia: Temple University Press.

Erlich, Mark, and Jeff Grabelsky, eds. 1988. "Up Against the Open Shop: New Initiatives in the Building Trades." *Labor Research Review 12* (Fall).

Grabelsky, Jeffrey. 1995. "Lighting the Spark: COMET Program Mobilizes the Ranks for Construction Organizing." *Labor Studies Journal* 20, no. 2 (Summer): 4–21.

Grabelsky, Jeffrey, and Richard Hurd. 1994. "Reinventing an Organizing Union." *Proceedings of the Forty-Fourth Annual Meeting of the Industrial Relations Research Association.* Madison, Wisc.: Industrial Relations Research Association.

"Gulf Coast Staffing/Retention: Cause and Mitigation." 1996. Report commissioned by Brown and Root, Fluor Daniel and H. B. Zachry. January 17.

International Brotherhood of Electrical Workers COMET (Construction Organizing Membership Education Training). 1991. *Trainer's Manual.* Handout #1.

Kennedy, Ted. 1992. "Managing Change in the Twenty-First Century." Speech to Engineering and Construction Conference of the American Institute of Chemical Engineers, San Francisco, September 15.

Korman, Richard, and David Kohn. 1995. "Running Short of Skilled Hands." *Engineering News-Record* 234, no. 2 (January): 8–9.

Krizan, William G. 1995. "Fourth Quarterly Cost Report: Labor-Craft Shortages Creeping In." *Engineering News-Record* 235, no. 26 (December 25): 34–35.

———. 1996. "Open Shop Loosens Purse Strings." *Engineering News-Record* 236, no. 25 (June 24): 31.

Mangum, Garth, et al. 1995. "Losing Ground: Lessons from the Repeal of Nine 'Little Davis-Bacon' Acts." University of Utah, February.

"More Construction for the Money: Summary Report of the Construction Industry Cost Effectiveness Project." 1983. The Business Roundtable, January.

Northrup, Herbert R., and Howard G. Foster. 1984. *Open Shop Construction Revisited.* Philadelphia: University of Pennsylvania Press.

"One Union—One Voice." 1990. Training videotape, United Brotherhood of Carpenters and Joiners of America.

Pleasure, Robert, and David Jonathan Cohen, eds. 1997. *Construction Organizing: An Organizing and Contract Enforcement Guide.* Silver Spring, Md.: Labor's Heritage Press.

Powers, Mary Buchner. 1996. "Groups Grapple With Training." *Engineering News-Record* 236, no. 8 (February 26): 9.

Schneirov, Richard. 1993. *Pride and Solidarity: A History of the Plumbers and Pipefitters of Columbus, Ohio, 1889–1989.* Ithaca, N.Y.: ILR Press.

Tomsho, Robert. 1994. "Labor Squeeze." *Wall Street Journal,* January 27, section A, p. 1.

Town and Country Elec., Inc. 1995. 116 S.Ct. 450, 150 LRRM 2897.

"Unnatural Disaster." 1995. Videotape produced by the California Building and Construction Trades Council.

"Wage Hikes Hit Rock Bottom." 1985. *Engineering News-Record* 214, no. 2 (January 10): 60.

Winston, Sherie. 1997. "The New Unionism: Building Trades Sharpen Skills, Toughen Tactics and Organize." *Engineering News-Record* 239, no. 9 (September 1): 28–31.

INTERVIEWS

Balgenorth, Robert. 1997. California Building and Construction Trades Council President. April 7.

Dart, Joe. 1997. Massachusetts Building and Construction Trades Council President. April 7.

Furman, Marc. 1996. United Brotherhood of Carpenters and Joiners of America, Southern California/Nevada. August 22.

Kieffer, David. 1996. Former Laborers International Union of North America Organizer; Current Staff, Organizing Department, AFL-CIO. August 22.

Maddaloni, Martin. 1997. General President, United Association of Journeymen and Apprentices of the Plumbing and Pipe Fitting Industry of the United States and Canada. September 9.

Nichols, Tim. 1997. Director of External Relations for the AFL-CIO's Building and Construction Trades Department. June 12.

Rudicil, Jim. 1997. Director of the Building Trades Organizing Project in Las Vegas and Former IBEW Construction Organizing Director. August 29.

Sullivan, Gerald. 1996. Business Manager, United Association Local Union 130. August 22.

10

POLITICAL WILL, LOCAL UNION TRANSFORMATION, AND THE ORGANIZING IMPERATIVE

Bill Fletcher, Jr. and Richard W. Hurd

B eginning in the mid-1980s under President John Sweeney, the Service Employees International Union (SEIU) purposely has struggled with the question of how best to stimulate the renaissance of the U.S. labor movement. Sweeney increased the national staff from about twenty to more than two hundred, selecting progressive unionists from within the SEIU and from other unions. By design, members of the staff were younger and more venturesome than their counterparts at other national union headquarters (Piore 1994, 527). While grappling with the day-to-day challenges of conducting SEIU business, the staff never lost sight of the objective of serving as a catalyst for change. A consensus emerged that rebuilding the labor movement would require massive efforts to organize the unorganized, and that SEIU should lead the way.

Over time the international shifted attention and resources into an aggressive organizing program. Simultaneously, Sweeney and organizing director Andy Stern led what might be described as an ideological offensive to win support for organizing from activists and elected leaders at all levels of the union. The results of this initiative are well-known—a combination of organizing, affiliations, and mergers made SEIU the fastest- growing union in the country, with membership more than doubling during a period when most unions experienced substantial declines. In short, "SEIU has been able to grow significantly because the leadership encourages new ideas and risk taking, supports new programs, and promotes organizing" (Needleman 1993, 361).

As part of its ongoing commitment, SEIU has devoted increasing attention to the challenge of getting local unions to embrace organizing and to allocate sufficient resources to the task. In this context, the union's 1992 national convention adopted two key resolutions: one to affirm the centrality of organizing, the second to assist leadership development with targeted educational programs (Needleman 1993, 362). In the months following the convention, a discussion unfolded among national staff regarding appropriate steps required to assist local union leaders committed to change. Although internal organizing and initiatives to develop leadership skills among women and people of color were encouraged, the highest priority was afforded to external organizing. The objective was to expedite a dramatic reorientation toward external organizing at the local level. Because SEIU is decentralized with significant local union autonomy, buy-in from local leaders was viewed as essential to assure organizing on the scale required to maintain steady growth and thereby enhance the union's power.

The discussions among national staff came to be defined as "local union transformation" and ultimately focused on the issue of representation. If local resources are to be freed for external organizing, then it follows that representational functions will be affected. A decision was reached to examine the actual steps that SEIU locals were taking to alter their methods of representation. A staff working group was established to explore this issue. Particular attention was devoted to identifying practices that would fulfill representational obligations and save resources.

In 1994 the international contracted with Cornell University's School of Industrial and Labor Relations to help it look more deeply at this question. SEIU chose to do this through a concrete examination of the experiences of several local unions. The staff work team began with something of a buckshot approach, sharing anecdotal information about a range of innovations. Attention was then narrowed to a manageable number of representative locals, covering all U.S. regions and representing all SEIU industries, and with a variety of experiences. Twelve "best-practices" locals were selected for in-depth analysis. The choice of these locals did not reflect a value judgment on locals not chosen, nor was the choice the result of a scientific method. Rather, the work team looked at a variety of different experiences that might help it think through which steps could be taken to shift resources in SEIU locals, with the ultimate objective being greater resources allocated to organizing. This essay focuses on the specific practices of eight of these locals, although it is based on all twelve cases, plus interviews and discussions with representatives from at least ten other national unions.[1]

The Representational Dilemma

The locals cited below have utilized a variety of different approaches vis-à-vis representation. In some cases they have revised practice as a result of a conscious decision that greater resources need to be allocated to organizing (internal and/or external). In other cases, changes have been introduced in order to foster the type of organizational culture that the leadership is attempting to develop. In still other cases, practices have been adopted as part of an attempt to make procedures more efficient. For purposes of the best-practices project, SEIU decided to examine different aspects of the representational process without any prejudgment regarding the intent of the change or procedure introduced.

One problem that has gripped the U.S. union movement has been how to address effectively and appropriately the issues of individual instances of workplace injustices (alleged and real). Some unions, including locals within SEIU, have made the decision to allocate the bulk of their resources to handling such cases; specifically, they have used staff to handle all levels of the grievance procedure from the first step through arbitration. In other cases, locals have immense legal bills from law firms retained to handle arbitrations. This approach often has been pursued at the expense of other activities of the locals, including organizing. It is this which generally is referred to as the *servicing model of unionism*. Under this model the local chooses to do everything through their staff structure *for* the individual worker rather than encouraging the worker to engage in work site struggles along with other union members. This implies, in essence, a prioritization and a resource choice. "Servicing," as a term, in some respects misdescribes and caricatures some of the day-to-day representational work necessary for a local union to sustain itself. To avoid confusion, we do not deal at length here with "servicing" but rather with how local unions represent their members. Although representation includes bargaining as well as the grievance procedure, this study focuses on the grievance system. The intent has always been to examine bargaining as a subsequent part of this same project.

In an attempt to counter the "servicing" approach, some unions, including many locals within the SEIU ranks, have moved to alter their representational practices and to place greater emphasis on internal organizing. This emphasis on mobilization is often called the *organizing model of unionism*. As part of the research reported here it was found that (1) there is not necessarily a common definition of the "organizing model" and (2) among those locals that have formally adopted this approach, there is not necessarily an allocation of resources to external organizing. In short, the "organizing model" generally is very successful in actually mobilizing the existing members, but it is often staff-intensive (at least in the beginning) and does not automatically translate into external growth.[2]

For this reason, attempts to discover means of streamlining the representational process in order to access greater resources for external organizing is only one part of the overall equation. The other part appears to be the need for a consciously developed external organizing plan, with the required resources and personnel. Combining the two into an overall strategic plan for the local and subsequently implementing that strategic plan can provide the basis for forward motion. In the absence of such a comprehensive approach, a local may find that it obtains and devotes resources to mobilizing and energizing its current membership (an activity that must continue to take place), but with no new growth. By implication, the "organizing model" alone could result in a scenario where the labor movement would continue its decline although it would decline militantly. If organized labor is to escape oblivion, it must find ways to access resources in order to grow as a percentage of the overall working class.

LOCAL UNION TRANSFORMATION IN A HISTORICAL CONTEXT

There have been significant efforts over the years to address the dilemma caused for labor by the lack of growth. The dramatic crisis reflected in the United States by the absolute decline of membership in the 1980s elevated concern with the problem. Such concern inevitably took political form and ultimately contributed to the successful challenge led by John Sweeney culminating in his election as president of the AFL-CIO. The relevant question, of course, is whether this is too little too late. The jury remains out on that, but it can be said that a serious look is being taken at the way some unions do their work. The local union transformation project advanced by SEIU has been one part of the process.

With the selection of Andy Stern as Sweeney's successor at SEIU and the advent of the Stern administration, transformation work has gone into a higher gear. Stern is placing an emphasis on getting local unions to become organizing locals. This effort involves assuring that locals actually place significant resources into *external* organizing, that they have a real organizing plan (with clear targets), and that they place a person in a position of responsibility to direct the organizing program (an organizing director). Although we do not discuss that effort here, we view it as essential that local union transformation be effectively integrated into any attempt by a national union to elevate the importance of external organizing.

A useful perspective on the problems and possibilities associated with organizational transformation is offered by John Kotter in a *Harvard Business Review* article (Kotter 1995). Although he bases his observations on the experiences of large corporations, we believe that many of the lessons he draws are applicable to unions. SEIU has found that transformation work involves actually convincing locals of its necessity. Along the lines of Kotter's observations,

Stern is impressing upon the locals a sense of real urgency to elevate the importance of organizing and introduce the structural changes this implies. At the same time, introducing such changes necessitates preparing for, discussing, and implementing approaches to representation that are different from current practice in most of organized labor. It is with this in mind that the work of the best-practices project and local union transformation have been so important. While one cannot inoculate an organization against all of the expected repercussions of dramatic change, through examining history one can anticipate the form and content of many eruptions.

The remainder of this essay reports on the actual experiences of SEIU locals included in the best practices project. The information was gathered in visits to each local where on-site interviews were conducted with elected leaders, staff, and activist members. The interviews were supplemented with internal documents provided by the locals and data on membership trends compiled by the international. First we will review practices designed to reduce the grievance and arbitration burden that confronts every local we visited. Then we will describe efforts by several locals to mobilize their members as part of a search for alternative ways to conduct representational work. Next comes what we view as the most essential ingredient to successful transformation: cultivating support for change among union members. The essay will conclude with our reflections on the lessons offered by the best-practices project.

ESCAPING THE GRIEVANCE AND ARBITRATION QUAGMIRE

The grievance and arbitration process creates a dilemma for local unions. On the one hand, an independent grievance system defines the union role of protecting against arbitrary management. On the other hand, most grievances address problems of individual workers and draw the union's attention away from collective concerns. More to the point for local unions committed to transformation, grievances and arbitrations can swallow up resources and staff time needed for other pursuits, particularly external organizing. The locals in the best practices project have experimented with a variety of approaches designed to streamline grievance handling. Although there is no easy escape from the grievance quagmire, this section reviews some of the more promising methods.

Centralization

One option is to centralize control of the process. The basic idea is to move away from the typical practice where each representative is assigned specific units and has independent responsibility for all grievances and arbitrations. A centralized system has the potential to introduce efficiencies, for example, by balancing the grievance load or by avoiding duplication of effort in grievance preparation. Some locals have introduced computerized systems that they use to track grievances, to determine trends, and to prepare for arbitrations. The two best-practices locals with computerized systems have not yet experienced any dramatic change in how they perform representational work, although one of them is using the information to target areas for internal organizing. While computerized grievance handling is being refined, a different approach to centralization has immediate potential.

District 925–Seattle, which represents clerical and technical workers at the University of Washington, introduced a new system in 1991. When a member with a problem calls the office, he/she is greeted by an answering machine, "We are in the field organizing, call your steward or leave a message." Office manager Cindy Cole screens all messages and returns calls from members to gather information or answer questions. If a member reports a possible grievance, Cole meets with the representative responsible for that worker's department and a steward is selected to handle the case. Next Cole contacts the member with the steward's name and phone number, and the representative talks with the steward. The steward sends a pregrievance letter that explains the member's responsibility to gather information that will help in evaluating the complaint.

Once the member has forwarded background information, including his/her personnel file, a description of the relevant event(s), and names of witnesses, the steward reviews the case with the representative. Together they make a "realistic assessment" to determine whether a contract violation has occurred; then the steward works with the member if filing a grievance is appropriate. The primary role of the representative is to answer stewards' questions and to monitor time lines. The steward assures that the member receives the pregrievance letter and takes responsibility for handling of the grievance. The member does the preparation work and coordinates with the steward. The pregrievance letter serves two purposes: it informs the member of his/her rights and obligations, and it protects the local from duty of fair representation complaints.

District 925–Seattle has used this system for five years. Its implementation was facilitated by Cole's experience; she had been with the local as a clerical employee since 1984 and over time had gradually taken responsibility for answering members' questions about the contract. In spite of her competence, members were initially "flabbergasted" when the local "turned on the answering machine." Eventually, however, they have adapted and complaints have all but disappeared. Steward Susan Williams summarizes her peers' attitude toward the shared responsibility in the grievance-handling system, "I believe in empowering people—if they don't want to do the work, I can't help them." Pat Harrison reports that in his unit, "People don't even think of calling the office—they go straight to the steward."

Although representatives monitor timelines and get regular updates from stewards, they are relieved of a considerable burden because all direct communication with the member is handled by Cole and the steward. According to staff director Kim Cook, "The constant pressure to talk with members about their complaints is a problem for a lot of locals; we just do not do it." The advantage of this system, as summarized by organizer-representative Joan Weiss, is that "it allows us to spend more time in the field developing leaders, educating members and organizing." Although staff still handle most appeals, the end result is that the grievance load has declined noticeably and the local focuses on helping people with real grievances. As District 925 president Debbie Schneider sums up the underlying philosophy, "The job of the union is to build greater power in the workplace, not to protect whiners."

Screening

A second option for improving efficiency is to establish a formal grievance screening process. An effective screen can assure that time and resources are not wasted on frivolous grievances, or on grievances that offer little hope of a positive result based on precedents established in prior cases. By formalizing the screening process, some locals have introduced a degree of impartiality into the decision, which reduces complaints from members whose potential grievance or arbitration has not been pursued. One best-practices local introduced a screening process primarily to reduce a major grievance and arbitration backlog. The backlog was cut by 80 percent, and staff time and resources were reallocated to internal and external organizing. However, a logjam need not be the motivating force, as the following case demonstrates.

Local 617 in Newark represents public school, day care, and housing authority employees. The local's long-standing grievance committee must approve every formal grievance before it is filed. The committee includes one elected member from each of the local's five major units plus the chief steward; it meets every Tuesday night. A member with a problem first will be assisted by a shop steward or business agent (BA) who will attempt to resolve the situation informally. If the member is at fault, the union attempts to counsel him/her to take responsibility or, if necessary, refers the member to an appropriate social service agency. If there is a possible breach of the contract or disciplinary procedures, and if informal resolution is not possible, the member must stop by the union office after work and complete a complaint form (an experienced staff member is always available to lend assistance). The complaint form is referred to the appropriate BA, who investigates the case. The member and the BA then attend a grievance committee meeting together. As BA Raqman Muhamad describes the process, "The grievance committee grills them and lets them know whether the grievance is legitimate." This process not only helps the local screen grievances, it also gets the members to take responsibility. And as executive vice president John (J. J.) Johnson emphasizes, "If you can get members to the union office, you get more participation in the local."

Staff Specialization

A third option for freeing resources from the grievance and arbitration quagmire is staff specialization. The typical local expects staff representatives to perform a broad range of functions, including internal organizing and mobilization, support for the external organizing program, political action, attendance at labor-management meetings, and contract negotiations. The reality is that an inordinate amount of time and energy is devoted to individual members' complaints, problems, and grievances. While many other duties are loosely defined with flexible deadlines, grievances are very specific tasks with clear timelines. Furthermore, results are easily monitored—the number of grievances settled, the number of arbitrations won, and the number of phone calls to the union office from disgruntled members. There is a natural tendency for staff to focus on grievances and put other work aside.

Several locals have concluded that the only way to assure appropriate staff attention to other functions, particularly those related to organizing, is to assign all grievance and arbitration work to a limited number of representatives. The other members of the staff are thereby freed to focus on external organizing, internal organizing, or other priority activities. According to one local leader, "The idea . . . is to reduce the number of people spending time on the grievance mill and the bosses' agenda and put a majority of field staff on our agenda." In some locals staff lawyers or experienced representatives handle all arbitrations. In other cases specialization has been facilitated by hiring members as part-timers to assist with grievances. A couple of these locals have experienced adjustment pains, as staff have to "scramble to keep up with grievances" and resort to "damage control." The lesson is that because of potentially troublesome side effects, it is important to establish a clear link between specialization and the new initiatives it facilitates.

Local 509, which represents Massachusetts Social Service workers, has attempted for several years to increase staff attention to internal organizing and mobilization. However, a heavy load of grievances and arbitrations has prevented individual staff members from sustaining consistent action. As representative Judy Davis describes the situation, "I really couldn't do [internal] organizing because there was always a crisis; I would have an office ready to go, then be pulled away [to deal with a grievance or arbitration] and things would fall apart." After extensive discussions among the staff, in 1995 the local decided to introduce specialization. Two positions were created—field representative/litigator and field representative/organizer—each with its own job description. The litigator specializes in grievances, appeals, and arbitrations and is responsible for the attendant preparatory work as well as coordinating with the employee(s) involved. The organizer concentrates on recruitment, leadership development, membership participation, and work site actions.

The local's full-time field representatives self-selected in equal numbers for the two specialties, working in pairs with one litigator and one organizer serving the same constituency. Each pair works out its own division of labor, but the standard is for the litigator to handle discipline and discharge cases plus clear individual grievances, while the organizer takes care of group grievances and anything that can be resolved through internal organizing.

During an initial adjustment period complaints from members increased because they didn't understand the change, and litigators were swamped while they figured out how to prioritize and reorganize their own time allocation. Now, however, the consensus is that the new system is working well. Litigator Darrel Cole explains, "The change has allowed me to focus on the part of the job I like the best. . . . Trying to do both was tough; this is a better way." Organizer Judy Davis reports, "I'm actively dealing with twelve offices. The members I'm seeing are really pleased, and I'm excited about it." The new system is working best where chapter officers are taking on more work. Most of them have accepted increased responsibility with enthusiasm. As chapter president Marilyn Souza sees it, "The local is emphasizing internal organizing because we need it. Without internal organizing we are just a union in name."

Delegation

A fourth option for more efficient delivery of grievance and arbitration services is delegation. The idea is to free staff time from the daily grind of grievances by assigning responsibility to stewards. Although in most instances the staff representative continues to monitor all grievances, stewards take over much of the work, especially during the early stages of the process. Delegation is effective only if stewards have the commitment and skills to do the job. This requires an aggressive outreach effort to recruit activists who are motivated and have leadership potential, plus an education and training program to prepare stewards for the task at hand. Although delegation encounters resistance from stewards reluctant to accept increased responsibility and from staff who have a hard time letting go of grievances, most locals that have tried it have benefited substantially.

Local 1199WV represents twelve thousand health care and social service workers in West Virginia, Kentucky, and Ohio. The local has long had a commitment to organizing, but many of the staff representatives were bogged down in grievances. In 1994 a decision was reached to take advantage of a strong delegate system (delegates are elected leaders who function as stewards) by introducing a new committee structure in each chapter. Under the new structure, each of the local's 140 chapters has a grievance chair (the equivalent of a chief steward) plus five standing committees: organizing, political action, labor solidarity, civil rights, and health and safety. The priority in implementing the new structure was to recruit a grievance chair, selecting from those already capable of handling grievances at the second step. This criteria is crucial because grievance chairs are responsible for all third step hearings.

In support of the increased expectations placed on delegates, Local 1199WV created a new position for training director. A former organizer for the local coordinates two-day trainings for each of the six areas of responsibility. The grievance chair training focuses exclusively on step-three grievances and is open to two delegates from each chapter. Although grievance chair and organizing chair training have been given priority, the local has also offered sessions on political action, health and safety, labor solidarity, and civil rights. The new structure frees staff organizers to concentrate on leadership development and organizing, while retaining responsibility for arbitrations and contract negotiations. Eighteen months after the new structure was introduced the grievance chairs were handling all step-three grievances in about 80 percent of the chapters, and organizing committees were active (that is, actually doing organizing) in about half of the chapters.

Rank-and-file leaders and staff are enthusiastic about the impact. Delegate Larry Daniels explains, "Now with the committee structure we do it ourselves. . . . The boss has to deal with people in the chapter so the power is here rather than an outside force." Ohio team leader Dave Regan reports, "Becky and Jennifer [staff organizers] haven't been to a grievance meeting in six months, which means that we are functioning at a higher level." This is echoed by Teresa Ball: "This is the most exciting thing we've done in the thirteen years I've been here; it frees us to do organizing which is fun work."

Internal Organizing and Mobilization

Most of the best-practices locals have endeavored to involve members more actively in the life of the union. Some locals have made this effort a focal point of their transformation work. The idea that revitalization of the labor movement can be achieved best by mobilizing current members has often been associated with the "organizing model" of unionism. In this section we make no effort to evaluate the validity of the "organizing model" per se, but rather present four examples of locals that have benefited from effective programs of internal organizing and mobilization. (Those interested in the "organizing model" debate should read Fletcher and Hurd 1998.)

Local 73 in Chicago has a long history as an organizing local. However, over time the local became more and more staff-driven. As President Tom Balanoff describes the situation, "The members didn't believe in the union . . . [so] we decided to concentrate on union building, communication and struggle." The effort to recapture member commitment has been rooted in contract campaigns. For each negotiation the local establishes a contract action team and uses tactics such as sticker days, group grievances, phone line jamming, and public rallies. These campaigns have helped build rank-and-file leadership, and creative actions taken by a militant minority have helped rekindle enthusiasm. By tying contract negotiations to activism and putting people in the streets, Local 73 is making significant strides. According to service representative Al Pieper, "People are progressing and starting to see things from a different paradigm; . . . they are gaining knowledge by going through struggle."

Local 200A in Syracuse also has concentrated on contract campaigns as an opportunity to mobilize members. The leaders and staff of the local have explicitly rejected the insurance agent approach to unionism, and, as President Marshall Blake explains, they are determined to "engage members in maximum struggle, to move to the highest level of collective struggle." Faced with the reality of many units (most of them small) and multiple negotiations each year, making contract campaigns the focal point of mobilization efforts was a logical choice. Members' interest is heightened at contract time at any rate, and they have responded with high-energy volunteering to distribute contract surveys one-on-one, participating in work site actions and union button campaigns, ratcheting up grievance filings and Occupational Safety and Health Act (OSHA) complaints, and thereby letting the boss know that the workers are the union. Although activism inevitably wanes when the contract is settled, the members are changed by the process. Kathy Tucker, unit chair at Carthage Hospital, describes the effect: "We are no longer timid; we're not always active, but we're always ready." Staff representative Coert Bonthius explains that this process works even though it requires more time and effort than traditional servicing: "Efficiency is inconsistent with this approach, but people feel connected and we have a stronger union."

Local 503 (Oregon Public Employees Union) represents twenty-two thousand state and local government employees. With fewer contracts to negotiate than some of the locals in other sectors, the OPEU has been able to devote ongoing attention to internal organizing. This commitment moved to a new level as the local prepared for the 1995 negotiations and a potential strike. The centerpiece of the initiative was a comprehensive internal organizing campaign under the theme "Strike Back '95." The organizing began more than a year before the OPEU's contract with the state expired. Staff member Suzanne Wall describes the process as "a good example of adopting a model of external organizing and bringing it into internal organizing." Field staff titles were changed to internal organizers, and they were required to canvass every workplace and track the commitment and activism of every member. When the process started, the local conducted a poll and found that less than half of the members would support a strike. When a vote was held as contract expiration approached after more than a year of internal organizing, 93 percent voted to strike. Then, when the OPEU staged the first statewide public strike in Oregon history in May 1995, more workers went on strike than were members of the union. Executive director Alice Dale concludes that "the strike built this union; we took a quantum leap forward."

The OPEU internal organizing program was initially resisted by staff, not because they were being asked to mobilize the members and build support for a strike but because they were required to chart every workplace and implement a detailed tracking system. However, as team leader Bill Uehlein reports, "Because of the tracking and canvassing we know which people have done what. . . . This got people to look at their jurisdiction more carefully, to look at holes and find people to fill them. . . . The strike helped staff understand why the thorough quantifiable monitoring."

Work site organizers worked closely with internal organizers in the canvassing process. Stewards took on more responsibility over time, and starting in January 1995 handled all step-3 grievances. The OPEU differs from some other locals because staff time freed from grievances as a result of this delegation is not diverted from established units. Rather, internal organizers focus on mobilizing members around workplace issues, political action, and external organizing campaigns. As executive director Alice Dale asserts, "We are militant, politically active and very field oriented. . . . We involve local people; we reward staff for building membership and leadership development; and activists who want training get it."

202

Local 1985, the Georgia State Employees Union (GSEU) functions without the benefit of a collective bargaining law, so its representational work has to be innovative. Furthermore, the effectiveness of the representational effort is essential since there is no union security. With no right to negotiate a contract, the local has promoted its members' interests with an innovative program of workplace actions, demonstrations, and an aggressive political operation. The driving principle for the GSEU as summarized by executive director Tyrone Freeman is "People come first, everything goes back to the members." Much like the locals just described that mobilize members during contract campaigns, GSEU relies on creative tactics as its primary representational set of tools—petitions, arm bands, pins, marches, and rallies. The local also files grievances through the state's merit system, but even here the preferred course of action is not traditional; with the assistance of an organizer, a member with an issue is encouraged to find six others affected by it and then file a group grievance. Another focal point of GSEU's representational effort is its extensive grassroots political program; the local sponsors legislative forums around the state, conducts voter registration drives, and holds regular lobby days bringing members to Atlanta to testify on key legislation. The entire political program is designed to "take it back to the members." Political director Andy Freeman describes the symbiotic relationship: "Moving legislators towards our agenda helps recruit members, and because we don't provide traditional services we need numbers to accomplish things politically."

BUILDING SUPPORT FOR TRANSFORMATION

Member buy-in is essential for sustainable transformation. Restructuring grievance and arbitration work can save resources, and alternative approaches to representation can build power. But without member enthusiasm, these innovations are likely to slip away and be replaced by a traditional insurance agent relationship. The servicing magnet is extremely powerful, especially in locals whose members have not been asked to assume responsibility. Best-practices locals have taken a variety of steps to build political will, and a few of them have proven to be extraordinarily effective.

Asserting a Vision

Transformation requires total commitment from the top of the local. If the local's leader equivocates, staff and members also will be cautious, which will undermine potential for positive change. In most of the best-practices locals the leaders have elucidated and supported a vision of the union's potential. The

203

vision itself has to make sense to the members based on the objective conditions they face, and the way the vision is communicated will naturally fit the style of the leader. A few examples will demonstrate a range of possibilities.

Tyrone Freeman, executive director of Local 1985 (GSEU), took his current position in 1995 after serving as organizing director for two years. Local 1985 has focused on organizing throughout its eleven-year existence, and Freeman has retained that concentration. He has secured enthusiasm and generated activism by connecting the organizing mission to empowerment of the members. According to the current organizing director Katie Foster, "Ty has made the member the most important aspect of what we do." Freeman personally attends leadership meetings every other month at each chapter and listens to concerns, ideas, and feedback. Executive board member Margaret Moss describes the effect of Freeman's presence in the field: "The union should be honest with members so they can trust what you say; people trust Tyrone because when you talk, he listens." First vice president Tom Coleman enthusiastically concurs: "Now that Tyrone is out there, we don't mind challenging [management]; you see the executive director doing things right, it energizes everyone." Freeman himself describes why he spends time with the members: "It's all related to educating them why the whole local is centered around organizing."

Tom Woodruff, president of Local 1199WV,[3] has secured support for an aggressive organizing program with a single and consistent message: "This is a fight over the distribution of wealth. The only way we can change our members' lives is to help workers get a fair share of what they produce." The connection to organizing is reinforced at every staff meeting and every executive board meeting by sharing victories. A few notes from the opening discussion at the local's July 1995 executive board meeting should demonstrate the effect:

> Tom Woodruff: "Victories!"
> Executive board member: "I don't know what you've been doing, but we really kicked butt . . . " [greeted by hoots, hollers and cheers]
> Tom Woodruff: "Victories!"
> Executive board member: "We won 40 to 36. Management said the union walked in like we owned the place. Well DUHHH! We do own the place . . . "
> Tom Woodruff: "Victories!"
> Executive board member: "We adopted Greenbrier Manor nursing home [as an organizing target]. We walked in and the administrator ran into her office and locked the door. We were in there for 45 minutes talking with people . . . "

By starting all meetings with an opportunity to share victories, Woodruff reinforces the message that permeates all of the local's work: organizing has the potential to change society. This vision of a union leading the fight for economic justice and winning has really caught on with members. Jennifer Schmidt, who recently left her job as a dietary worker in a mentally retarded and developmentally disabled (MRDD) facility represented by 1199WV to take a job on the local's staff, captures the effect: "We deal with the distribution of wealth. You have to have conversations with people about power and numbers. . . . Victories are shared . . . members have said that they want to be different. They take pride that our union is out front."

In her eleven years as executive director of Local 503 (OPEU), Alice Dale has led the union by the force of her own drive to dramatically higher levels of militance and member involvement. She believes that it is essential to "put members in an uncomfortable position" by requiring them to confront the boss rather than relying on union staff. As described by Bill Uehlein, team leader in the union's Portland office, the OPEU continually asks, "How do we move people in a united way to operate at higher and higher levels of militancy?" Dale's vision is not limited to confrontation and struggle though; she also advocates grassroots control because "the members are the union." Dale's intensity has energized the membership. Internal organizer Guy Schneider describes an "exciting democratic process that is absolutely member-driven." He concludes, "We've moved a long way because of struggle; there's a feeling out there that you've got a union." In May 1995, 90 percent of Oregon's seventeen thousand state employees participated in the OPEU's first statewide strike, fulfilling Alice Dale's ideal as recalled by Tim Pfau (a longtime rank-and-file leader who recently joined the staff as an internal organizer): "Where has the mob gone? I must catch up with them, I am their leader."

Tom Balanoff was elected president of Local 73 in 1994. He sets an example by being out front in the local's bargaining, organizing, and political initiatives. Balanoff wants the local "to push heavy in terms of solidarity, to develop a reputation for being there," and he actively promotes "real trade union values—solidarity of class and collective action." He has relied on his own charisma to drive the process. When Hospital Corporation of American ceased dues deductions at Michael Reese Medical Center during contract negotiations in 1995, Balanoff led a group of seventy activists into the hospital to collect dues. Balanoff went straight to the clerical offices adjacent to the hospital administration, climbed on top of a desk (which elevated his six-and-a-half-foot frame to near ten feet), and announced "I'm your union president!" When asked by the management to leave, he refused: "I'm talking with my members." By the time Balanoff and his Local 73 team left the hospital nearly an hour later almost everyone was wearing a union button. The action helped turn the tide, and the contract was resolved. Balanoff has relied on this type of leadership to win the enthusiastic backing of members and a diverse staff, most of whom worked for the union before his election. Al Washington puts it simply, "Tom gets involved." Eli Medina observes, "Any program Tom has implemented has worked." Gloria Richard shares the excitement, "We're a great union; we make it happen."

The techniques used by these four remarkable leaders are instructive. But leadership transcends technique or personal style. What is crucial is that each of them has demonstrated commitment to a vision that has inspired members and staff and has won their support for transformation. None of the four pretend to be changing the locals on their own; they are all committed to developing members as leaders. The reality, though, is that leadership with a clear vision and diligence is essential to successful transformation.

ENGAGING MEMBERS AND STAFF

The experiences of the best-practices locals demonstrate that transformation is enhanced when members and staff are given encouragement, opportunities, and challenges that stimulate political growth. Some locals affirm the importance of engaging in struggle, others endorse radicalizing members or raising the level of class consciousness within the local. Most openly reject the insurance agency style of unionism and explicitly promote a vision of a labor movement founded on collective values and committed to economic and social justice. Best-practices locals have used various approaches to raise consciousness. Some brief snapshots will reflect the broad range of options.

Some locals have implemented communications programs to promote change. Local 73 has hired a communications specialist to conduct educational work and consciousness raising through the local's newspaper and site-specific newsletters and leaflets. The newspaper highlights militant actions and broad coalitions but is effectively limited to one directional communication. The quarterly site-specific newsletters and targeted leaflets go further, stimulating discussion and debate among members and work site leaders about the role of the union. Local 509 faced internal opposition to a proposed campaign to organize workers in private sector social service agencies, who were viewed suspiciously by members employed by the state of Massachusetts. The local was able to defuse this narrow self-interest through an informal communications effort, which politically educated elected rank-and-file leaders by engaging them in a series of discussions over an eighteen-month period and eventually won support for the organizing campaign.

Other locals have developed educational programs for the purpose of elevating political awareness. Local 503 (OPEU) trains members in media communications techniques and encourages them to take an assertive role around the state. As a result members have been speaking out on political issues important to the union on radio talk shows, in letters to the editor, and through news interviews. Local 1199WV has established the position of labor solidarity chair in each of its units and offers the chairs training on how to enlighten members about the importance of solidarity and how to involve them in activities that support the broader labor movement. Local 1985 (GSEU) uses a "train the trainer" approach with staff, who then deliver training at chapter meetings around the state on topics such as organizing and grassroots political action.

Some locals believe that actual engagement in struggle is the best way for members and staff to understand the importance of building an aggressive labor movement. Locals such as 200A engage members in contract campaigns not just to improve bargaining outcomes but to increase militancy and help members appreciate the value of collective struggle. Other locals endeavor to involve members in militant action around organizing. This approach is a hallmark of the Justice for Janitors campaigns in two of the best-practices locals. One local recruits volunteers from organized units for its "brigade," which engages in civil disobedience and other actions in support of the local's organizing program. Part of the objective is to get members to take the activism back into their workplaces. The other local turns out members for demonstrations in support of external campaigns in part so that they will "see it working, feel the power, and understand the need for organizing."

Coalition building that actively involves members and staff also has been an important part of the transformation process in many locals. Chicago's Jobs with Justice coalition has been revitalized by Local 73, whose members participated along with three thousand other unionists in a jobs march, established solidarity committees to support locked-out Staley workers, and helped kick off a living wage campaign in Illinois. Marshall Blake of Local 200A was recently elected president of the Syracuse Central Labor Council based on a platform of increased activism. Subsequently, busloads of 200A members joined with others in the labor community to protest the Republican right's "Contract with America" when Newt Gingrich came to Syracuse to deliver a speech.

Although a variety of approaches have been used by best-practices locals in an effort to achieve political commitment to transformation, there is a consistent theme. A progressive ideology is necessary for any local that hopes to win and maintain support from members and staff, especially where transformation involves long-term commitment to an aggressive organizing program. The initiatives described in this section have heightened political awareness among those members who have participated personally or who have been touched directly. A few quotes from staff members and rank-and-file activists from best-practices locals reflect the potential:

> "The more we link with community, with where members live, the more we can get members active and the more power we gain."
> "One thing I feel about OPEU, we're doing the right thing by pushing the envelope of social and economic justice."
> "Coming up against the real estate interests people have a sense of their strength, of what they can do. Nobody else is doing that, teaching that the way we are."
> "You get knowledge going through struggle. I've learned so much about politics, government, being active."
> "We're much bigger players than we were nine years ago—we're organized, have a militant reputation, the members are more active."

In spite of the progress, for many locals questions remain concerning how to reach a critical mass of members and how to make political commitment self-perpetuating. The next section turns to three locals that are attempting to address these questions with comprehensive programs.

Cultivating the Will to Organize

Local union transformation is difficult to sustain in the face of strong internal opposition, and the process makes no sense if, once recast, the local stagnates or reverts to old practices. To endure, transformation must be supported enthusiastically by rank-and-file activists, staff, and members. Several best-practices locals that have been able to maintain momentum have paved the way by developing a culture of organizing.

Local 1985 (GSEU) directs all of its energies in support of organizing. All field staff are referred to as organizers, and they are constantly reminded that their job is to organize. According to Tyrone Freeman, "servicing is not a concept we allow." Organizer Michelle Castleberry confirms the maxim: "Business agent is bad language around here. You just don't grow with a business agent's attitude." The abstention from servicing is facilitated by delegating responsibility to members and hiring part-time grievance technicians and, more important, is understood in the context of empowering members. This connection is endorsed by the elected executive board, as explained by Vice President Tom Coleman: "The executive board assures that dues money is being used in a responsible manner for organizing and building power. . . . The organizer's job is to organize. Chapters are run by the members."

A central component of the local's effort to establish political will is an organizing program run by the members. Member-to-member organizing is coordinated by the statewide organizing committee, whose thirty-five members include the eight-person executive board plus twenty-seven rank-and-file recruiters. As described by Mona Washington, their job is "phone banking, recruiting, leafleting, marching, and talking union all the time." By centering the whole local on organizing, Local 1985 has achieved phenomenal growth from 3,800 dues-paying members in 1993 to nearly 7,000 in 1996, all of it one new member at a time. Political director Andy Freeman describes the union's direction in three words: "Organize, organize, organize."

District 925–Seattle also operates in the public sector and for many years was an open shop. During the 1980s the local pursued a super servicing approach but was unable to attract and retain members, and by 1990 only about 28 percent of bargaining unit employees were paying dues. In 1991 a decision was reached to shift directions and become an organizing local. The decision was communicated openly to members. All committees were disbanded and replaced by a thirty-member organizing council. Every meeting of the council and the local included training on some aspect of organizing, and every decision was considered based on its contribution to building the union. It was during this changeover that the local turned on the answering machine at the union office.

For more than five years 925–Seattle has been in a campaign mode, continually assessing all members and targeting nonmembers, contacting each new employee three times, and working out weekly organizing plans and numerical goals for each staff member. The systematic organizing diligence has paid off: membership hit 40 percent in 1992, the local won a super majority fair share vote in 1994, and current membership stands at over 70 percent with nonmembers paying an agency fee. While continuing the systematic assessment and recruiting in the established bargaining unit, in 1995 the local initiated a campaign to organize nonrepresented clerical, research, and technical workers also employed by the University of Washington; by 1996 the campaign had produced representation election victories in several small units.

Although District 925–Seattle's diligence and systematic commitment to perpetual organizing is impressive in its own right, it could not have survived without support from the membership. By openly discussing the decision to abandon the super servicing approach the local laid the groundwork to build a different culture. There was vocal opposition to the change from some staff, some elected leaders, and some members. But they were publicly confronted by rank-and-file leaders committed to organizing and were eventually silenced. Office manager Cindy Cole recalls, "We worked hard to educate members what it means to be an organizing local, because we had to make the change to survive." Staff organizer Joan Weiss relates her own conversion: "I was a steward in the old model and did a lot of servicing. I was kind of old school, chasing ambulances. The discussions in 1991 on the change from servicing to organizing convinced me that in reality it's not helping people that builds the union." Steward Joanne Factor sums up the local's creed, "Strength doesn't come from individual grievances but from getting better contracts. That's why we're an organizing union."

The priority of Local 1199WV has never been in doubt. Teresa Ball has worked for 1199WV for thirteen years and reports, "We've always been an organizing local. It's organize or die." Maintaining and strengthening this commitment has required continual attention. As President Tom Woodruff reports, "We have concentrated on how to build the political will to institutionalize a methodical, disciplined organizing program so we don't have to keep re-creating it." Experience has convinced Woodruff that "members will spend more money to build a powerful organization and get ahead." Or as former organizer and current training director Al Bacon emphasizes, "Organizing is about protecting the members we have; you have to organize for power." The attention to building political will and the consistency of the organizing message have paid off in member support for a steadily expanding organizing budget. In 1989 the local made a specific commitment to spend 25 percent of revenue on organizing; in 1990 members voted to increase dues and to support 35 percent for organizing; in 1994 members voted for another dues increase and the executive board earmarked 50 percent for organizing. These decisions have been embraced by the members because they have been reached democratically. The dues increase votes both passed with 65.7 percent support.

The democracy extends to the 140-member executive board, which has better than one representative for each 100 members. Executive board member Larry Daniels captures the rank-and-file spirit with this personal affirmation: "I love my union—-it enables me to get my fair share, it's democratic, it enables me to express my own ideas and beliefs." This kind of spirit is enhanced by a no-holds-barred style that excites the members. Ohio area director Dave Regan proclaims, "Let it rip and we'll win more than we lose." Organizer Rachel Brickman agrees, "The most exciting thing about being here is that time after time we risk everything; we're constantly putting it on the line." This aggressiveness changes people, as attested to by Jennifer Schmidt who moved from the rank-and-file onto the staff, "It's great to see people grow, especially women who stand up and take on the world."

For the past five years Local 1199WV has helped send this spirit back into the shop with its organizing internship program. Six interns at a time take five-week leaves to work on campaigns, where they are exposed to all aspects of organizing. The experience has been that when the interns go back to their chapters they bring enthusiasm with them and usually become the chapter's organizing chair. At the local's July 1995 executive board meeting recent interns were awarded newly designed red T-shirts with a union logo on the front and a graphic on the back: a foot with the toe angled up and flames coming out from the heel proclaiming "Kicking Ass for the Working Class!" A soft-spoken woman who had been reticent a few minutes earlier when reporting an organizing victory seemed to grow a foot as she walked back with her T-shirt and announced in a powerful voice "I'm wearing this to work on Monday!"

ANALYSIS AND CONCLUSIONS

Local union transformation is essential at this critical juncture in the evolution of the U.S. labor movement. Revitalization of the entire movement can succeed only if there is a dramatic shift in orientation at the local level. In this context, it is essential that national union leaders and the AFL-CIO assist and encourage local leaders in part by helping to clarify the qualities and characteristics of transformed locals and by offering a vision of what they are capable of accomplishing.

We have concentrated on three interrelated aspects of local union transformation—streamlining and redefining representational work, mobilizing members, and winning support for durable change. The practices we have described are not intended as panaceas but as examples of the type of experimentation that is necessary as we search for new methods that facilitate growth rather than block it. The following observations embrace the SEIU tenet that external organizing must be the top priority and consider all best practices in light of their potential contribution to this objective.

New Approaches to Representation

The most promising practices aimed at breaking out of the grievance and arbitration morass have a common ingredient: responsibility is pushed down to lower levels. Members are expected to take more responsibility for their actions (no more whining!), and where injustices have occurred they have an obligation to assist with the preparation of their cases. Stewards and other rank-and-file leaders (unit chairs, chapter officers, chief stewards) need to perform their tasks independently without dumping everything on staff representatives. For their part staff must let go, get out of the way, and let members and stewards take over.

211

Of course, revising practice is not easy, and a few cautions are in order. Centralization should be implemented not as a control process but as a way to systematize grievances so that members and stewards know exactly what is expected of them. Screening can help weed out weak and inappropriate grievances but only if the process is understood by the membership and viewed as impartial. Specialization should not be introduced merely as an expedient to free resources for external organizing or other functions; members need to see some direct evidence that the change can benefit them—for example, increased staff activity in the field doing mobilization work. And most important, delegating responsibility will succeed only if supported by education, on-the-job training, and mentoring.

Two of Kotter's warnings about the failure of transformation efforts are relevant here: obstacles to change must be removed, and during transition periods short-term wins are vital (Kotter 1995, 64–5). Every local we visited encountered resistance to change, from staff wedded to their roles as grievance and arbitration experts and from members comfortable with their passivity. There seems to be no good alternative other than getting the elephants out of the way, and to do this, support for transformation from activist members is essential. There is no more effective way to silence opposition than to win something now and herald it—a successful action or strike, an organizing victory that makes sense to members (for example, a previously nonunion competitor in close proximity), even a third-step grievance win by a steward.

Although the SEIU best-practices project offers a useful glimpse at how some locals have altered how they handle grievances and arbitrations, we want to emphasize that there are no easy answers. What is needed is a willingness to break away from stale methods and to take risks with new approaches to representational work. Other aspects of representation also need to be examined, such as labor-management meetings and especially contract negotiations. In local unions with multiple contracts, bargaining accounts for a significant share of the work of many union staff. This is especially true where there are no industrywide or areawide agreements. Those locals will need to examine how to bargain in a way that supports organizing and look for innovations that contribute to the accumulation of power for workers on a much larger scale than is now common.

The Limits of the "Organizing Model"

In grappling with the challenges of reforming representational practices, all of the SEIU best-practices locals have come face-to-face with the reality of limited member involvement in the union. If locals hope to shift resources into external organizing, they must reduce resources devoted to other pursuits. As we have just argued, the most promising new approaches to grievance handling involve delegation of responsibility. The need to engage members and mobilize them to contribute more energy to their union is obvious. The experiences of those locals that have made mobilization and internal organizing their priority are instructive and yet sobering.

In order to move beyond the committed core of activists, several locals (as described above) have devoted considerable effort to tapping the energies of a broader cross section of members. The efforts have typically involved borrowing techniques from external organizing and applying them internally, thus the common use of "organizing model" to describe this initiative. These "organizing model" locals have succeeded in raising the level of participation and activism, and as a result have enhanced their power in the workplace. In addition, internal democracy has blossomed and commitment to the union has deepened.

However, this success has come at a considerable cost and, as we have argued elsewhere (Fletcher and Hurd 1998), there are significant limitations to this strategy. Implementation of the "organizing model" is likely to be very staff-intensive, at least at the beginning. It is critical that union leaders not act under the illusion that by adopting approaches that focus on member activism this, in and of itself, will free staff time for external organizing or other priorities. It does not necessarily work out that way. To a great extent these locals are challenging long-standing cultures and practices. Given the nature of the political and economic climate in which we live, change will rarely be spontaneous, thus continual attention from staff representatives will be required in order to achieve the desired mobilization.

We do not take issue with the necessity of member mobilizations, greater internal democracy, or the need for workers to be organized in order to fight for the issues that they consider critical. However, we conclude that mobilization will not—on its own—result in a greater impulse among members to support *external organizing* nor will it contribute directly to external organizing itself. The approaches followed by "organizing model" locals do, in many cases, help them reallocate resources, but that reallocation does not necessarily involve assigning priority to external organizing. Such a prioritization must be a political choice by the leadership of the local. Winning member enthusiasm for external organizing is distinct from the challenges of internal mobilization.

Building Support for Transformation

The most important ingredient of local union transformation is buy-in from members and staff. Without cultivation of political will as part of the process, backsliding is almost inevitable. Since most members have never known any style of unionism other than the "servicing model" or insurance agent approach, the natural tendency is to view change skeptically and to accept retrenchment passively. Because staff typically are more experienced with traditional servicing than with either organizing or alternative forms of representation, their comfort level and competencies are also more in tune with a union that acts like an insurance agency. In short, the servicing magnet is exceedingly powerful because it is easier for almost everyone to think of representation the old way. As Kotter warns, "Until changes sink deeply into a [union's] culture, a process that can take five to ten years, new approaches are fragile and subject to regression" (Kotter 1995, 66).

Transformation has more staying power when there is wide acceptance of a new vision. To achieve this, persistence and a comprehensive program are key. In particular, Kotter warns against "under communicating the vision by a factor of ten" (Kotter 1995, 63). Some leaders of best-practices locals encountered resistance when they moved quickly to shift priorities and resources toward external organizing without first winning members' support. Other local leaders misinterpreted activism by a militant minority as an endorsement for change, when in reality most members and staff retained commitment to traditional approaches and rebelled when they realized what was happening. We conclude that external organizing can be established as an ongoing priority only with a clear and consistent message plus vigilant attention to building political will.

There are several layers to local union transformation. For one thing, locals must balance the necessities of external organizing with the necessity to respond to internal pressures for continued representation. In other words, streamlining representational practices needs to be done in such a way that members are convinced that they are not being abandoned on the altar of external organizing. It is counterproductive to fantasize about members' militance, commitment to progressive change, and competence to accept increased responsibilities. Hardheaded assessment and carefully crafted strategic plans are absolute necessities.

This is why we have devoted attention to grievance and arbitration practices with the potential to save resources. The efforts reflected in these innovations signify an intent to accomplish representation, but to do the work in a different way. The locals cited here have been attempting to build greater ownership of the union by the members and to break the members from the sense that the union, as an institution, is an insurance agency or law firm.

Additionally, building support for transformation must be founded on a clear *leadership consensus*. In the absence of a unified leadership vision as to the objectives of transformation, the steps to be taken and the risks involved, the potential for splits and factionalism are great. Unity of will is especially important, because transformation means new responsibilities for union staff and activists. Inevitably a whole new set of expectations arise for staff representatives, including a different role in the grievance procedure, expectations to organize internally and stimulate member activism, and the reassignment of staff to external organizing. Likewise, new expectations are placed on union activists, including greater responsibility for work-site-based struggles, for grievance handling, and for new member recruitment and orientation. In addition, selected activists are likely to be encouraged to participate in external organizing and to take a more visible role in the larger community.

The one issue that haunts this entire matter is whether any of this new work, best practices, and so forth, can actually help to *recreate* a labor movement in the United States. We certainly have no answer to this, but we would say that should organized labor fail to experiment with new forms of representation with the intent of reallocating resources toward external organizing, then the obvious conclusion is that the union movement, as we have known it, will cease to exist by the early part of the twenty-first century.

Building support for transformation must be recognized as integrally connected to member education. Transformation is not a matter of altering a few practices but really goes to the ideological foundation of U.S. trade unionism. To succeed, it requires education, discussion, and struggle around questions of local union structure, representational responsibilities, the organizing imperative, and alternate visions for the future. New efforts by the AFL-CIO to promote economics education for union members illustrates the recognition by the federation's new leadership that a more global approach to education must be adopted if successful mobilizations and member ownership of unions are to materialize. As with the AFL-CIO, so it is also true with local unions. To transform the practice of local unions, the members must be convinced that such changes are necessary and urgent, and they must be given the opportunity to acquire the leadership and representational skills required. To paraphrase Machiavelli, revolutions that come only from the top have a tendency to be swept quickly away for lack of a firm foundation.

NOTES

1. Portions of this essay are extracted from the final report prepared for the SEIU on the "Best Practices" project. However, the introduction and conclusion and analytical comments throughout are those of the authors and do not represent the opinions of SEIU.

2. For a more comprehensive discussion of this topic, see Fletcher and Hurd 1998.

3. After the election of Andy Stern as president of SEIU in April 1996, Woodruff moved to the international staff as director of local union organizing.

References

Fletcher, Bill, and Richard Hurd. 1998. "Beyond the Organizing Model: The Transformation Process in Local Unions." Pp. 37–53 in *Organizing to Win,* ed. by Kate Bronfenbrenner et al. Ithaca, N.Y.: ILR/Cornell University Press.

Kotter, John. P. 1995. "Leading Change: Why Transformation Efforts Fail." *Harvard Business Review* 73, no. 2 (March–April): 59–67.

Needleman, Ruth. 1993. "Building an Organizing Culture of Unionism." Pp. 358–66 in *Proceedings of the Forty-Fifth Annual Meeting of the Industrial Relations Research Association,* ed. John F. Burton, Jr. Madison, Wisc.: Industrial Relations Research Association.

Piore, Michael. 1994. "Unions: A Reorientation to Survive." Pp. 512–41 in *Labor Economics and Industrial Relations,* ed. Clark Kerr and Paul D. Staudohar. Cambridge, Mass.: Harvard University Press.

11

CRITICAL JUNCTURE: UNIONISM AT THE CROSSROADS

Michael Eisenscher

In 1995 the AFL-CIO conducted the first contested election for national labor federation leadership since John L. Lewis unsuccessfully challenged Samuel Gompers for command of the AFL in 1921 (Widick 1964, 170–71). The contest occurred in the wake of decades-long decline for organized labor—falling union density; eroding real wages and living standards; growing income inequality; corporate restructuring and downsizing; deindustrialization, capital flight, and globalization; and declining political influence. Union density has been dropping continuously since the mid-1950s merger of the AFL and CIO. Private sector density is lower today than at any time since the first decade of this century (Goldfield 1987, 10, tab. 1; Hirsch and Macpherson 1996; Troy 1965, 1, tab. 2). The real wonder is that it took so long for a revolt in the house of labor.

The triumphant slate of John Sweeney, president of the Service Employees (SEIU); Richard Trumka, president of the Mineworkers (UMWA); and Linda Chavez-Thompson, vice president of the State, County and Municipal Employees (AFSCME) offered a promised reform and renewal. Their program, "A New Voice for American Workers," called for a dramatic increase in resources for organizing; more focused efforts in the political arena; new programs to increase union effectiveness in dealing with multinational corporations; new forms of international labor cooperation and solidarity to respond to globalization and capital mobility; an expanded, more persuasive public relations effort to better communicate labor's message and to reestablish its credibility; and internal reforms to improve labor's relevance to a diverse and changing workforce ("New Voice" 1995).

The election of the Sweeney slate has heartened those who recognized that the labor movement had to make dramatic changes if it was to be effective with employers and relevant as a social force. As the Sweeney administration implements its program for rejuvenation of the AFL-CIO, it has given encouragement to forces of reform and renewal within each of its affiliated unions. The process has opened space for debate and initiatives for change with potentially far-reaching and perhaps unintended effects. The Sweeney team moved decisively to implement the changes they proposed. They crisscrossed the country, meeting with local and state labor leaders and union activists, listening to their ideas for change. This effort at inclusion, their openness, and more aggressive leadership have energized the labor movement and rekindled confidence on the part of labor's allies—and also raised the expectations of many union members.

Unlike Lane Kirkland, who avoided media exposure with almost allergic disdain, the Sweeney team has aggressively pursued public venues to advocate for working people. They made the axiom "America needs a raise" a compelling issue in the 1996 election-year debates.[1] They centered labor's 1996 political campaign on issues as well as candidates and focused labor's resources to defeat some of its staunchest political enemies (Bernstein, Borrus, and Dunham 1997, 36–37). They reached out to academics, inviting both ideas and criticism through a series of labor-university teach-ins, and to students through programs like Union Summer and an expanded Organizing Institute internship program (Hamilton 1996; Hornblower 1996; Lerner 1991/92, 83–91; Murolo 1996; Sugrue 1996; Tomasky 1997).

However, I argue that reform must go beyond greater activism, militancy, and even greater involvement. Increasing membership participation over the long run should lead to increasing membership *control* if participation is to mean something more than disempowered submission to the designs of an insular bureaucracy. The battle for union democracy is an integral part of the effort to rebuild labor's ranks and influence. *Activism and empowerment must be wed if unions are to be transformed and labor rejuvenated.*

In confronting more powerful economic and social forces, democracy is an instrument for building solidarity, for establishing accountability, and for determining appropriate strategies—all of which are critical to sustaining and advancing worker and union interests.[2] *Union democracy is not, however, synonymous with either union activism or militancy.* Members can be mobilized for activities over which they have little or no control, for objectives determined *for* them rather than *by* them. The quality of democratic participation and the consequences of that participation for the operation and strategic direction of unions are vital to union success and labor's continuing relevance. There are, of course, numerous examples from labor history of less than democratic leaders and labor organizations who nonetheless led struggles that contributed mightily to labor's

218

advance. (John L. Lewis and the Steelworkers Organizing Committee of the CIO are examples.) Yet the standards and expectations for democratic participation are higher today than they were earlier in this century, and rejuvenation that only reinvigorates a hierarchical bureaucratic structure is likely to be unsustainable over the long haul even if it provides some short-term relief.

Like democratic governance of society (or of the workplace), democratic control of unions by their members serves both moral and instrumental objectives. Rule of, by, and for a union's members is as fundamental to a meaningful theory of democratic union governance as related concepts of governance are to democracy in the polity. Union members ought to be owners and cocreators of their own labor organizations. All too frequently today union leaders speak in the name of their members but actually act in service to their own institutional and bureaucratic interests, for many are only loosely accountable to their membership.[3]

At issue is not a diminution of the role of leadership but rather a change in the relationship between leaders and members—one that holds leadership accountable, keeps them accessible, and allows ultimate authority to rest with and be exercised by an informed and motivated membership. Unions also need to expand both their horizons and their constituency to rebuild a social movement that acts and speaks for broad class concerns as well as particular workplace or occupational interests of its members. A movement that is focused primarily on meeting the immediate workplace needs of a shrinking base of members invites being viewed by most others as a "special interest." This requires that the labor movement become more inclusive, broaden its definition of membership, reach out to previously underrepresented constituencies, and establish new relationships with community allies.

Without a unifying vision motivated by clearly defined core values and a conception of its role in society, labor will be unlikely to develop coherent strategies for revitalization. Achieving these objectives will require what amounts to a fundamental transformation of the organizational culture of most unions. Long-held ideological assumptions and deep-seated practices need to be reexamined and critically challenged. This transformation is captured in part by the contrast between the "service model" of unionism that became dominant after World War II and what some have come to describe as the "organizing model."[4]

Russo and Banks (1996) describe the distinction between the servicing and organizing models as follows:

> In the Service Model: 1) union leaders solve problems for members; 2) the
> union relies on the grievance and arbitration procedures; 3) membership is

passive or limited to responses to leader requests for cooperation; 4) members rely on specialists, experts, and union staff; 5) the union develops secretive and closed communication channels; 6) union structures are centralized and top heavy; 7) the union grows dependent on and is reactive to management; 8) distinctions are made between internal and external organizing activities.

The Organizing Model: 1) stimulates and involves members in problem-solving in group process or collective actions; 2) is not limited to the bargaining process; 3) is committed to education, communications, and member participation in the union; 4) develops and depends on members' skills and abilities; 5) shares information and develops open communication channels; 6) has a decentralized organizational structure; 7) operates independently of management, and is proactive; 8) makes no distinction between internal and external organizing activities.

John Sweeney speaks eloquently about strengthening unions as institutions and their role in society through greater involvement of union members (Sweeney 1996a, 1996b, 1997b).[5] But what he describes is greater member mobilization in support of goals decided from above, not expanded member involvement in union governance and strategic decisions. Mobilization from the top with only token input and control from the bottom perpetuates an activist version of service model unionism rather than building democratic empowerment of union members. This "mobilization model" ("Organizing Model of Unionism" 1991) is distinct from the organizing model described by Russo and Banks, even though it is frequently called that.[6]

Some proponents of mobilization treat union democracy as little more than a feedback mechanism—one that can be achieved by relying on polls and focus groups to monitor the sentiment of the members without actually increasing their direct involvement in decision making. This has its parallel in the corporate community where mechanisms for encouraging worker "voice" stop short of giving workers more actual *power* over the terms and conditions of their labor (Eisenscher 1995). Such voice frequently becomes little more than management's echo.

As part of its reforms, the new leadership has created a number of new institutes, departments, centers, offices, and programs within the federation's central bureaucracy (AFL-CIO 1997; Moberg 1997; "New Voice" 1995); they have also eliminated and consolidated others.[7] The "new" AFL-CIO seeks to expand organizing dramatically. It has created a new organizing department, expanded its Organizing Institute, and encourages its affiliates to invest 30 percent of their income in organizing. (Most currently spend 2–5 percent

[Silverstein 1997; Greenhouse 1997.]) However, union members, committed to their organizations and labor's cause, have always been labor's most effective organizers. This kind of commitment is encouraged by leadership that values and welcomes effective membership control over their organizations rather than by leaders acting as brokers for worker interests (or their own). The new leadership calls for greatly expanded use of volunteer member-organizers but appears to make no connection between expanding the base of member-organizers and expanding the realm of member involvement in the democratic governance of the unions they are asked to build.

The crisis confronting labor cannot be resolved merely by reallocating resources to organizing, as important as that may be. While many of its reforms are worthy, the changes announced to date fail to address some of the more difficult institutional challenges associated with transformative reform. Some reforms actually perpetuate service model practices by reemphasizing the directing role of staff and centralized leadership rather than by nurturing "leadership from below."

THE POSTWAR LABOR-MANAGEMENT "ACCORD"

The New Voice ticket hasn't critically questioned most of the institutional practices and ideological assumptions embedded in the organizational culture of the post–World War II labor movement. During this period, labor moved away from its New Deal heritage of evangelizing social movement unionism in favor of a more narrow focus on collective bargaining, political brokering, internal control, and institutional concerns (Leahy 1989; Moody 1996; Nissen 1990a, 1990b). The shift made labor more insular and conservative, eroding its moral influence and ultimately its organizational capacities. A deeper appraisal would have required a critical reexamination of the postwar labor-management "compact" (sometimes termed "social contract" or "accord") that provided the ideological bulwark for nearly fifty years of service model business unionism. It would have considered ways in which control over the affairs of unions shifted to an increasingly hierarchical, insular leadership and growing, largely unelected staff bureaucracy (Leahy 1989; Moody 1996; Nissen 1990a, 1990b; Gordon, Edwards, and Reich 1982).

Under the postwar accord, management accepted organized labor's legitimacy, and bargaining over periodic economic gains for workers derived from expanding markets and growing productivity. Unions pursued narrow bargaining objectives, emphasizing wage-benefit demands over social solidarity and social rights. Workers could expect greater job security and a generally increasing standard of living. Union survival was no longer at constant risk;

dues check-off and union security provisions stabilized labor institutions; a growing economy assured their own growth. Labor accepted management's control of the enterprise; capital's prerogatives—decisions over investment, technological change, plant location, pricing, and products—were to be exercised exclusively by management. Union leaders took more responsibility for control and discipline of the rank and file as workplace disputes were channeled into bureaucratic multilevel grievance and arbitration procedures that removed their resolution from the workplace and the direct involvement of affected workers into the union office and the hands of staff and leadership. Union bureaucracies accordingly mushroomed. Multiyear contracts with binding no-strike provisions replaced annual bargaining rounds. Labor embraced U.S. global hegemonic ambitions and Cold War aims as its own. Indeed, the entire accord was predicated on U.S. global dominance and control of both international markets and geopolitics. By the late 1960s, however, circumstances changed; profit rates were in decline; capital acted to restore accumulation, which required changing the terms of the "deal" (Bowles, Gordon, and Weisskopf 1990, 53–57, 66–72; Green 1980, chs. 6–7; Marshall 1987, 9–11; Nissen 1990a, 1990b). Capital's unwillingness to maintain the accord is at the heart of labor's present crisis.

The "Decline of Democracy": Not Just a Civic Issue

In his acceptance speech, John Sweeney spoke of the "decline of democracy in America" ("In Their Own Words" 1995). He was referring to democracy in the public sphere. Throughout his campaign, however, little if anything was said about democracy in the labor movement itself. The Sweeney administration points to the need for greater membership participation but does not examine the causes of faltering member involvement in their unions. Changes proposed by the new leadership will not in themselves increase member participation in union decision-making processes or improve the accountability of leadership and the responsiveness of union representatives to the needs of union members. In other words, they do not get at the underlying connection between the members and their union, and the ways in which those connections have frayed over time (Heckscher 1988, 27–29; Matles and Higgins 1974; Widick 1964).

Many union members today treat their unions as if they were vending machines. They make monthly deposits of dues and expect to have to do no more than pull a lever when they need assistance. This is both encouraged by and helps sustain the service-model union, which turns grievances into "cases" and struggles for workplace justice into legal contests between union staff or attorneys and employer industrial relations managers and management lawyers. It fuels a bureaucratic penchant for control among union leaders every bit as powerful as management's obsession with control. In many unions, sparse attendance at union meetings serves leadership's interests in control, as do skimpy explanations of the terms of complex and sometimes controversial contract settlements.

PRICE OF POLITICAL DEPENDENCY: THE CHARITY OF STRANGERS

A thorough reappraisal would consider labor's continuing attachment to and reliance upon a Democratic Party that gladly takes labor's dollars and relies on election day union voter mobilizations, while continuing to serve its corporate clients and other wealthy political investors (Ferguson 1995; McClure 1995b; Moberg 1995; Tasini 1995; Wypijewski 1995). Reflecting labor's flagging political influence, the federation uncritically embraced Bill Clinton for reelection without extracting a single significant political concession (Farrell 1996; "In Their Own Words" 1995, 60; Wypijewski 1995). While it concentrated on issues education during the 1996 campaign, targeting vulnerable anti-labor (mostly Republican) candidates, it exercised little if any influence over the selection of candidates who ran against them. Labor's ability to discipline supposed "friends" who later renege on pledges to support labor's agenda has been reduced to its use of media to embarrass and harass rather than its ability to field and elect its own candidates (Bernstein, Borrus, and Dunham 1997; Moberg 1997). The Sweeney administration's concept of "independence" does not extend to a capacity to field its own candidates or to act outside the framework of wealth-dominated two-party politics. This leaves labor dependent on party political leadership whose loyalty to labor's agenda and workers' interests is tenuous and opportunistic, and subordinate to powerful financial interests over which unions have no control (Ferguson 1995; Slaughter 1997). Unions need to broaden their concept of politics beyond endorsements, PAC contributions, lobbying, media blitzes, and election-day voter mobilizations to develop workers' full participation in civic life and to strengthen their independent role in the polity. This can only happen if labor has an accurate analysis of the sources and exercise of power in American political life, and an understanding of the institutional forces that affect its own exercise of power.

IN THE SERVICE OF THE STATE: GOVERNMENT-CERTIFIED SOLIDARITY

The Sweeney administration has taken important steps to reorganize the federation's international operations, consolidating a number of separate programs and institutes into a single department under new leadership. The federation's decades-long preoccupation with communism, which kept it from even speaking to many unions around the world, is yielding to a focus on international solidarity based on unity among workers who face common multinational corporate adversaries, without regard to political or ideological orientation (Brecher and Costello 1996; Moberg 1997). The New Voice leadership, however, has made no commitment to break labor's reliance on direct and indirect government funding or to acknowledge and repudiate federation involvement with U.S. government intelligence agencies. It is time for the federation's leadership to reexamine and acknowledge the AFL-CIO's cooperation and collusion with U.S. government intelligence services in destabilizing and deradicalizing foreign labor movements (Bacon 1996; Brecher and Costello 1996; McClure 1995a, 1995b).[8] Labor's anticommunist preoccupations caused it to sacrifice its political independence as it eroded labor's tolerance for internal dissent (Fellner 1990a, 102). The confidence that workers' movements abroad can have in the U.S. labor movement would be immeasurably strengthened by a candid reappraisal.

SPEAKING FOR WORKERS—LIVING LIKE BOSSES

"Double-dipping" is one manifestation of business unionism that has dramatically undercut labor's standing with both union members and unorganized workers alike (Greer et al. 1994). Indeed, during the campaign, it was revealed that between 1981 and 1994 John Sweeney himself drew "consulting fees" amounting to nearly $450,000 after leaving the presidency of SEIU Local 32-B in New York to become the national union's top officer ("Union Boss" 1995, A-9; McClure 1995c).

Union executive salaries and allowances place most leaders in the lower economic echelons of corporate executives, giving credence to the pejorative "union bosses" (Bernstein 1985, 102). In an era of declining real incomes for most workers, the gulf between the lifestyle and economic standing of labor's leadership and that of the workers that unions seek to organize makes a mockery of labor's claim to egalitarianism and its aspirations for a less economically polarized society. For union leaders to decry excessive corporate executive pay (AFL-CIO 1996, 7–8) while collecting salaries and perks that allow them to live like corporate executives probably appears morally hypocritical to many workers (even though *Fortune 500* executives enjoy compensation that is many times what union leaders receive). In decrying growing income inequality, union leaders must be seen as part of the solution, not part of the problem.

BEYOND THE MOBILIZATION MODEL TO TRANSFORMATIONAL UNIONISM

There are many factors that have influenced labor's four-decade decline.[9] Some are external and largely beyond the immediate direct influence of union members and leadership, but others are endogenous. Many barriers to rebuilding the labor movement can only be removed by radically expanding the involvement of union members and unorganized workers in determining the strategic role and direction that unions pursue. To accomplish such involvement, however, will require a "transformation" in organizational practices that goes beyond new tactics and strategies to shift authority downward in the organization by bringing the membership into both activity *and* decision making.[10] Achieving this transformation requires that unions expand their function beyond collective bargaining (Tasini 1995, 41–47). Unions should seek to act not only for dues-paying members but also for those yet to be hired and those who no longer work. They must speak, bargain, and act in the interests of the entire working class if they want to be identified in the minds of workers as their most effective and dependable advocates. It appears that John Sweeney has recognized this challenge. The New Voice program says, "The labor movement must speak forcefully on behalf of all working people," and calls upon the federation to become "the fulcrum of a vibrant social movement, not simply a Federation of constituent organizations" (Brecher and Costello 1996, 13, 19). Richard Bensinger, Sweeney's director of the newly reconstituted organizing department, has said the labor movement should "become a moral force in society" and "use [its] power to fight for all workers" (Moberg 1997, 27). The Sweeney team must now translate those affirmations into concrete actions.[11]

SHUFFLING THE DECK WON'T CHANGE THE CARDS

Deep, transformative institutional and cultural changes require more than merely changing officials. The Teamsters are a case in point. The election of Ron Carey as president only opened the possibility of change. The struggle to transform the culture of the union will remain an ongoing challenge for years to come.

Impediments to labor revitalization are located within institutional practices and an organizational culture in which ideological conformity to the status quo within unions are transmitted from one generation to the next. Reform can be initiated or accelerated by effective leadership, but transformation cannot be achieved by leadership initiative alone. The most dramatic change will come when rank-and-file union members who want a more energized, aggressive, independent, and democratic labor movement drive the process of renewal.

THE CHALLENGE OF DIVERSITY

As the racial, ethnic, and gender composition of local unions comes to reflect the demographics of the workforce, an additional challenge presents itself to unions, whose leadership remain overwhelmingly white and predominantly male (Cobble 1993; Fellner 1989, 1990a, 1990b; Gooding and Reeve 1993; Bennett 1995, 4–5; Roby 1995).[12] The Sweeney slate struggled to change the composition of the AFL-CIO General Executive Council. Important changes made it more diverse and representative of union membership. The election of Linda Chavez-Thompson to a newly created executive vice presidency made her the first woman or person of color to hold a high federation post. Together minorities comprise 27 percent of the new council, compared to 17 percent in the old (Kelber 1995, 2). Yet these are advances that are distant from the lives of most workers. Only when the leadership of their own unions reflects the diversity of the their workplaces will unions be perceived to be truly representative. Transformation requires advancing women, minorities, and youth to leadership.

Even in unions that have adopted mobilization strategies, too often a largely white male English-speaking bureaucracy leads an immigrant, non-white, non-English-fluent, often mainly female membership. Members are mobilized and represented by union staff who may never have worked in the industry, were hired from outside the union's ranks, and often have little or no prior union (or even work) experience. They may be unable to communicate with members in a language they understand, and they may answer to a union administration that is itself distant from the lives of the members it leads (Fellner 1989, 1990b). Few would dispute the need for competent able union staff, but the question is what relationship staff have to members, as well as whether union staff are recruited and trained from among the ranks of the members themselves (Early 1996). At issue is whether newly organized units are allowed and assisted to develop indigenous leadership, as opposed to having "professional" staff dominate the affairs of the union.

The case of SEIU Local 399 in Los Angeles is instructive. The local has twenty-five thousand members, primarily in health care, janitorial, and other service industries. It is a local deeply involved in the much-heralded Justice for Janitors campaign, which has been responsible for rebuilding SEIU's membership in the building service industry (Blackwell 1993; Lerner 1991/92; Waldinger et al. 1997). Justice for Janitors has been a laudable effort on the part of SEIU to recover its base and influence in the building service industry. It has also contributed to rebuilding labor-community alliances, projecting labor activism and relevance in the media, defending the rights of immigrant workers, and highlighting the growing disparity between the working poor and the wealthy in society.

Local 399 successfully mobilized its members, its community and labor allies, and unorganized workers themselves to confront the powerful building owners in places like Century City, the site of a now-infamous police assault against peacefully demonstrating immigrant janitors who were seeking union recognition (Multiracial Alliance 1995; Bacon, 1995; Colatosi 1990).

Despite Local 399's reputation for progressive militancy and worker activism, the union has been torn by a bitter internal battle between a segment of dissatisfied union members and the local's leadership. A rank-and-file caucus, the Multiracial Alliance, reports that "for years, behind this facade of activism, bitter contradictions flourished between the union's administration and the membership. . . . The leadership excluded from decision-making those very workers who helped build the union" (Multiracial Alliance 1995).

The Multiracial Alliance charged that the local's executive board was dominated by union staff members. The Alliance ultimately organized a slate of candidates and conducted a successful campaign that swept reform candidates into twenty-one of twenty-five elected union leadership posts. Informed observers note that staff divisions and political rivalries greatly exacerbated internal political differences (author's interviews, December 9–11, 1995, and January 11–14, 1996, anonymous by request). When the newly elected majority on the executive board sought to make personnel and policy changes, the incumbent president insisted that he alone had the authority to determine staff assignments (Bacon 1995; Colatosi 1990).[13] This confrontation between old guard and newly elected leaders paralyzed the local, leading SEIU to place the local in trusteeship (Bennett 1995). Elected leaders were removed; a number of staff were fired. Appointed administrators now run the local.[14]

MOBILIZATION AND MILITANCY DO NOT GUARANTEE DEMOCRATIC CONTROL

Justice for Janitors is a paradigmatic case of the mobilization strategy. What this case illustrates is that a mobilization form of unionism need not be any more democratic than a more traditional service-model business union. In Local 399, militant mobilization did not provide members with greater democratic control. The leadership and staff determined the priorities, developed the strategy, and defined the objectives. Members were expected to be active, but only as directed by leadership.

One characteristic of the service model is the dominance of unelected staff. Operations are nominally overseen by an elected executive board, but in some regional or statewide unions it may be so large or meet so infrequently as to be ineffective as a real oversight body. In practice, the organization is run by a few officers or the executive director with a hired staff. This resembles a mutual insurance company in which a professional staff administers the affairs of policyholders, dispensing benefits on an as-needed basis. Power and authority remain centralized in leaders' hands, and that concentration of power often creates a self-perpetuating elite.

No change process is likely to be sustained that does not involve transferring to union members the power to determine the strategic direction and objectives of their organizations. What is required is a change that is deeply rooted in and energized by the union's membership, and processes and structures put in place to protect and reinforce membership control, regardless of who serves in leadership.

The engine of labor renewal is the creation a of movement for democratic participation by union members. Elements of such a movement already exist and are gathering strength. They may be found in movements such as Teamsters for a Democratic Union (TDU), the New Directions movement in the United Autoworkers (UAW), Black Workers for Justice in the South, and in other national and local reform efforts (Moody 1988). The election of the Sweeney leadership at the AFL-CIO will likely encourage others as rank-and-file expectations are raised and confidence in the possibilities for change grows. Even in the most democratic organizations, there is an important role for rank-and-file caucuses, networks, and movements. They replenish the democratic vision and serve as guarantors of the exercise of democratic rights; they remind even good leadership in whose interests leaders serve and to whom they must answer. The extent to which fundamental change occurs or new leaders are coopted by or incorporated into the prevailing culture will be determined by the strength and level of development of rank-and-file movements pressing for democratic renewal, not just by the commitment of individual leaders to change.

Union Staff and the Democratic Imperative

If the shift in leadership of the AFL-CIO creates an opportunity for change, it also poses a challenge. The challenge is not simply in deciding who should lead but in determining what relationship one will have to the processes that must occur down below. This may pose difficult choices for those who make labor their life's work. Union staff find themselves torn between their commitments to the principles of democratic unionism, their loyalty or obligation to leadership, and their own power, authority, economic security, and future careers in the labor movement. When the participatory democratic potential of a labor organization is fulfilled, its staff are more likely to be liberated from bureaucratic roles and may find greater fulfillment than they would as agents of a hierarchical bureaucracy. As members assume greater responsibility, union staff obtain the opportunity to make a more creative and enduring strategic contribution by bringing members forward rather than by acting as their unelected agent, advocate, or champion.

One does not have to overidealize the desirability of or potential for rank-and-file control of unions to see that the present operation of many unions is often widely at variance with some of the most elemental principles of democracy. Without democratic control by and accountability to the members, there is considerable danger, if not likelihood, that the next generation of labor leaders will only replicate the institutional practices of those that preceded it. These practices are not just individually chosen, they are also institutionally constituted and culturally conditioned. If organized labor is to survive as something more than a niche or marginal social factor in the next century, a much deeper process of change and renewal is called for.

WILL THE WORKPLACE OFFER MORE PARTICIPATION THAN THE UNION?

It is widely argued that we now live in a postindustrial, postfordist,[15] globally integrated economy, one in which the production and distribution of information and services, not just manufactured goods, are value-adding activities that employ a large and growing proportion of the workforce (Bell 1973; Block 1990; Marshall 1987; Toffler 1980; Touraine 1971). Despite the hype, manufacturing still matters, and a substantial amount of activity in the service sector is directly tied to manufacturing activities (Cohen and Zysman 1987; Piore and Sabel 1984). But there is no doubt that we live in a very different world from that of the 1930s, or even the 1970s. Industrial restructuring, the expansion of contingent labor, globalization of production, introduction of new technologies in production of goods, services, communications, and transport, and changes in the demographics of the labor force all combine to dramatically and, in most cases, irrevocably alter the terrain on which organized labor operates.

Unorganized workers and union members alike have been introduced to new forms of workplace participation and responsibility that push decision making down, remove layers of bureaucracy, seek to engage workers in the objectives of the enterprise, and endeavor to secure from them identification with and commitment to corporate goals (Cooke 1990; Eisenscher 1995; Kochan, Katz, and Mower 1984; Parker and Slaughter 1994; Siriani 1987).

Whatever one thinks of this process, it should be clear that union members will not for long accept the notion that they can have more responsibility for the day-to-day operation of their workplace than they have over the day-to-day affairs and governance of their own organizations. Unorganized workers will find little appeal in unions that appear far more bureaucratic and hierarchical and far less participatory than their own workplaces (even if one accepts that most workplace participation they are offered is of a shallow, powerless sort) (Greer et al. 1994, 11–17).

LOCAL UNIONS: THE ENGINE OF TRANSFORMATION

The local union continues to be the most vital institution through which members can assert their democratic will, exercise control, and realize the goals of union revitalization. What remains is to restore it as a living organism of discussion, debate, education, and struggle over the policies and practices that guide the life of the union and establish its objectives and priorities. National unions should be structured to give life to the democratic potential of their local organizations. The experiences of central labor bodies in Atlanta, Milwaukee, San Jose, and elsewhere suggest that central labor councils also have great potential as agents of labor renewal (Gapasin and Wial 1996). The New Voice program recognizes this fact and the Sweeney administration has begun to reorganize to enable them to play that role. Among its new initiatives is a "Union Cities" program intended to raise the visibility and expand the role of central labor bodies and reconnect them to the communities in which they function (AFL-CIO n.d.[b]; Brecher and Costello 1996; Moberg 1997).

LEGAL REFORM AND TRANSFORMATION: THE UNIONS SHOULD LEAD

Transformation cannot be legislated, but that does not mean there is no place for legislative reform. It is evident to many that if democratization of unions is key to unleashing the creative power of labor's base (or as a value for its own sake), it is unlikely to occur in some unions absent a major revolt from below or prodding from outside—or both. While legal reform may not be sufficient, it may be necessary to kick-start the engine of renewal.[16] Rather than abdicate the terrain of membership interests to the National Right-to-Work Committee, employers, and a handful of liberal civil libertarians, the demand for democratic reform should become the property of all those who claim an interest in labor's future. The labor movement itself would be wise to embrace a program of reforms around which a struggle can be waged both within unions and in the legislative arena. It is unlikely to do so, however, without considerable prodding from within and without.[17]

There is no structural "quick-fix" that will ensure democratization, but there are union practices that contribute to the opportunity for rank-and-file control, such as:

- direct election of all officers;[18]
- secret-ballot referenda of all affected workers to authorize a strike, suspend a strike, or ratify a contract;
- member ratification of all side-agreements, and memoranda of understanding between the union and management negotiated during the term of an agreement;
- membership right by petition for a special "no-confidence" vote on the performance of unelected staff who are responsible for negotiating and administering agreements that affect them.

These proposals are illustrative but hardly inclusive. It should also be recognized that any structural reform can be frustrated or corrupted. Without an active, vigilant rank and file, no amount of structural reform will produce a more democratic organization.

BEYOND INTERNAL DEMOCRACY: A BROADER CONSTITUENCY AND SOCIAL AGENDA

Much has been written about the changing composition of the workforce and structure of the labor market—growing diversity, increasing participation of women, the crucial role of immigrants, the rise of contingent work arrangements, the employment shift from manufacturing to services, the increasing importance of "knowledge" workers, creation of networked production arrangements, outsourcing, and other manifestations of restructuring (Cobble 1993; Gooding and Reeve 1993). Attention to the constellation of practices that constitute what has come to be known as "high-performance" work organization (HPWO) has grown to near-faddish proportions. Without overstating the penetration of these practices, changes are nonetheless taking place in the way work is performed, the way it is organized, and in some respect in the very nature of work itself (Appelbaum and Batt 1994; Heckscher 1988; Levine 1995).

The labor movement has been divided over how to respond to these developments (Baugh 1994; Parker and Slaughter 1994; Siriani 1987). Its response, such as it is, has been primarily in those workplaces where unions already have collective bargaining rights, affecting only those workers for whom the unions already negotiate. Unions have been even slower to address the needs of the 85 percent of workers who are unrepresented, and in particular the more than 40 percent of private-sector workers and millions more public employees who are not even covered by the National Labor Relations Act (NLRA) or other labor laws (Eisenscher 1995, 8). By some estimates, one-quarter of the U.S. workforce is employed in "contingent" jobs that are either excluded entirely under current labor law or exist at the margins of traditional workplace organization ("New BLS Data" 1996, 1; Appelbaum 1992). This proportion will continue to increase into the next century.

Revitalization that focuses only on labor's existing membership base will be inadequate to meet the challenge workers confront or to reverse labor's decline. Unions will have to break out of the constraints imposed by traditional organizing units dictated by the National Labor Relations Board (NLRB). The narrow objective of winning representation elections and negotiating collective bargaining agreements for those units will no longer suffice. The labor movement will have to develop more creative organizing strategies in addition to more flexible forms of membership and representation to reach segments of the workforce that find themselves outside the law, beyond customary bargaining units, in nontraditional work arrangements, and in occupations and industries that have heretofore received little attention from organized labor. Addressing workplace needs themselves will have to be redefined to break the bounds imposed by statutory dictates of what is and is not a "mandatory subject of bargaining." Labor will have to master a range of new skills to be able to represent workers in diverse and changing employment situations effectively and to challenge and bargain with employers over issues that have heretofore been considered sacrosanct managerial prerogatives (Banks 1991/92; Oppenheim 1991/92).[19]

Labor will also have to become more adept at bargaining with the state over issues of classwide concern to workers. This reinforces the need to develop a capacity to operate independently within the major parties and in third-party or independent political arenas. This will require a level of political agility, flexibility, and creativity that has not been characteristic of union political action in the postwar era.

This broader view of labor's constituency and mission will require significant expansion of labor education and union training programs within and outside union ranks. Such education, however, must not be limited to narrowly devised "skills" training. What unionists need in addition is education for strategic planning, political and economic analysis, and critical thinking. Early initiatives of the newly formed education department appear to move the federation in just that direction.[20]

NEW CONNECTIONS TO COMMUNITIES

The pressures for change are having their effect in the house of labor. Activist movements like Jobs with Justice (Banks 1991/92; Early and Cohen 1994) and Justice for Janitors are rekindling the kind of member activism that is reminiscent of the prewar labor movement. These are movements the success of which is determined by the breadth and depth of support they can build both among union members and within the communities in which they function (Banks 1991/92).

Responding to labor's crisis, some unions have already begun to explore alternative strategies that redefine the relationship between labor and its community. It became abundantly clear in the 1980s to those unions that relying on the procedures of the NLRA and NLRB no longer protected workers in the course of organizing, and as often as not did not result in collective bargaining agreements. (See, for example, Crump 1991/92). In the wake of the firing of striking members of the Professional Air Traffic Controllers Organization (PATCO), employers increasingly turned to permanent striker replacements to break strikes and to decertify unions. Organized labor searched for alternative organizing and bargaining strategies. Unions began to organize to be able to demand recognition outside the procedures of the NLRA. They turned to "inside strategies" and corporate campaigns to resolve disputes and win new contracts ("New Tactics for Labor" 1985, "No More Business as Usual" 1993; Press 1996).

These strategies place a greater premium, however, on alliances with forces outside the union. Unions will have to rebuild relationships with community constituencies in ways that transcend the self-serving, short-term instrumental coalitions that have too often typified labor's relationships with nonlabor groups. The process of reaching out to community allies and developing new kinds of working relationships has already begun, particularly among those unions (often at the local level) that have already concluded that survival demands that they act in new ways—ways that are at variance with the practices that have been in place through most of the postwar era.

Labor-community alliances, like Jobs with Justice, expand the realm of solidarity beyond the labor movement to the community. In building labor-community solidarity movements, they create new levels of mutual obligation that compel unions to broaden their horizons beyond workplace, craft, or industry to incorporate the needs of entire communities, including traditionally nonunion elements within them. As unions attempt to balance their collective bargaining objectives with these broader social goals, it is likely that conflicts will arise that test the strength of these new relationships. Community participants who are motivated by broad social justice goals are compelled to infuse their objectives with concrete analyses of the economic sources of injustice, which will bring them to confront the nature of economic exploitation and quality of employment available to workers in their communities. This will, in turn, force them to address the conduct of employers, some of whom may have previously been the source of financial support for social programs of these religious, charitable, social action, nonprofit, and other community organizations. In other words, these coalitions confront their participants with difficult but valuable and potentially transformative challenges, among which is the challenge to build into new organizing and coalition strategies participatory democratic practices that institutionalize membership control and involvement in nonelitist, nonhierarchical organizations that reach out to and draw in a wider constituency.

THE SHAPE OF THE FUTURE

Among the things we bequeath to our children are our class traditions, our political culture, and the legacy of our struggles (the lessons we learn from our own experiences—our victories and our defeats—and the lessons we pass on from our parents' generation). Will unions pass on the culture of self-sacrifice, struggle, solidarity, and community inherited from the 1930s and 1960s generations, or transmit the prevailing culture of individualism, bureaucratic hierarchy and autocracy, and acquisitive consumerism embedded in society and reinforced by the business/service-model of unionism? The future of the labor movement will be shaped by the answer.

NOTES

1. Falling real incomes is only one of the reasons former secretary of labor Robert Reich has dubbed American workers the "anxious class" (Taylor 1995). As a symbolic expression, this federation slogan tends to reduce the concerns of working Americans to a simple economic prescription. Yet America also needs more decent jobs, justice, economic equality, health care, child care, elder care, and democracy in the workplace.

2. I am grateful to Elly Leary, national cochair of the New Directions Movement of the United Auto Workers, for drawing this point to my attention in an E-mail communication on March 4, 1996.

3. The liberal concept of democracy is of "a representative system in which law and public policy are made by officeholders who have won freely contested elections. . . . The system is founded upon the assumption that citizens are aware of their self-interest

and are able to pursue it through their vote" (Bachrach and Botwinick 1992, 20). In their now classic institutionalist treatment *Labor and the American Community* (1970), Bok and Dunlop propose a very similar definition of union democracy: "the term 'democracy' refers to the processes that keep union leaders responsive to the members: principally the elections by which union leaders are chosen and union policies are ratified by the rank and file" (70). In this view, members vest authority in their leaders through a system of "representative government." In my view this is a very constricted view of democracy. As used in this chapter, I refer to a far more participatory concept of democracy in which members have an active role in collectively governing their union. In this view, democracy involves individual self-development in which self-interest is expanded to encompass "an identification with and a commitment to the well-being of others" (Bachrach and Botwinick 1992, 20–21). This meaning is at the heart of solidarity, which is the glue that binds workers to one another. I propose that unions ought to operate in such a way as to encourage the widest distribution of power and responsibility to members who have a corresponding responsibility jointly with their elected leaders and appointed staff for the strategic direction, objectives, and goals of the organization. The difference between these two views of democracy is best illustrated in an example suggested by Mike Miller, executive director of ORGANIZE Training Center (private communication, June 7, 1997):

Union "X" could have elected stewards and officers who militantly advocate in behalf of aggrieved members. Local monthly meetings consider resolutions on a wide range of social and political topics over which there is vigorous debate. Officers are elected in lively contested elections, without a taint of corruption or unfair electioneering. The union periodically mobilizes its members for voter registration, election day voter mobilization, and legislative lobbying activities. Union "X" is a paradigm of representative democracy.

Union "Y" has no elected stewards and only appointed business agents to handle grievances. Their commitment to workplace rights is questionable. Meetings are run, when they are held at all, autocratically and to the extent the union takes positions on issues, they are usually conservative and narrowly self-interested. Elections are either uncontested or dominated by the incumbent machine that controls the process to make an effective challenge difficult if not impossible. By the standards of representative democracy, Union "Y" would be considered undemocratic.

From the view of participatory democracy, however, neither are fully democratic. In Union "Z," elected stewards organize their coworkers for collective actions to resolve disputes, if possible, before they even become grievances. Together they create a "point-of-production" environment in which workers regularly contest management prerogatives to expand their own control over their work environment and to gain their dignity in the workplace. In their community, these workers are encouraged by their union to organize for civic action in their neighborhoods, for electoral participation, or for other purposes. Between union meetings, members participate in a range of committees and task forces addressing both workplace and social/civic problems. Resolutions not only relate to positions on issues but serve as a mechanism for democratic decision making about actions the workers resolve to take together. Leadership helps facilitate and implement member participation in effectuating those decisions. Union "Z" is a participatory democratic organization.

4. Conrow (1991) also discusses an "organizing" model of unionism. The entire issue of *Labor Research Review 17* in which her article appears is devoted to the subject of "An Organizing Model of Unionism." While associated with a bottom-up approach to contract administration, this model is also key to organizing the unorganized and mobilizing a union's forces to win collective bargaining struggles. It also makes possible a different way in which unions can do politics and influence public policy. (See as well, "No More Business as Usual" 1993, and "Labor and Political Action" 1994, both in *Labor Research Review*.)

5 The new general executive council adopted a mission statement that includes a commitment to "change our unions to provide a new voice to workers in a changing economy." In a letter to affiliates issued in January 1997, John Sweeney said, "The federation has committed itself to speak for working people every day at every level of our world economy, as well as to transform the role of the union from an organization that focuses on a member's contract to one that gives workers a meaningful say in all the decisions that affect our working lives—from capital investments, to the quality of our products and services, to how we organize our work." In furtherance of that goal, the AFL-CIO established the "Center for Workplace Democracy" (AFL-CIO 1997; AFL-CIO n.d.[a]; Sweeney 1997b).

6. Stephen Lerner, an architect of SEIU's Justice for Janitors campaign and key advisor to the newly established AFL-CIO Organizing Department, elucidated this "mobilization" approach in an article that appeared in the *Boston Review* in 1996 (Lerner 1996). In the *Review's* next edition, it was followed by responses from a dozen respondents representing a range of views.

7. Suzanne Gordon (1995), speaking of the New Voice program, observes, "For every union problem, there's a new Washington solution—an institute, a task force, a monitoring project, a clearinghouse, a policy center, a training center, a center for strategic campaigns, a new organizing department (with an office of strategic planning), a strategic planning process ('Committee 2000'), two or three campaign funds, and a 'strike support team of top people' from various union staffs. . . . Except in the section on organizing and the role of the labor councils, there's no emphasis in the Sweeney proposals on bottom-up initiatives."

8. Lest anyone think that labor's foreign intrigues ended with the collapse of the Soviet Union, see Bacon (1995) on the operations of the AFL-CIO inside the current Russian labor movement. On labor and foreign policy, see Ginger and Christiano 1987, 723–69; Thompson 1980, 185; Wheaton 1980, 426; Brecher and Costello 1994, 15; and Morris 1967.

9. There is an extensive literature that examines structural, institutional, demographic, and other exogenous influences on unionization. This essay focuses on those that are

internal to the labor movement. For a more wide-ranging discussion, see, for example, Aronowitz 1983; Cornfield 1987; Craver 1993; Goldfield 1987; Kochan 1986; Kochan, Katz, and McKersie 1994; Mishel and Voos 1992.

10. While his work has been directed primarily at management, Peter Senge (1990) suggests some lessons equally applicable to union leadership regarding the transformation of institutions into "learning organizations."

11. The new leadership has taken some steps already toward realizing that ambition. It has created a new women's department, opened dialogue with academics and community groups, raised the profile of issues that affect all working families in the last elections, established a new education department charged with making popular economics education accessible to more working people, and officially embraced Jobs with Justice, a labor-community coalition that had operated outside the orbit of the federation under Kirkland (Banks 1991/92; Brecher and Costello 1996; Moberg 1997; Slaughter 1997). The federation also took steps to bring more diversity to its general executive council. These measures together, however, only begin a process that has far to go to meet the challenges labor faces.

12. In 1994, women of all races and men of color constituted 50.3 percent of all U.S. union members, up from 43 percent in 1985 (Roby 1995, 66). That same year, of 92 AFL-CIO unions, two were headed by black men, three by white women, and 87 by white men (68).

13. The Multiracial Alliance did not run a candidate against the incumbent president, Jim Zellers.

14. Following an extended trusteeship, the janitorial members of Local 399 were split from the local and assigned to SEIU Local 1877. Local 1877 had been a San Jose area local that had gone through its own internal upheaval that brought Mike Garcia to its presidency as part of a reform effort. Garcia implemented an aggressive Justice for Janitors campaign that is credited with rebuilding the union's membership and power in the Silicon Valley. Garcia became involved in Local 399 during its trusteeship. In extending his local's jurisdiction to all of California and assigning Local 399 building service members to it, SEIU has created a structure that will be well insulated from rank-and-file challenge, given the difficulties of mounting an effective statewide challenge in a place as large as California by a mostly immigrant workforce employed by a large number of small, dispersed building contractors.

    Andrew Stern was elected to replace John Sweeney as president of the SEIU. Stern had been the union's director of organizing under Sweeney and is credited with increasing its membership by several hundred thousand. In an unexpected move, Stern announced that SEIU would abandon its confrontational Justice for Janitors strategy in Washington, D.C., in favor of a more cooperative relationship with building owners. Whether this reversal of course will extend to the Justice for Janitors campaign generally remains to be seen (Swoboda and Haggerty 1997).

15. "Fordism" is a term used loosely to describe the dominant system of twentieth-century assembly-line mass production. It incorporates deskilling and division of labor

associated with Frederick Taylor's "scientific management" and hegemonic forms of industrial organization consisting of large integrated corporations, the dominance of basic industrial sectors in the economy, and mass consumption of mass-produced goods (Sayer and Walker 1992, 194). Postfordism is therefore characterized by flexible production methods, with rapid changeability of both products and production processes enabled by computerization; smaller, more specialized firms, with greater reliance on subcontracting and contingent forms of employment; greater attention to demand variations and niche marketing; and collective social and institutional order in place of hierarchical control (Storper and Walker 1989, 152).

16. While the role of the rank-and-file reformers and Teamsters for a Democratic Union cannot be underestimated, Ron Carey would not be president of the International Brotherhhood of Teamsters (IBT) today were it not for the intervention of the government and courts. Legal reform has a place in the larger struggle for democratic renewal.

17. In the present political climate, and given the makeup of Congress, a focus on legislative reform that simply reopens the Landrum-Griffin workers' rights provisions would likely be an invitation to an even more reactionary law than is now in effect. Unions, however, can take initiatives that lay the groundwork for future federal reform by strengthening member rights provisions of their own constitutions and by-laws.

18. Direct elections of national union officials is not a panacea and can itself be subject to undemocratic features or practices. To be able to run a national election campaign, candidates must have or create a national campaign structure, raise substantial sums, have the freedom to travel and access to members, and have resources to produce and distribute campaign materials. Incumbents in such elections have an advantage, just as they do in congressional elections. But in unions where convention delegates have traditionally elected top officers and in which members have little effective voice, a change to direct elections, properly monitored, can break open the iron grip an entrenched autocratic leadership may have, or minimally induce incumbents to be more responsive to the needs and concerns of members by virtue of having to campaign for their votes.

19. Perhaps the most ambitious initiative of the Sweeney administration has been its programs designed to expand organizing of unorganized workers dramatically. In addition to the newly created Organizing Department and Organizing Institute, the federation launched a Union Summer program, Senior Summer program, Field Mobilization Department, and an Office of Strategic and Cooperative Campaigns. Further, it has said that all departments and programs sponsored by the federation will be integrated to be mutually supportive of the organizing objectives (AFL-CIO 1997; Brecher and Costello 1996; Moberg 1997).

20. The Sweeney administration created a new education department under the direction of Bill Fletcher. Fletcher has reached out to labor educators and their professional associations to assist in designing the federation's program, with particular

attention to providing union members with a working understanding of the economy and the economic forces that affect them and their jobs. A joint Economics Education Working Group was created to help develop a "multi-year, multi-level economics education program" that "resonate[s] with the experience of [members'] daily lives" (Fletcher 1996a, 1996b).

REFERENCES

AFL-CIO. 1996. "America Needs a Raise." Washington, D.C.: Department of Economic Research, AFL-CIO. February.

———. 1997. "Highlights of Major 1997 Program Initiatives." Report issued by AFL-CIO in Washington, D.C.

———. n.d.(a). "Mission and Goals of the AFL-CIO." Report issued by AFL-CIO in Washington, D.C.

———. n.d.(b). "Union Cities, Strong Communities." Report issued by AFL-CIO in Washington, D.C.

Appelbaum, Eileen. 1992. "Structural Change and the Growth of Part-Time and Temporary Employment." Pp. 1–14 in New Policies for the Part-Time and Contingent Workforce, ed. Virginia L. duRivage. Armonk, N.Y.: M. E. Sharpe.

Appelbaum, Eileen, and Rosemary Batt. 1994. The New American Workplace— Transforming Work Systems in the United States. Ithaca, N.Y.: ILR Press.

Aronowitz, Stanley. 1983. Working Class Hero: A New Strategy for Labor. New York: Pilgrim.

Bachrach, Peter, and Aryeh Botwinick. 1992. Power and Empowerment: A Radical Theory of Participatory Democracy. Philadelphia: Temple University Press.

Bacon, David. 1995. "The AFL-CIO in Moscow: The Cold War That Never Ends." Covert Action 54 (Fall): 52–57.

———. 1996. "Sweeney's Quandry: Will the AFL-CIO's New Leaders Change Its Old Cold War Policies?" Dollars and Sense 203 (January/February): 12–13, 34–35.

Banks, Andy. 1991/92. "The Power and Promise of Community Unionism." Labor Research Review 18 10, no. 2 (Fall/Winter): 17–31.

Baugh, Robert. 1994. Changing Work: A Union Guide to Workplace Change. Washington, D.C.: Human Resources Development Institute, AFL-CIO.

Bell, Daniel. 1973. The Coming of a Post-Industrial Society: A Venture in Social Forecasting. New York: Basic Books.

Bennett, Iris. 1995. "Los Angeles Workers Fight for Union Democracy." Labor Page, December, 4–5.

Bernstein, Aaron. 1985. "Why Union Bosses Are Also-Rans in the Big-Buck Derby." Business Week, May 6, 102.

Bernstein, Aaron, Amy Borrus, and Richard S. Dunham. 1997. "Labor's Last Laugh." *Business Week,* June 2, 36–37.

Blackwell, Elise. 1993. "A Commitment to Organizing: Justice for Janitors." *Beyond Borders* 1, no. 2 (Spring): 16–33.

Block, Fred. 1990. *Post-Industrial Possibilities: A Critique of Economic Discourse.* Berkeley and Los Angeles: University of California Press.

Bok, Derek, and John T. Dunlop. 1970. Labor and the American Community. New York: Simon and Schuster.

Bowles, Samuel, David M. Gordon, and Thomas E. Weisskopf. 1990. *After the Wasteland: A Democratic Economics for the Year 2000.* Armonk, N.Y.: M. E. Sharpe.

Brecher, Jeremy, and Tim Costello, eds. 1990. *Building Bridges: The Emerging Grassroots Coalition of Labor and Community.* New York: Monthly Review.

————. 1994. *Global Village or Global Pillage.* Boston: South End.

————. 1996. "A 'New Labor Movement' in the Shell of the Old?" *Labor Research Review 24* (Summer): 5–25.

Cobble, Dorothy Sue, ed. 1993. *Women and Unions: Forging a Partnership.* Ithaca, N.Y.: ILR Press.

Cohen, Stephen S., and John Zysman. 1987. *Manufacturing Matters: The Myth of the Post-Industrial Economy.* New York: Basic Books.

Colatosi, Camille. 1990. "Police Give Janitors No Justice." *Labor Notes* 136 (July): 1, 14.

Conrow, Theresa. 1991. "Contract Servicing from an Organizing Model." *Labor Research Review 17* 10, no. 1 (Spring): 45–59.

Cooke, William. 1990. *Labor-Management Cooperation.* Kalamazoo, Mich.: W. E. UpJohn Institute.

Cornfield, Daniel B., ed. 1987. *Workers, Managers, Technological Change: Emerging Patterns of Labor Relations.* New York: Plenum.

Craver, Charles B. 1993. *Can Unions Survive?* New York: New York University Press.

Crump, Joe. 1991/92. "The Pressure's On: Organizing without the NLRB." *Labor Research Review 18* 10, no. 2 (Fall/Winter): 33–43.

Early, Steve. 1996. "New Organizing Should Be Member-Based." *Labor Notes* 205 (April): 12.

Early, Steve, and Larry Cohen. 1994. "Jobs with Justice: Building a Broad-Based Movement for Workers' Rights." *Social Policy* 25, no. 2 (Winter): 7–18.

Eisenscher, Michael. 1995. *Cooperation, Competition, and Company Unions: Teaming Up for the Twenty-First Century Workplace.* Paper for a conference of the Society for the Study of Social Problems, Washington, D.C., August 19. Distributed by Sociological Abstracts, Inc., San Diego, Calif.

Farrell, John Aloysius. 1996. "AFL-CIO Backs Clinton-Gore, Pledges $35m for Democrats." *Boston Globe,* March 26.

Fellner, Kim. 1989. "In Search of the Movement: 1960s Activists in Labor." Manuscript. In possession of author.

———. 1990a. "An Uneasy Marriage in the House of Labor." *American Prospect* 2 (Summer): 93–105.

———. 1990b. "Women Still Have No Standing in Unions." *New York Times,* September 3.

Ferguson, Thomas. 1995. *Golden Rule: The Investment Theory of Party Competition and the Logic of Money-Driven Political Systems.* Chicago and London: University of Chicago Press.

Ferguson, Thomas, and Joel Rogers. 1979. "Labor Law Reform and Its Enemies." *Nation* (January 6): 1, 17–20.

Fletcher, Bill. 1996a. "A Draft Vision Document for the Ec. Ed. Project." Memorandum to participants in the December 17 Economics Education Working Group. Photocopy in possession of the author. December 6.

———. 1996b. "Economics Education: What is Our Message, What Are Our Goals?" Draft "Vision Document" attached to Fletcher 1996a. Photocopy in possession of the author. 11 pp.

Gapasin, Fernando, and Howard Wial. 1996. "The Role of Central Labor Councils in Union Organizing in the 1990s." Paper presented at the AFL-CIO/Cornell University Research Conference on Union Organizing, Washington, D.C., March 31–April 2.

Ginger, Ann Fagan, and David Christiano. 1987. *The Cold War Against Labor, Volumes 1–2.* Berkeley, Calif.: Meiklejohn Civil Liberties Institute.

Goldfield, Michael. 1987. *The Decline of Organized Labor in the United States.* Chicago: University of Chicago Press.

Gooding, Cheryl, and Pat Reeve. 1993. "The Fruits of Our Labor: Women in the Labor Movement." *Social Policy* 23, no. 4 (Summer): 56–64.

Gordon, David, Richard Edwards, and Michael Reich. 1982. *Segmented Work, Divided Workers.* New York: Cambridge University Press.

Gordon, Suzanne. 1995. "Is Sweeney's `New Voice' a Choice or an Echo?" *Labor Notes* 199 (October): 12–13.

Green, James R. 1980. *The World of the Worker: Labor in Twentieth-Century America.* New York: Hill and Wang.

Greenhouse, Steven. 1997. "AFL-CIO Puts Recruiting at Top of Agenda." *New York Times* [electronic edition], February 17.

Greer, Margolis, Mitchell, Burns and Associates, Inc. 1994. "Being Heard: Strategic Communications Report and Recommendations" Report prepared for the AFL-CIO. March 21.

Hamilton, Martha M. 1996. "Labor Gets a Young Look." *Washington Post,* September 1, p. H1, Section F.

Heckscher, Charles C. 1988. *The New Unionism: Employee Involvement in the Changing Corporation.* New York: Basic Books.

Hirsch, Barry T., and David A. Macpherson. 1996. *Union Membership and Earnings Data Book 1995: Compilations from the Current Population Survey.* Washington, D.C.: Bureau of National Affairs.

Hornblower, Margot. 1996. "Labor's Youth Brigade." *Time,* July 15, 44–45.

"In Their Own Words." 1995. *Boston Globe,* October 29.

Kelber, Harry. 1995. "AFL-CIO Charts New Course under Sweeney after Convention Makes Major Changes." *Labor Educator* 4, no. 6 (November/December): 1–2.

Kochan, Thomas A., ed. 1986. *Challenges and Choices Facing American Labor.* Cambridge, Mass.: MIT Press.

Kochan, Thomas A., Harry C. Katz, and Robert B. McKersie. [1986] 1994. *Transformation of American Industrial Relations.* Ithaca, N.Y.: Cornell University Press.

Kochan, Thomas, Harry C. Katz, and Nancy Mower. 1984. *Worker Participation and American Unions: Threat or Opportunity?* Kalamazoo, Mich.: W. E. UpJohn Institute for Employment Research.

"Labor and Political Action." 1994. *Labor Research Review 22* 13, no. 1 (Fall/Winter). 112pp.

Leahy, Dan. 1989a. "'The Deal Is Dead.'" *Bulletin.* Pacific Northwest Newspaper Guild, July, 6–9.

———. 1989b. "'The Deal Is Dead.'" *Bulletin.* Part II. Pacific Northwest Newspaper Guild, August, 6–9.

———. 1990. "'The Deal Is Dead.'" *Bulletin.* Part III. Pacific Northwest Newspaper Guild, January, 11–13.

Lerner, Stephen. 1991/92. "Let's Get Moving! Labor's Survival Depends on Organizing Industry-wide for Justice and Power." *Labor Research Review 18* 10, no. 2 (Fall/Winter): 1–15.

———. 1996. "Reviving Unions: A Call to Action." *Boston Review Reprint* 21, nos. 2, 3/4 (April/May, Summer): 1–5.

Levine, David. I. 1995. *Reinventing the Workplace: How Business and Employees Can Both Win.* Washington, D.C.: Brookings Institution.

Marshall, Ray. 1987. *Unheard Voices: Labor and Economic Policy in a Competitive World.* New York: Basic Books.

Matles, James J., and James Higgins. 1974. *Them and Us, Struggles of a Rank-and-File Union.* Englewood Cliffs, N.J.: Prentice-Hall.

McClure, Laura. 1995a. "AFL-CIO: A New Era?" *Labor Notes* 201 (December): 1, 10–11.

———. 1995b. "Lapdog Politics Lead Nowhere." *McClure's Labor News* 3, no. 1 (January): 1–3.

———. 1995c. "Turmoil at the Top: Shaking Up the AFL-CIO." *Dollars and Sense* 201 (September/October): 8–9, 39–40.

Mishel, Lawrence, and Paula B. Voos. 1992. *Unions and Economic Competitiveness.* Armonk, N.Y.: M. E. Sharpe.

Moberg, David. 1995. "Twilight of the Idle." *In These Times,* March 20, pp. 20–23.

———. 1997. "The Resurgence of American Unions: Small Steps, Long Journey." *WorkingUSA,* May, 20–31.

Moody, Kim. 1988. *An Injury To All: The Decline of American Unionism.* London: Verso.

———. 1996. "U.S. Labor Wars: Bottom to Top." *New Politics* (Winter): 81–91.

Morris, George. 1967. *CIA and American Labor: The Subversion of the AFL-CIO's Foreign Policy.* New York: International Publishers.

Multiracial Alliance. 1995. "What? The Members Want to Run the Union?" *Labor Notes* 197 (August): 3–4.

Murolo, Priscilla. 1996. "What Kind of Alliance?" *Radical Historians* 75 (December): 1, 4, 15–16.

"New BLS Data: 26 Percent of American Workers are Contingent Workers." 1996. *Contingent Worker News* 1, no. 1 (January).

"New Tactics for Labor." 1985. *Labor Research Review* 7 (Fall): 114pp.

Nissen, Bruce. 1990a. "A Post-World War II 'Social Accord?'" Pp. 173–207 in *U.S. Labor Relations 1945–1989: Accommodation and Conflict,* ed. Bruce Nissen. New York: Garland.

———. 1990b. *U.S. Labor Relations, 1945–1989: Accommodation and Conflict.* New York: Garland.

"No More Business as Usual: Labor's Corporate Campaigns." 1993. *Labor Research Review 21* 12, no. 2 (Fall/Winter). 106pp.

Olmos, David R. 1996. "Coalition Seeks Initiative to Limit Power of HMO Industry." *Los Angeles Times,* January 18.

Oppenheim, Lisa. 1991–92. "Women's Ways of Organizing: A Conversation with AFSCME Organizers Kris Rondeau and Gladys McKensie." *Labor Research Review 18* 10, no. 2 (Fall–Winter): 45–49.

"An Organizing Model of Unionism." 1991. *Labor Research Review 17* 10, no. 1 (Spring). 98pp.

Parker, Mike, and Jane Slaughter. 1994. *Working Smart: A Union Guide to Participation Programs and Reengineering.* Detroit: Labor Notes.

Piore, Michael J., and Charles F. Sabel. 1984. *The Second Industrial Divide: Possibilities for Prosperity.* New York: Basic Books.

Press, Eyal. 1996. "Union Do's: 'Smart Solidarity.'" *Nation* (April 8): 29–32.

"Rebuilding the American Labor Movement: A New Voice for American Workers. A Summary of Proposals from the Unions Supporting John J. Sweeney, Richard Trumka, and Linda Chavez-Thompson." 1995. June 28. 8 pp. Document circulated by unions supporting AFL-CIO leadership candidates Sweeney, Trumka, and Chavez-Thompson. Photocopy in possession of the author.

Roby, Pamela. 1995. "Becoming Shop Stewards: Perspectives on Gender and Race in Ten Trade Unions." *Labor Studies Journal* 20, no. 3 (Fall): 65–82.

Russo, John, and Andrew Banks. 1996. "Teaching the Organizing Model of Unionism and Campaign-Based Education: National and International Trends." Paper presented at the AFL-CIO/Cornell University Research Conference on Union Organizing, Washington, D.C., April 1.

Sayer, Andrew, and Richard Walker. 1992. *The New Social Economy: Reworking the Division of Labor.* Cambridge, Mass.: Blackwell Publications.

Senge, Peter M. 1990. "The Leader's New Work: Building Learning Organizations." *Sloan Management Review* (Reprint Series) 32, no. 1 (Fall): 7–23.

Silverstein, Stuart. 1997. "Unions Putting Hard Labor into Recruitment." *Los Angeles Times* [electronic edition], February 18.

Siriani, Carmen, ed. 1987. *Worker Participation and the Politics of Reform.* Philadelphia: Temple University Press.

Slaughter, Jane. 1997. "The New AFL-CIO's First-Year Report Card—Sweeney: Pass, Fail or Incomplete." *Against the Current,* March/April, 7–10.

Storper, Michael, and Richard Walker. 1989. *The Capitalist Imperative: Territory, Technology, and Industrial Growth.* New York and Oxford, U.K.: Basil Blackwell.

Sugrue, Thomas J. 1996. "The Long Road Ahead." *Radical Historians* 75 (December): 1, 13–15.

Sweeney, John. 1996a. "Labor's Role in a Meaningful Society." *Tikkun* 11, no. 4 (July–August): 37–39.

———. 1996b. "Responses." *Labor Research Review* 24 (Summer): 26–29.

———. 1997a. Correspondence to affiliated unions regarding the Center for Workplace Democracy. January.

———. 1997b. "Time for a New Contract." *Dissent* (Winter): 35–36.

Swoboda, Frank, and Maryann Haggerty. 1997. "Janitors' Union Ends Strikes, Picketing." *Washington Post,* May 16.

Tasini, Jonathan. 1995. *The Edifice Complex: Rebuilding the American Labor Movement to Face the Global Economy.* New York: Labor Research Association.

Taylor, Robert. 1995. "Anxious Times." *Financial Times,* February 3.

Thompson, Peter. 1980. "Bilderberg and the West." Pp. 157–89 in *Trilateralism,* ed. by Holly Sklar. Boston: South End Press.

Toffler, Alvin. 1980. *The Third Wave.* New York: William Morrow.

Tomasky, Michael. 1997. "Waltzing With Sweeney." *Lingua Franca*, February, 40–47.

Touraine, Alan. 1971. *The Postindustrial Society.* New York: Random.

Troy, Leo. 1965. *Trade Union Membership, 1897–1962.* New York: National Bureau of Economic Research.

"Union Boss Gets Salary from His Old Local." 1995. *San Francisco Chronicle*, August 25.

Waldinger, Roger, et al. 1997. "Justice for Janitors." *Dissent* (Summer): 37–44.

Wheaton, Lisa. 1980. "'Democratization' in the Dominican Republic." Pp. 419–34 in *Trilateralism*, ed. by Holly Sklar. Boston: South End Press.

Widick, B. J. 1964. *Labor Today: The Triumphs and Failures of Unionism in the United States.* Boston: Houghton Mifflin.

Wypijewski, JoAnn. 1995. "Labor's Challenge." *Nation* (November 20): 595–97.

CONTRIBUTORS

STEWART ACUFF is the president of the Atlanta Labor Council AFL-CIO. His background is in community organizing and as a union organizer and union leader in the Service Employees International Union. He has published articles in *Southern Changes, Atlanta Constitution, Labor Research Review,* and *In These Times.*

LARRY COHEN has served since 1986 as assistant to the president and director of organization for the Communications Workers of America (CWA). He has been involved in organizing new units, adding more than 100,000 CWA members. Previously, Cohen was assistant to the vice president, CWA District 1, and New Jersey area director. He is also a founder and national steering committee member of Jobs with Justice (JWJ), a national workers' rights coalition of labor and community organizations.

BRIAN R. CORBIN has worked for more than ten years as the diocesan director of Social Action of Catholic Charities of the Diocese of Youngstown, Ohio. He received his bachelor's degree from the School of Philosophy of the Catholic University of America and is completing a doctorate in political science at the Massachusetts Institute of Technology. Corbin has written several articles on the Catholic Church's ideas and role in economic justice and community development. He has served on various national, state, and local religious and public commissions and boards dealing with fair housing, human relations, health, and community development.

STEVE EARLY has spent the last twenty-five years working as a labor educator, journalist, lawyer, organizer, and union representative. He has been a Boston-based international staff member of the Communications Workers of America (CWA) since 1980. He serves on the policy committee of *Labor Notes* and is an editorial board member of *New Labor Forum*.

MICHAEL EISENSCHER is a veteran labor organizer, consultant to unions, and doctoral candidate in Public Policy at the University of Massachusetts—Boston. He resides in Oakland, California, where he is coordinator of the Project for Labor Renewal, a program of the Organizers Training Center in San Francisco.

MARK ERLICH is the senior assistant administrator of the New England Regional Council of Carpenters. A member of the Carpenters Union since 1974, Erlich worked as an apprentice, journeyman, foreman, and superintendent before becoming program director of the Massachusetts Building Trades Council in 1988, being elected business manager of Carpenters Local 40 in 1992, and moving to the Regional Council in 1997. In addition to his career in the trades, he is the author of two books, *With Our Hands: The Story of Carpenters in Massachusetts* and *Labor at the Ballot Box,* as well as many essays and articles on labor history and contemporary union issues.

BILL FLETCHER, JR. is the education director of the AFL-CIO. He previously served as the assistant to the president for the Services Employees International Union. His past union staff experience includes a stint as the organizational secretary/administrative director for the National Mail Handlers Union and as an organizer for District 65–United Auto Workers in Boston. He is the author of numerous articles published in a variety of newspapers and magazines and is the coauthor of the pictorial booklet *The Indispensable Ally: Black Workers and the Formation of the Congress of Industrial Organizations, 1934–1941.*

JEFF GRABELSKY is the director of Cornell University's Construction Industry Program. He develops and delivers education and training programs for building and construction trades unions and provides research and technical assistance in all aspects of union affairs. He is a member of the International Brotherhood of Electrical Workers and is a former organizer for that union. He is also on the faculty of George Meany Center and trains organizers for many international unions. He is the author of the trainers manual for the Construction Organizing Membership Education and Training (COMET) Program, which is currently being used by the national AFL-CIO Building and Construction Trades Department and many state councils. He travels throughout the United States and Canada working with building trades unionists and conducting a wide variety of training and education programs.

RICHARD W. HURD is a professor of Labor Studies at Cornell University's School of Industrial Labor Relations (ILR). He is coeditor of *Restoring the Promise of American Labor Law* and *Organizing to Win.* Hurd had published dozens of papers in books and professional journals, among them "Contesting the Dinosaur Image: The Labor Movement's Search for a Future," "Reinventing an Organizing Union: Strategies for Change," and "Beyond the Organizing Model."

PHILIP J. MCLEWIN is a professor of economics at Ramapo College of New Jersey, a public liberal arts college. He specializes in labor economics and has published articles on the Paterson, New Jersey, silk industry in *The Review of Radical Political Economics.* Since 1983, he has been president of the Bergen County Central Trades and Labor Council, AFL-CIO. He is an original member appointed by AFL-CIO President John Sweeney to the National Central Labor Advisory Committee that developed the *Union Cities* initiative. McLewin is also a founding board member of the American Labor Museum, an original board member of New Jersey Citizen Action, vice president of New Jersey Industrial Union Council, and founder and president of United Labor Agency of Bergen County, Inc.

DAVID MOBERG is a senior editor of *In These Times.* His writings on labor have appeared in many journalistic and scholarly outlets. His research on the global economy and worker rights is supported by a grant from the John D. and Catherine T. MacArthur Foundation.

BRUCE NISSEN is assistant director of the Center for Labor Research and Studies at Florida International University in Miami. He has been a union activist and labor educator for many years. His recent authored and edited works include *Unions and Workplace Reorganization; Fighting for Jobs: Case Studies of Labor-Community Coalitions Confronting Plant Closings; Grand Designs: The Impact of Corporate Strategies on Workers, Unions, and Communities;* and *Theories of the Labor Movement.*

WADE RATHKE is the chief organizer of Local 100, Service Employees International Union, AFL-CIO, and has been since the local was founded in 1980 in New Orleans, Louisiana. Rathke is a member of the international executive board of SEIU and serves as secretary-treasurer of the Greater New

Orleans AFL-CIO. He is also the founder and chief organizer of the Association of Community Organizations for Reform Now (ACORN), a national community organization with close to 100,000 lower income and working family members.

SETH ROSEN is the administrative assistant to the vice president of District 4 of the Communications Workers of America (CWA). In that capacity, he oversees the organizing, mobilization, and community action programs of CWA District 4. As the district organizing coordinator, he set up the District 4 organizing network. Rosen has also been an activist with Jobs with Justice (JWJ) and is the director of the Cleveland Area Workers Rights Board of JWJ.

JOHN RUSSO is the coordinator of the Labor Studies Program in the Warren P. Williamson Jr. College of Business Administration. Russo received his doctorate from the University of Massachusetts, Amherst, where he served as a postdoctoral research fellow at the Labor Relations and Research Center. He is also a cofounder and the director of the Center of Working-Class Studies at Youngstown State University. The center is an interdisciplinary center for research, teaching, and community activity on working-class life, work, culture, and thought. Russo has written widely on labor and social issues and is recognized as a national expert on labor unions. For his research and community activities, Russo has been awarded distinguished professorships in both scholarship and public service by YSU.

EVE S. WEINBAUM is education director and political organizing director for the southern region of UNITE, the Union of Needletrades, Industrial and Textile Employees. She travels around nine states of the southeastern United States working with union members and activists. She received her Ph.D. in political science from Yale University.

INDEX